The Divergent Dynamics of Economic Growth

This book explains how changing technology and economizing behavior induce vast changes in productivity, resource allocation, labor utilization, and patterns of living. Economic growth is seen as a process by which businesses, regimes, countries, and the whole world pass through distinct epochs, each one emerging from its predecessor and creating the conditions for its successor. Viewed from a long-run perspective, growth must be characterized as an explosive process marked by turbulent transitions in social and political life as societies adapt to new opportunities, the demise of old ways of living, and the vast increase and redistribution of human populations. The book is based on a new and unique synthesis of classical economics and contemporary concepts of adaptation and economic evolution. Although it is grounded in analytical methods, the text has been stripped of all equations and with few exceptions is devoid of technical jargon.

Richard H. Day is Professor of Economics at the University of Southern California. He cofounded the distinguished *Journal of Economic Behavior and Organization* with Sidney Winter in 1980 and served as its editor until 2002. Professor Day's first book developed a class of recursive programming models for simulating production, investment, and technological change. This work became the basis of a dynamic theory describing economic change when agents are boundedly rational, when economic behavior is adaptive, when markets work out of equilibrium, and when economic structure evolves. Professor Day went on to investigate chaos and multiphase dynamics in competitive markets, stock market prices, business cycles, and growth when significant nonlinearities are incorporated. His findings were published in two volumes titled *Complex Economic Dynamics: Volume I: An Introduction to Dynamical Systems and Market Mechanisms* (1994); *Volume II: An Introduction to Macroeconomic Dynamics* (2000). His ongoing research investigates core macroeconomic issues for private enterprise and public policy as well as the implications of behavioral economics for macroeconomic theory, modeling, and policy.

The Divergent Dynamics of Economic Growth

Studies in Adaptive Economizing, Technological Change, and Economic Development

RICHARD H. DAY

University of Southern California

PUBLISHED BY THE PRESS SYNDICATE OF THE UNIVERSITY OF CAMBRIDGE
The Pitt Building, Trumpington Street, Cambridge, United Kingdom

CAMBRIDGE UNIVERSITY PRESS
The Edinburgh Building, Cambridge CB2 2RU, UK
40 West 20th Street, New York, NY 10011-4211, USA
477 Williamstown Road, Port Melbourne, VIC 3207, Australia
Ruiz de Alarcón 13, 28014 Madrid, Spain
Dock House, The Waterfront, Cape Town 8001, South Africa

http://www.cambridge.org

© Richard H. Day 2004

First published 2004

Printed in the United Kingdom at the University Press, Cambridge

Typeface Minion 10.5/13 pt.   *System* LaTeX 2_ε [TB]

A catalog record for this book is available from the British Library.

Library of Congress Cataloging-in-Publication Data
Day, Richard Hollis, 1933–
The divergent dynamics of economic growth : studies in adaptive economizing,
technological change, and economic development / Richard H. Day.
p. cm.
Includes bibliographical references and index.
ISBN 0-521-83019-2
1. Economic development.   2. Technological innovations – Economic aspects.
3. Evolutionary economics.   I. Title
HD82.D373   2003
338.9–dc21   2003046060

ISBN 0 521 83019 2 hardback

Dedicated to My Sisters

LYLA AND SYLVIA

*Whom I adored as a child
and who have been a
continual source of
encouragement ever since*

Contents

Preface

This volume is based on a series of essays written during the last four decades. In looking it over, I find that even the oldest paper included in the collection is even more relevant today than when first published. For example, one essay observed that

invention, innovation, and diffusion of new products, new inputs, new production, marketing, and decision-making methods . . . are leading now, as they have in the past, to overlapping, imbalanced waves of development, to counterpoints of growth and decline as old modes of production and consumption are abandoned in favor of more competitive alternatives and as established mores give way to new patterns of living.

These facts are sometimes recognized by politicians and general commentators, but often too late to plan effective action to alleviate their social effects. The recent onset of the energy crisis underscores this fact. It seems to have been recognized long after it was in the making; little seems to have been done to prepare for it; few agree on its importance, or, conceding its importance, few agree on what to do about it.[1]

The crisis referred to occurred in the 1970s, but the assessment made of it in that early paper could apply with equal force to the current controversy over energy, which seems to have been as little anticipated and as little understood now as the one three decades ago. Indeed, technical change and social transformation are proceeding still more rapidly and with even more massive consequences than was the case a quarter of a century ago. Almost all regions of the world are now entrained in a worldwide process of economic development. Like it or not, globalization is a reality. Sooner or later, the dynamic view presented in these essays will have to be more widely utilized if we are to understand, anticipate, and survive the undesirable consequences

---

[1] Day (1980).

of growth and if we are to learn either how to suppress or to live comfortably with the explosive growth in human numbers.

Early in my career I felt myself, quite immodestly I admit, to be creating a new synthesis of classical, neoclassical, and modern developments in economic thought with a class of "recursive programming models" based on adaptive economizing behavior. I felt my mission to have been that of providing a better characterization of economic change. As time went by, I realized that some of my predecessors and contemporaries had anticipated insights that had seemed entirely my own and had already written about them or were in the process of doing so: Alcian, Cooper, Simon, Cyert, March Hayek. Another such scholar is Sidney Winter, who observed in a recent conversation that such convergencies understandably occur to those who stand on the shoulders of the same giants. My giants in economics included Smith, Malthus, Cournot, Walras, Marshall, Keynes, Schumpeter, and Chamberlin.

I was also inspired by the mid-twentieth-century giants, including Samuelson, Frisch, Haavelmo, Koopmans, Georgescu-Roegen, Marschak, Goodwin, Modigliani, Arrow, Debreu, and Leontief, who were refining, generalizing, and extending economic theory and introducing new ideas and methods that could serve as a foundation for further improvements in understanding this immensely difficult subject – especially Leontief, my "Doktor Vater" – who once paid me the highest compliment I ever received: "We think alike," he said.

Leontief, whose fame rested on the development of input–output analysis, wrote his thesis on dynamics and later produced several seminal essays devoted to issues involving economic growth and development.[2] He also championed the view that economics should be grounded in observation and data, not just in the estimation of model parameters but in the assumptions and structure of the theory itself. Many years later when I saw him not long before his death, I reminded him of that remark made at the conclusion of my thesis defense and told him how much it had meant to me. He replied, "It is important to think about things in the right way." I think I have done so in this book, and it is a sufficient reward for a lifetime of work to believe that he would have thought so, too.

Thus, my approach developed out of the work of many others but emphasized aspects of the subject that were not recognized or stressed by the great body of the discipline for a long time. In recent years that has changed. The

---

[2] Leontief (1966).

subject is once again being enriched by the development and application of many new ideas and methods. For that reason it is possible (and I hope) that the ideas and methods outlined in these essays will receive a warmer welcome and a wider audience now than they did when they first appeared. And I do believe that the synthesis of classical, neoclassical and adaptive, evolutionary points of view is still novel and has yet to be explored to the extent needed.

While my own ideas were developing – in some ways far removed from current fashion – I received crucial support at various times from several institutions and individuals: John Kenneth Galbraith, whose recommendation made possible my thesis research described in Chapter 4; Guy Orcutt and Charles Holt, Directors of the Social Systems Research Institute at the University of Wisconsin; the late Theodore Heidhues of the University of Göttingen; Jean-Pierre Aubin, founder and long-time director of the *Centre Researche de Mathematique et la Decision*, the University of Paris IX-Dauphine; the late J. Barkley Rosser and Steve Robinson, Director and Associate Director, respectively, of the Mathematics Research Center at the University of Wisconsin; Kenneth Arrow and Dale Jorgenson, who arranged a productive stay at Harvard; Jay Forrester, who provided a congenial atmosphere in his Systems Dynamics Group at MIT; Gunnar Eliasson at the Institute of Social and Economic Research (IUI) in Stockholm; the Electric Power Research Group under the leadership of Al Halter; Al Hirschman, who made possible a year in academic nirvana at Princeton's Institute for Advanced Study; the late Richard Goodwin, Giulio Pianigiani, Lionello Punzo, and my friends and colleagues at the University of Siena; Ari Kapteyn, who was responsible for another year in academic nirvana at the Institute for Advanced Study in Wassenaar; the Fulbright Foundation for granting me a visiting distinguished professorship at the European University Institute in Florence; and for continuing support through thick and thin at the University of Southern California.

Several of the chapters are based on collaboration with my graduate students at the University of Wisconsin or subsequently at the University of Southern California. They are acknowledged in the usual way at the head of the chapters to which they contributed. But I want to emphasize the teamwork that involved them and others of their contemporaries who collaborated with me. At Wisconsin they included Che Tsao, Inderjit Singh, William K. Tabb, Masatoshi Abe, Peter Kennedy, John Austin, Malcohm Lindsay, Jon Nelson, Mohinder Singh Mudahar, Yiu-Kwan Fan, Milton Mitchel, and Hugo Cohen; at Southern California, Frederico Segura, Kenneth Hanson,

Tzong-Yau Lin, Weihong Huang, Gang Zou, Zhigang Wang, Jean-Luc Walter, Zhang Min, and Oleg Pavlov.

Through it all I also had the assistance of extremely competent secretary/administrative assistant/word processors; at Wisconsin, Stephanie Bullis and Linda Anderson, and as with all of my work during the last two decades, Barbara Gordon Day who prepared this manuscript, tirelessly reconstituting it in response to numerous revisions and finding ways to encourage the necessary efforts on both our parts.

In editing the book virtually all of the mathematical notation and equations have been removed. Some technical terms remain, but most readers will have an intuitive understanding of them. In any case, I hope you are motivated to proceed in spite of them because the forces under consideration sooner or later influence all of us directly or indirectly.

References

Day, R. H. 1980. "Technology, Population and the Agro-Industrial Complex: A Global View," Chapter 10 in R. H. Day and N. Kamrany, *Economic Issues of the 80s*, Johns Hopkins Press, 1980.

Leontief, W. W., 1966. *Essays in Economics: Theories and Theorizing*, New York: Oxford University Press.

Acknowledgments and Comments

Chapter 5

Incorporates substantial parts of the following three papers with permission of the publishers:

"A Dynamic Model of Regional Agricultural Development," with I. J. Singh, *International Regional Science Review*, 1, Spring 1975.

"A Microeconomic Chronicle of the Green Revolution," with I. J. Singh, *Journal of Economic Development and Cultural Change*, 23, June 1975.

"Factor Utilization and Substitution in Economic Development: A Green Revolution Case Study," with I. J. Singh, *Journal of Development Studies*, April 1975. (© The University of Chicago.)

The complete study was published as *Economic Development as an Adaptive Process: A Green Revolution Case Study*, Cambridge University Press, 1974 which was based on Inderjit Singh's University of Wisconsin doctoral dissertation.

Chapter 6

Incorporates parts of the following papers with permission of the publishers:

"Recursive Programming Models of Industrial Development and Technological Change," with M. Abe, W. Tabb, and C. Tsao, in Carter and Brody (eds.), *Input–Output Techniques*. (In honor of Wassily Leontief), Vol. 1: Contribution to Input–Output Analysis, North-Holland Publishing Company, 1970.

"A Class of Dynamic Models for Describing and Projecting Industrial Development," with Jon Nelson, *Journal of Econometrics*, May 1973.

"Behavioral, Suboptimizing Models of Industrial Production, Investment and Technological Change," with Masatoshi A. Abe, Jon P. Nelson, and William K. Tabb, Chapter 4 in Day and Cigno, *Modelling Economic Change: The Recursive Programming Approach*, Elsevier North-Holland, Inc., 1978.

The empirical aspects of these papers were initially developed in the Wisconsin doctoral dissertations of the several coauthors.

Chapter 10

This essay was originally presented at the Columbia University Conference on "Managing Planet Earth," April 1997. The computations were performed by Oleg Pavlov. Since it was written, a very detailed technical analysis has appeared in Chapters 19–24 of Day, 1999, *Complex Economic Dynamics*, volume 2, The MIT Press, Cambridge. A further development of the model that contains various improvements can be found in Day and Pavlov, 2001, "Qualitative Dynamics and Macroeconomic Evolution in the Very Long Run," Chapter 4 in L. Punzo (ed.), *Cycles, Growth and Structural Change*, Routledge, London.

ONE

The Adaptive, Evolutionary Theory of Divergent Economic Growth

In law eternal it lies decreed
that naught from change is ever freed.
Boethius, *The Consolation of*
Philosophy

1.1 Reconsidering Economic Theory

Informing the central message of Adam Smith is the recognition that no one understands everything but private individuals in the pursuit of self-interest can contribute to the advantage of others even though they may not intend to do so and may not concern themselves with the economy as a whole. A system of private property and market competition is needed to make this possible: Private property empowers the individual and creates scope for discretion in coping with local situations, that are what each individual knows best; market competition provides incentives for individuals to expand their potential and exercise effective choices. In setting forth this vision of the competitive process, Smith and his followers explicitly recognized that producers and consumers adapt their behavior to price signals that reflect imbalances in supply and demand.

A century after Smith, Léon Walras formalized the idea of a balance or equilibrium in supply and demand and specified two complementary mechanisms of out-of-equilibrium adjustment: consumers' *tâtonnement* (literally, "groping in the dark"), involving price adjustments in response to

Reprinted in part from *The Limits of Government: On Policy Competence and Economic Growth*, G. Eliasson and N. Karlson (eds.), City University Press, Stockholm, 1998 with permission of the publisher.

1

discrepancies in supply and demand, and producers' *tâtonnement*, involving quantity adjustments in response to profit opportunities. He emphasized that such a system of dynamic relationships would not converge to a general equilibrium but would oscillate around one, sometimes approaching a steady state (like a "glassy sea") and sometimes exhibiting more or less turbulent fluctuations (like an "ocean storm").

Thus, from the beginning of the discipline's "modern" era, two complementary streams of thinking have flowed through the domain of economic theory – one characterizing and deriving properties of economic equilibrium, the other characterizing and deriving properties of disequilibrium. Both are found running through all the great classical and neoclassical founding fathers and in the great economists of the twentieth century, including (among many others) Wicksell, Keynes, Schumpeter, Hicks, and Hayek.

Equilibrium concepts are sometimes argued to be most relevant for studying the "long run," that is, for identifying and analyzing the state toward which an economy must presumably be heading. But even a cursory glance at history tells us that human development has approximated an equilibrium state only occasionally – and then only temporarily. Rather, at any one time, history is more meaningfully described as a process of moving away from an equilibrium, and any equilibrium toward which it may be moving at the moment is itself changing with no possibility of ever catching up. If this is true, then it is remarkable that, during the last quarter century, economists – especially growth theorists – have come increasingly to rely exclusively on the concepts of economic equilibrium. It seems to me high time to reverse this disciplinary trend. Accordingly, the essays in this volume are offered in the hope of reinstating a more realistic approach that better answers the questions of if, why, and how economies develop?

But suppose one already has an adequate descriptive history of what has happened. Why, once that knowledge is acquired, does one need a theory or model to characterize it? Just what does a theoretical model add to the story that the facts already tell? First of all, the model itself is not a descriptive history but a hypothetical framework of cause and effect. This framework characterizes specific relationships among the variables that tell the development story. Second, if the causal framework produces data that correspond to historical facts, then we are permitted to entertain the possibility that we understand why those facts came about as they did and not some other way. Third, with this kind of understanding, useful clues about the future may be inferred. Of course, the model variables and the causal relationships merely approximate their real-world counterparts; moreover, the model-generated histories are not expected to recreate all the details of place or time. But we do demand that the histories mimic the real-world process in some of its most salient features.

1.2 An Overview of the Essays

The essays collected in this volume all deal one way or another with three intertwining themes.

1. New technology and economizing behavior induce vast changes in productivity, resource allocation, and labor utilization.
2. These changes have made possible an explosion in human numbers, drastic changes in resource utilization, and massive relocation of people from rural regions to concentrated urban centers.
3. To understand these developments scientific economic theory needs to incorporate concepts of adaptive, economizing, and structural evolution.

The reorientation of economics around these themes does not require abandoning economic optimization and equilibrium theory, for that theory makes possible a rigorous definition of what perfect coordination is and what practical and theoretical problems arise when coordination is not perfect. For this reason, equilibrium and disequilibrium are dual theoretical concepts; that is, one implies the meaningfulness of the other. The former describes how economies would function if everyone's actions were perfectly coordinated and no one had an incentive to modify the distribution of wealth or his or her behavior; the latter characterizes how economies really function.

The second chapter emphasizes the global context of human development. From that point of view – from the world as a whole and the history of our species over its entire span – economic growth is an explosive process. It involves increasing population, intensifying resource utilization, frequent restructuring of production, redistribution of populations, and changes in consumption and behavioral patterns. For the world as a whole, and at the scale of the lifetime of the earth, population, production, and resource utilization form spikes. Within these spikes, individual cultures and political units emerge, each depending on some dominant way of life that flourish, decline, and disappear. On the scale of the last two centuries, the period accounting for almost the entire "height" of the human trajectory, overlapping waves of individual technologies appear with successive waves rising far above their predecessors before they too fall as new waves supersede them. From this very long run perspective, economic development is a counterpoint of growth and decay with the pace and magnitude of change accelerating.

Chapter 3 reviews the fundamental theoretical and methodological concepts that will be exploited in the remaining essays for understanding the development story. These concepts are based on empirical characteristics of actual economizing activity. A general analytical framework is outlined and examples of adaptive economic models are briefly reviewed – in particular the class of "recursive programming" or "adaptive economizing" models.

The essays in Part II deal with microeconomic transformations involving rapid technological change in specific, narrowly defined agriculture regions and industrial sectors. These transformations provide coherent economic histories of specific settings of time and place. From the theoretical point of view they constitute tests of adaptive economizing theory, of the recursive programming methodology, and the role of multiphase dynamics in describing structural transitions. The implications extend far beyond the specific circumstances investigated. Thus, the dynamic microeconomic theory, properly constituted to represent the realities of human decision making and the strategic details of production technologies, provides a coherent and substantially correct explanation of the macroeconomic effects of the forces at work at the microeconomic level and how the social landscape of a region or industry is transformed within a fraction of a century.

The essays in Part III are concerned with the macroeconomic effects of accumulating change within a national economy or the entire world over long periods. Methodologically, it involves a progression from the microeconomic studies of individual, specialized sectors to the study of development on a grand scale over a century, several centuries, or over many millennia. Chapter 8 describes a hypothetical economy using a multisector model that generates capital accumulation and technological change in industry and agriculture. The corollary is the industrialization of agriculture and the urbanization of population – a process that occurs, once started, primarily within one generation. It mimics in macroeconomic terms the transition process described in microeconomic terms in Part II that has taken place already or is well under way in virtually every region of the world.

Chapter 9 considers economic growth and the switching of economic distribution systems during the transition to market-oriented production in the manorial economies of the middle ages. At this level of theorizing, inferences are entirely qualitative. Nonetheless, the analysis shows how growth can lead an economy away from a given system and into another with very different economic characteristics. This exercise also explains how noneconomic events – in this case the early fourteenth-century plague – can alter the chain of events and bring about a temporary restoration of an earlier regime.

From the long run of three quarters of a century or of several centuries in Chapter 9, Chapter 10 is concerned with the very long run, that is, the evolution of the world through the great socioeconomic epochs from hunting and food collecting through settled agriculture, the city-state, trading civilizations, the nation-state, and into the present global-information-based economy. The analysis suggests that the global forces operating over the very long run have implications for the short run – in terms of imminent, potentially catastrophic problems and the crucial focal points for solving them.

Economic theory provides a way to think about and understand economic aspects of experience. On the basis of that understanding, it provides a rational way to influence actions. If mental images of theory do not adequately reflect what is really "out there," then action may be ineffective or counterproductive. Survival may be jeopardized. The research described in Parts II and III led me very early on to see economic optimizing and equilibrium theory (by themselves) as inadequate mental images of the real economic world. The individual case studies suggest a general, unified system of thought that provides an enhanced basis for thinking more broadly about economics, society, and human development. That unified system of thought is the subject of Part IV, which concerns the foundations for a general theory of economy and state based on principles of adaptation, multiphase dynamics, and evolution.

Chapter 11 describes the relationship of complex multiphase dynamics to concepts of punctuated equilibrium, endogenously generated structural change, and economic evolution, illustrating the general concepts using individual studies of Parts II and III as examples. Chapter 12 explains how cognitive limits and adaptive economizing behavior prevent perfect coordination among the parts of the economy; how the lack of coordination requires intermediating mechanisms of exchange and why conflict arises that requires institutions of civil order; how the creative faculty of mind perturbs the existing system, thus providing new opportunities and new solutions, which often generate unforeseen consequences; how the democratic system provides recourse to market and governmental coordination failures; and how, in response, policies that introduce new opportunities and constraints are innovated. Such new constraints and opportunities change the environment within which private economizing takes place. Thus, market and state coevolve.

1.3 The Recursive Programming Methodology

In the case studies of specific development periods and processes of Parts II and III, much use is made of a class of dynamic models referred to as "recursive programming" or "adaptive economizing." The term recur means "to come up again for consideration, thought or discourse" and "to occur again after an interval." Programming is a term used, more or less synonymously, for the constrained optimization problems that arise in many different theoretical and applied fields – especially in economics. Best economic choices or decisions are modeled mathematically in this way. Thus, recursive programming implies making "best" decisions again and again as time passes. I put best in quotes because, in line with the modes of economizing behavior, my models describe choices in a *neighborhood of current practice* based on a cautious response to estimates of future consequences using partial information and calculated for a finite, usually short, time horizon. The decision maker adapts recursively, more or less cautiously moving in the direction of what, on the basis of incomplete knowledge, seems like the "best way to go" and then reconsiders after time passes and new information has been revealed. In contrast to this usage, an important school of macroeconomic theorists uses the term "recursive methods" or "recursive models" to describe economic choices governed by a recursively applied, optimal strategy.[1] The latter is a mathematical rule that governs the decision maker's present situation and prescribes once and for all what is the best thing to do on the assumption of perfect knowledge of all possible consequences forever.

Recursive programs involve various constraints that may or may not be effective or limitational. If they are, they have a causal impact; otherwise, they do not. Moreover, the various activities about which decisions are being made may or may not be pursued. It is the local optimizing choice that determines which activities are undertaken and which constraints are binding. The currently pursued activities and binding constraints form a "causal structure." In the various models of this genre described nontechnically in subsequent chapters, the specific activities pursued and the specific constraints that are binding change from time to time, which is equivalent to a change in the structure of causal relationships characterizing the dynamic process over time. The period of time during which a given causal structure

---

[1] For the fundamental treatise, see Stokey and Lucas, 1989, *Recursive Methods in Economic Dynamics*, Cambridge: Harvard University Press. For representative recent contributions, see Cooley (ed.), 1995, *Frontiers of Business Cycle Research*, Princeton: Princeton University Press.

is effective is called a *phase, regime,* or *epoch.* The history of a given economic organization, sector, or economy as a whole is thus described in terms of the sequence of phases through which it passes. Structural change is modeled explicitly, and economic evolution is seen to consist of the endogenous generation of one structure after and "out of" another – in this way taking a giant step forward in the task of understanding economic development in rigorous theoretical terms.

1.4 Elements of the Argument

Before going into the individual studies, it may be useful to anticipate the basic concepts and overall theory that emerges from them.

1.4.1 Modes of Economizing Behavior

In addition to conscious comparison of alternatives, that is, rational choice, behavior in economic situations is governed by imitation, by "trial and error," and by accidental modifications of behavior that, in effect, constitute unintended "innovations." These, if successful, can be selected by others through imitation in the pursuit of advantage. Less successful behavior may be culled as experience accumulates. Obviously, of course, intended innovation guided by conscious design also contributes to the process, but the central point is the impossibility of acting optimally because of informational and cognitive limits and the possibility of improving performance nonetheless.

In addition to explicit or procedural optimizing, experimentation, trial and error, and imitation, I include as distinguishable (but perhaps not independent) modes of economizing following an authority, tradition, or habit, unmotivated search, and following a hunch. All of these modes – including procedural optimizing – share the characteristic that those who use them do not know and do not find out what is the best thing to do. At best, these people can only do their best as they are able to perceive or calculate it, and this may lead them to abandon optimizing behavior and engage in trial-and-error search, to imitate, to obey an authority, to repeat previous actions mindlessly, or simply to guess.[2]

---

[2] In his classic paper, Armen Alcian (1950) observed that [in the real world] "modes of behavior replace optimum equilibrium conditions as guiding rules of action." I have elaborated these "modes of economizing behavior" most recently in Day (1992). Pingle (1994, 1995) has shown how these modes arise in various laboratory experiments.

1.4.2 The Problems of Disequilibrium: Suboptimality, Mediation, Instability, and Inviability

Given these fallible modes of behavior, intelligent individuals have good reason to seek knowledge. But that is costly. It takes time and other resources. And it perturbs individuals from whatever positions they are in, which in turn perturbs the entire interacting system of which they are a part. That interacting system can strike an equilibrium, if one exists, only by chance, and the chance would be vanishingly small. If an equilibrium did result, no one would know it. Further efforts to understand the situation and to improve the possibilities would perturb the system out of the equilibrium again. For this reason alone, economic systems rarely, if ever, display the characteristics of perfect coordination.[3]

This is an implication of bounded rationality that has not yet received adequate attention. Certainly, the neoclassical economists did not deal with these implications. Subsequent writers who emphasized realistic behavior have often been too sanguine about the market's ability to overcome the difficulties it creates through its own internal workings. After all, markets are essentially a network of firms that mediate transactions for profit and whose managers are governed by the same modes of behavior that govern producers and consumers. If producers and consumers cannot perform equilibrium miracles, how then can market mediators? Of course, they cannot. Indeed, the economy as a whole can be viewed as a vast system of simultaneous experiments undertaking trial-and-error search. It is in Eliasson's (1996) felicitous phrase, "an experimentally organized economy."

The consequence of disequilibrium is serious at all times for some and at some times for many. If the agents are not in equilibrium, then they are out of it; and if they are out of it, some people cannot do what they want or hope to do. In extreme but not infrequent situations, survival may be threatened for individuals and organizations. Some may not survive. In short, economic selection, like its biological counterpart, is cruel: it expels its participants – those who cannot compete successfully lose their chance to do so. Thus, the system evolves in a fundamental way, that is, by changing its constituent "parts." Sometimes technologies or activities, or, more generally, ways of life are abandoned. Sometimes they are individual firms or other

---

[3] Through this discussion I have in mind a Nash equilibrium as in a Walrasian general equilibrium for a deterministic economy or in a strategy space when risk is present as, for example, defined by Hahn (1973). Note that defining an equilibrium does not establish existence.

organizations. These are impersonal components of the economy, but they are components made up of persons whose individual fortunes depend on the activities, ways of life, or organization of which they are a part. When a business firm is eliminated, the individuals involved will be forced to change in ways they never intended.

When expulsion by economic selection occurs relatively slowly and involves only a few activities and organizations at any one time, the individual consequences can be absorbed without great disruption. When expulsion occurs rapidly and involves many activities and organizations, the system as a whole begins to tremble.

1.4.3 Institutional Innovation and Government

Every now and then, economic systems are so thoroughly destabilized by disequilibrium developments that they collapse entirely, as occurred in Russia in the early part of this century, in Germany in the 1930s, and more recently in the Soviet Union. Other countries, for example Great Britain and the United States, have also experienced economic crises and periods of political turmoil. They have been more fortunate, however, having successfully avoided collapse. Their history is characterized instead by episodes of substantial change when existing market or government institutions are modified or new ones are created within the same overall conceptual structure of political and economic organization. These episodes are often followed by somewhat less dramatic periods of consolidation or partial retrenchment.

A brilliant analysis of the Anglo-American interaction of market and state is to be found in John R. Commons's no-longer-read masterpiece *Legal Foundations of Capitalism* ([1924] 1959) and in a somewhat more readable rendition edited by Kenneth Parsons titled *Collective Action* 1950. Commons's method was founded on the direct observation of market and government organizations in action, on a careful description of the origin and development of specific market and governmental institutions, and on a pointillist analysis of specific conflicts that arose among private and public agents in the process. He was able then to show in varied historical cases how specific privately organized economic activities could emerge as a result of private and public innovations as new opportunities opened up, how laws were modified or reinterpreted, and how new public agencies were created to deal with conflicts that occurred when the actions of some agents led to diminished payoffs to others.

Many of the opportunities and conflicts that trigger institutional innovations arise endogenously through the out-of-equilibrium working of the market system, as explained in the preceding section. The institutional changes then modify the economic environment of the private sector by redefining opportunities, constraints, and potential payoffs and by providing specific new mechanisms for resolving conflict and for mediating transactions. To characterize this interaction, I refer to it as the "coevolution of market and state." A very similar vision, also based on historical analysis, is the grand theory of Douglass North (1990).

Armen Alcian's papers are written within this tradition. Alcian argued that, until you know how the system works, you cannot understand how it can work well, that an understanding must rest on a recognition that nonoptimizing modes of behavior need to play a central role, and that the structure of property rights and the mechanisms of market and government selection are required to explain how individual fortunes and public welfare evolve. I emphasize the coevolution of market and government because changes in one virtually always directly involve or trigger changes in the other. As Alcian puts it, "there should be an evolutionary force toward the survival of larger clusters of certain types of rights in the sanctioned concert of property rights." He did not allude to Commons's brilliant analysis of the evolution of property as the chief medium through which the institutions of government and market coevolve in response to conflicting economic interests, but his own contribution, along with that of Coase, was instrumental in setting off an independent, somewhat parallel line of work that has sharpened our understanding of private property and how the real economic system works.

1.4.4 The General Theory of Market and State

I now present a brief outline of the theory of the coevolution of market and state that has its foundations in the "modes of economizing behavior" and in attempts to solve the disequilibrium problems.[4]

Because the system of individuals and of market and government institutions is never in equilibrium, for those whose plans are blocked various options have to exist for economic life to go on, such as doing without, drawing from inventories, queuing, or resorting to some contingent tactic

---

[4] The following summarizes the theory explicated in greater detail in Day (1987). I have produced numerous variations on this theme such as my 1992 paper.

that can "keep one going" for the time being until an alternative course of action can be identified and pursued. In short, *inconsistency forces unwanted change*.

To prevent such inconsistencies and unwanted changes, "markets" fulfill two very important functions. They intervene between agents who wish to exchange but who could not possibly expend the resources necessary to find one another. For example, when we want food, we do not seek out the farmer but take ourselves to a market (literally the "supermarket") where what we want is available without our knowing how, by whom, or even why it was provided. Food is there because we are willing to pay the cost of mediation provided by the merchant instead of paying a greater cost of finding the goods for ourselves. Likewise, the farmer no longer sends his milk in a pony cart driven by his child to dole out ladlefuls in crockery bowls to housewives along a route through the town but delivers his goods to a buyer, wholesaler, or processor without ever knowing the path by which the milk finds its way to someone's cereal bowl or who, indeed, will consume it. In addition to lowering the cost of exchange, markets buffer the discrepancies between demand and supply that follow from the aggregate of actions taken out of economic equilibrium and no one knows where that equilibrium is or how to get to it. Instead, they produce viability for individuals in an economy too complex to be perfectly coordinated by any individual or system, market-oriented or otherwise.

As the amounts and variety of goods have escalated, the role of market mediation has escalated until it is usual for marketing costs to exceed production costs – often by substantial margins. In principle, we could all be better off if we did not have to pay for all these people and resources expended in the marketing process – if only we could exchange costlessly in equilibrium. The resources saved could be used to produce more of the goods and services we really want; or we could enjoy more leisure. Since we cannot determine such a situation, we are better off paying the cost and giving up the idea that we could be better off without mediation. Thus it is that "markets" or, more generally, "market mechanisms" create viability. They make complex exchanges economically feasible and unwittingly coordinate individual decisions that would be inconsistent without them.

This, however, is not the whole story. Disequilibrium creates dynamic movements as producers, consumers, and mediators adjust prices and quantities in attempts to balance supply and demand. We know that these dynamic movements vary in magnitude, sometimes displaying modest fluctuations and sometimes substantial ones, and occasionally such great imbalances arise that the system of mediation that has evolved to date cannot continue to establish interagent viability. Among the effects at such times is the expulsion of large numbers of agents from the market; that is, participation in work, management, production, and consumption under prevailing conditions is blocked for many individuals, both business people and workers. When their numbers are large enough, they constitute a potential constituency and the imbalance spills over into the political system.

Government mechanisms have evolved to regulate private activity to reduce such occurrences, to lower their private and social costs, and to restore access to the system. These innovations in government have arisen in large measure as responses to the direct or indirect pressures created by the collective actions of individuals who have discovered common economic interests during times of duress. The mechanisms of modern democracy make such innovations possible within an evolving system of institutions and laws that can be created or redirected without overthrowing the entire system of government – or, so it has worked for more than two centuries. *Democracy lowers the violence of social conflict caused by economic imbalance by providing recourse for those expelled or threatened with expulsion from the market.*

This is not to say that any given governmental device or even the whole lot of such devices has been entirely successful. Indeed, there can be little doubt that many government regulations and activities have been counterproductive, moving the economy farther from desirable states than would have been the case without them. Moreover, it is correctly argued that, left to their own devices, private individuals and enterprises can, and often do, create sufficient new opportunities by adjusting themselves to aggregate imbalances, thus eliminating or drastically reducing the problems of individual inviability that disequilibrium conditions tend to cause.

But market capitalism is, if anything, an engine of rapid change. It can produce imbalances that can overwhelm its capacity for timely self-correction. When people are expelled from the system of markets, they have recourse in the system of government. Indeed, the mere perception of the possibility of expulsion is enough to motivate government innovations to modify the system and, once it is realized that the government not only creates but can influence, control, or even eliminate markets, the pressures to substitute a government agency for a private agency can proceed far enough to stifle the beneficial effects of market competition.

Thus it is that, in their coevolution, the institutions of market and of government have multiplied and elaborated their functions, evolving ever more complex public and private systems of mediation in response to the fluctuating imbalances among economic flows.

1.5 Remarks on the Literature

A similar interest in adaptive, evolutionary change and the methods of dynamic analysis that could be used in the theoretical study of complex dynamic processes emerged about the same time in the physical, engineering, and biological sciences as well as in the other social sciences. Many of the early works are briefly described in Chapter 3. The accumulation of all this – what has actually been a normal, if intermittent, outcome of the scientific enterprise – is sometimes described as a major paradigm shift in the way people now think about the world. Looking back, however, we can clearly see that there has been – at least since the early Greek philosophers – a stream of thought concerned with the unstable, divergent nature of life. These essays belong to that tradition.

As was made clear in the opening paragraphs and will be further explicated in later essays, the adaptive, evolutionary point of view is – so far as the discipline of economics is concerned – classical in its origin and was advanced by the greatest economists of the nineteenth and twentieth centuries. With the exception of Schumpeter and Keynes, however, it never competed on equal terms with the traditional emphasis on the ideas of individual optimality, interagent coordination (the balance of supply and demand), and social efficiency. Beginning with seminal contributions by Simon (1947), Alcian (1950), and Cooper (1951), a systematic basis for rethinking this emphasis was initiated. Further developments began to appear a few years later in the papers of Cyert and March, which were collected in their *Behavioral Theory of the Firm* (1963) and in two dissertations, my own, *Recursive Programming and Production Response* (1963), and Sidney Winter's *Economic Selection and the Theory of the Firm* (1964).

In 1974, a conference sponsored by the University of Wisconsin's Mathematics Research Center brought together several contributors who had emerged in the preceding decade, including Masanoi Aoki, Jean-Pierre Aubin, Sanford Grossman, Alan Kirman, Hukukane Nikaido, and Sidney Winter. This occasion provided an opportunity to set forth my own vision. Chapter 3 is the nontechnical version of that essay. At the time, it seemed that the discipline was poised for a major reorientation. Indeed, progress has continued, and now it can be said that the general approach advocated here is a major stream of economics, although sometimes under different terminological banners such as "computational," "learning," "behavioral" economics, complexity theory, or interacting agents. I will not attempt to provide a comprehensive survey of the now voluminous literature. A few selected contributions and collections, however, will indicate the extent of the ongoing work.

The volume I edited with Theodore Groves, *Adaptive Economic Models* (1975), was based on the Wisconsin conference previously mentioned.[5] I also edited a volume with Alessandro Cigno published in 1978 devoted to the recursive programming methodology. Nelson and Winter's *An Evolutionary Theory of the Firm* came out in 1982. More or less independent lines of related work exist in the fields of adaptive games, learning in micro- and macroeconomics, models of interacting agents, and especially various "Schumpeterian models" that usually involve computer simulations. Examples of books and collections of papers include Anderson, Arrow, and Pines (1988), Hanusch (1988), Heertje and Perlman (1990), Day and Chen (1993), Hodgson (1993), Dow and Earl (1999), Dopfer (2001), Punzo (2001), and Augier and March (2002).

A considerable body of literature is based on methods taken over wholesale from altogether distinct disciplines. Thus, the "system dynamics" school originated by Forrester (1961) is derived from physical conservational principles and engineering servomechanisms, while Prigogine's ideas have built on the dynamics of open physical systems far from equilibrium, i.e., those that absorb energy from – or radiate energy to – the "outside." See Prigogine (1993), also Lorenz (1963). More recent examples include Peter Albin's use of neural nets (1998) and Holland's genetic algorithms based on random crossover and recombination of strings of ones and zeros. Dawid (1999) describes how genetic algorithms have been used to model the generation of new behavioral rules in decision-making situations. For another example, Wolfgang Weidlich (2002) has exploited the master equations of thermodynamics to develop a general theory of sociodynamics, while Jean-Pierre Aubin (1997) has reoriented the pure mathematics of differential inclusions (or set valued dynamical systems), a field which he has greatly advanced, to the modeling of evolutionary systems in general and to economics in particular.

My impression is that few of these studies are based on direct observation of economic institutions or careful empirical testing using real-world data. As a result, much of this work seems to lie as far from reality as its equilibrium counterparts. Nonetheless, one must applaud the imaginative application

---

[5] The organizing committee included Jacob Marschak, Theodore Groves, and Steve Robinson.

of techniques developed in other disciplines and the resulting accretion of methods available for the study of economics. Too many examples of the successful importation of ideas from one field into another exist to discourage this practice.

My own approach evolved out of efforts to model specific development processes in particular regions and industries using direct observation and the best available data, as explained in Part II. The concept of adaptive economizing that I exploited in those studies was based on the same facts that form the basis of equilibrium economic theory: that we perceive alternative actions, that technology conditions the range of possibilities before us, that we form preferences among them, and that we try to do the best we can. But rather than assume equilibrium, I emphasized that all rational thought is conditioned by what we know about the present and past, by our hopes and expectations about the future, by our limited ability to solve the problems presented to us as life unfolds, and finally by the restraint we exercise in acting on such rational plans – restraint based not on probabilistic calculations but on the general (if not universal) advisability of caution in the face of uncertainty. In constructing these models, my collaborators and I researched the relevant trade journals concerning the technical specifications of production processes and interviewed decision makers in numerous farms and factories. Our in-depth observations and empirical results support the inference, or so it seems to me, that our approach is on the right track.

References

Albin, P. S. 1998. *Barriers and Bounds to Rationality: Essays on Economic Complexity and Dynamics of Interactive Systems.* Princeton: Princeton University Press.

Alcian, A. A. 1950. "Uncertainty, Evolution and Economic Theory." *Journal of Political Economy* 58(3):211–21.

Anderson, P. W., K. J. Arrow, and D. Pines (eds.) 1988. *The Economy as an Evolving Complex System.* Redwood City: Addison-Wesley Publishing Company, Inc.

Aubin, J. P. 1997. *Dynamic Economic Theory.* Berlin: Springer-Verlag.

Augier, M., and J. G. March (eds.) 2002. *The Economics of Choice, Change and Organization: Essays in Memory of Richard M. Cyert.* Cheltenham, UK: Edward Elgar.

Commons, J. R. 1924. *Legal Foundations of Capitalism.* New York: The Macmillan Co. Reprinted by the University of Wisconsin Press, Madison, WI, 1959.

Commons, J. R. 1950. *The Economics of Collective Action.* New York: The Macmillan Co.

Cooper, W. W. 1951. "A Proposal for Extending the Theory of the Firm." *Quarterly Journal of Economics* 65:87–109.

Cyert, R., and J. March. 1963. *The Behavioral Theory of the Firm.* Englewood Cliffs, NJ: Prentice-Hall.

Dawid, H. 1999. *Adaptive Learning by Genetic Algorithms.* 2nd Edition. Berlin: Springer-Verlag.

Day, R. H. 1963. *Recursive Programming and Production Response.* Amsterdam: North–Holland Publishing Co.

Day, R. H. 1975. "Adaptive Processes and Economic Theory." in R. Day and T. Groves (eds.) *Adaptive Economic Models.* New York: Academic Press.

Day, R. H. 1987. "The General Theory of Disequilibrium Economics and Economic Evolution." Chapter 3 in D. Batten, J. Casti, and B. Johansson (eds.) *Lecture Notes in Economics and Mathematical Systems: Economic Evolution and Structural Adjustment.* Berlin: Springer-Verlag.

Day, R. H. 1992. "Bounded Rationality and the Coevolution of Market and State." Chapter 4 in R. Day, G. Eliasson, and C. Wihlborg (eds.) *The Markets of Innovation, Ownership and Control.* Amsterdam: North-Holland in cooperation with IUI-Stockholm.

Day, R. H., and P. Chen (eds.) 1993. *Nonlinear Dynamics and Evolutionary Economics.* New York: Oxford University Press.

Day, R. H., and A. Cigno. 1978. "Modelling Economic Change: The Recursive Programming Approach." Chapter 1 in R. Day and A. Cigno (eds.) *Modelling Economic Change.* Amsterdam: Elsevier North-Holland Inc.

Dopfer, K. (ed.) 2001. *Evolutionary Economics: Program and Scope.* Boston: Kluwer Academic Publications.

Dow, S. C., and P. F. Earl (eds.) 1999. *Economics Organization and Economic Knowledge: Essays in Honor of Brian Loasby.* Volumes I and II. Cheltenham, UK: Edward Elgar.

Eliasson, G. 1996. *Firm Objectives, Controls and Organization.* Dordrecht: Kluwer Academic.

Forrester, J. W. 1961. *Industrial Dynamics.* Cambridge: MIT Press.

Hahn, F. 1973. *On the Notion of Equilibrium in Economics.* Cambridge: Cambridge University Press.

Hanusch, H. (ed.) 1988. *Evolutionary Economics: Applications of Schumpeter's Ideas.* Cambridge: Cambridge University Press.

Heertje, A., and M. Perlman (eds.) 1990. *Evolving Technology and Market Structure: Studies in Schumpeterian Economics.* Ann Arbor: University of Michigan Press.

Hodgson, G. M. 1993. *Economics and Evolution: Bringing Life Back into Economics.* Ann Arbor: University of Michigan Press.

Lorenz, E. 1963. "Deterministic Nonperiodic Flow." *Journal of the Atmospheric Sciences* Series II, 25:409–432.

Nelson, R. R., and S. G. Winter. 1964. *An Evolutionary Theory of Economic Change.* Cambridge: Harvard University Press.

North, D. C. 1990. *Institutions, Institutional Change and Economic Performance.* New York: Cambridge University Press.

Pingle, M. 1994. "Submitting to Authority: An Experimental Examination of Its Effect on Decision-Making." Unpublished manuscript.

Pingle, M. 1995. "Imitation versus Rationality: An Experimental Perspective on Decision-Making." *Journal of Socioeconomics* 24(2):281–315.

Prigogine, I. 1993. "Bounded Rationality: From Dynamical Systems to Socio-economic Models." Chapter 1 in R. Day and P. Chen (eds.) *Nonlinear Dynamics and Evolutionary Economics*. New York: Oxford University Press.

Punzo, L. F. (ed.) 2001. *Cycles, Growth and Structural Change: Theories and Empirical Evidence*. New York: Routledge.

Simon, H. A. 1947. *Administrative Behavior*. New York: Free Press.

Winter, S. G. 1964. "Economic Natural Selection and the Theory of the Firm." *Yale Economics Essays* 4:225–72.

PART ONE

GLOBAL TRENDS AND ADAPTIVE ECONOMICS

TWO

Global Trends, World Models,
and Human Adaptation

Warnings set forth by many scientists and popular pundits that an over-crowded, poisoned, and exhausted earth lies in wait for our grandchildren, perhaps even for our children, and our own old age are shrouded in controversy. Technological optimists, pointing to the accomplishments of the past, look for new materials and sources of energy; economic optimists, pointing to the amazing records of past growth and to the theoretical efficiencies of perfect competition, look for the market economy to induce appropriate technological changes and resource substitutions; social and political optimists, pointing to mankind's seemingly limitless adaptability, look for government policies, social reorganization, and modifications of individual behavior to alleviate problems as they arise.[1]

At various times and places in the world, however, local situations have approximated on a relatively small scale the conditions warned of by contemporary Cassandras. Certain well-known cities of the world have long been regarded as hideously overcrowded. Others have for short periods experienced alarming death rates from polluted air and water. The energy crisis has brought the potential effects of resource exhaustion home to people everywhere, and rapid, seemingly uncontrollable inflation reminds us that the

---

[1] Tobin and Nordhaus (1972), Kaysen (1972), Solow (1973).

Reprinted with permission from *General Systems Theorizing: An Assessment and Prospects for the Future*. Proceedings of the 1976 Annual North American Meeting, The Society for General Systems Research, Washington, DC. An early version of this paper, "Investment in New Technology and Social Change," was presented at the University of Bonn in the spring of 1968 and subsequently in a German version at the 20th International Economic Days, Vienna, 10 June 1968. It was written at the University of Göttingen when I was a Fulbright Lecturer and Visiting Professor on leave from the University of Wisconsin. The present version was written in 1975 while I was a visiting scholar in the Economics Department, Harvard University.

stable development of complex economies can scarcely be taken for granted. Even if – as some argue – crash programs for resource conservation, pollution abatement, and population control do not yet seem warranted, it is long since obvious that a better understanding of the global state of mankind is needed and that improved methods for projecting long-run development should receive high-priority attention.

These remarks outline some of the facts and issues of global development and suggest their relationship to the problems of change and to the methods appropriate for its study and control.

2.1 Past Trends in Global Development

It is now widely recognized that the economic development of mankind, conceived in its broadest terms, has proceeded through four more or less distinct epochs:

I. The food-collecting epoch preceding the development of the bladed tool about 50,000 B.C.;

II. The age of the hunting band, which gave way to civilization around 10,000 years ago when plants and animals were domesticated;

III. The agriculture-urban age involving the organized production of food and artifacts and a settling of people into farms or farming villages and cities;

IV. The scientific-industrial revolution of the past several centuries characterized by a radical increase in agricultural and industrial production using machines, mechanical power, and scientific methods of cultivation, husbandry, and fabrication.[2]

Each of these epochs involved an increase in food production and population. Prior to the domestication of plants and animals, the human population grew so slowly that, had it continued to grow as it had for millennia, it would have reached a total in our own time of a mere four or five million. With the establishment of agriculture, however, a new epoch of population growth ensued. Given humanity's dependence on animal power and its own labor – a dependence that continued throughout the Renaissance – the population during this age of agriculture and urbanization grew to about

---

[2] Sampedro (1967), Cipolla (1975).

140 million. Had this age continued, and on the assumption that it had not spread to the Western hemisphere, the population would not have surpassed 150 million or so by now. This is nonetheless a thirty- or fortyfold increase in human numbers compared with the age of hunting and fishing. During the fifteenth and sixteenth centuries, agriculture and city life spread to the New World. At the same time the foundations for the Industrial Revolution were laid in Europe. As it unfolded, population growth experienced a marked acceleration in part because of the extension of the urban-agriculture system to the new lands and partly because of the massive increase in agricultural productivity made possible by the Industrial Revolution.[3]

Malthus, writing early in the nineteenth century, estimated that the world population was about one billion and that it was doubling about once every quarter century. The latter figure overestimated the actual growth rate, which at the time was closer to a doubling every half century. The Malthusian figure has nearly been reached in our own time though. Indeed, recent figures stagger the mind; the world population is approaching a total of 4 billion at a rate of some 5000 net additions per hour![4]

The awesome nature of this phenomenon can perhaps be put into perspective best by shifting from a historical to an astronomical time scale. In the last decades, astronomers, through the most exacting kind of observation and calculation, have arrived at a theory of stellar evolution that tells us, among other things, that our own solar system came into being about four and a half billion years ago and that it has about an equal time before it perishes.[5] That theory is not our concern, but if we measure population from this astronomical perspective – from the beginning of the earth to the projected end of life on earth as we know it – we obtain the diagram shown in Figure 2.1.[6]

The long, slow, steady ascent of humankind from straggling bands of humanoids through all the great civilizations that have risen and

---

[3] Deevey (1971).

[4] Malthus ([1817] 1963).

[5] Jastrow (1967), Meadows (1967).

[6] In the intervening years since this essay was written, population has continued to explode: from the roughly 3.8 billion in 1975 to some 6.4 billion in 2002. On the scale shown, the spike is now well above the box, but the addition of one-third of a century to the width of the spike cannot be discerned. All the other trends mentioned have increased similarly. The controversy mentioned concerning global warming is still not resolved, but the energy crisis has reemerged, and attempts to deal with it are accelerating. The several stages of growth mentioned in the text are the subject of Chapter 10.

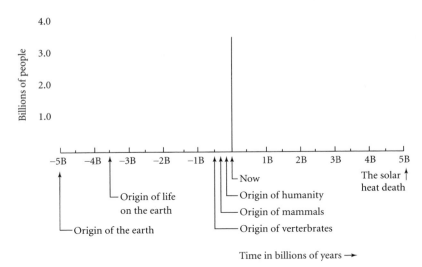

Figure 2.1. The human population explosion.

declined – indeed, the evolution of humanity and all the great epochs of its history and prehistory – are mere details disguised within the thickness of a vertical line!

Trends measuring economic activity, plotted on a similar scale, would have essentially the same shape: that of spikes whose height would for the most part be associated with the last century alone. Let us comment briefly on some of the more important of these trends.

The world production of crude oil and other fossil fuels is associated with, and underlies, similar trends in industrialization – the substitution of me-chanical power for animal power, the great reduction in manpower require-ments for producing food, and the migration of people from rural to urban settings. All of this amounts to an indirect industrialization of agriculture. Products manufactured in various industrial sectors use resources drawn from outside agriculture that are substituted for farm-produced inputs and rural labor. The resulting substitutions have taken place with amazing speed. For example, the tractorization of farming in the United States took a mere two decades. It displaced a primary source of power on which agriculture had been dependent for several centuries. A similar process has already been completed or is under way in many other parts of the world.[7]

---

[7] Pratt (1971, p. 243).

A corresponding expansion in world food production that enabled per capita food consumption to increase slightly for a time, even in the face of rapidly rising population, was associated with the "Green Revolution," which got under way in the United States a decade or two before it spread elsewhere. The increase, however, was temporary, and in spite of it the world as a whole has barely more than is needed for good nutrition. Industrialization and the growth in agricultural output notwithstanding, at least half of the world's population lives in calorie-deficient areas or on the edge of starvation even in the absence of unusual droughts.[8]

A trend of special interest is the one for fertilizers. Nitrogen fertilizers have been manufactured increasingly from ammonia compounds synthesized from natural gas whose growth trend is essentially like that for petroleum. But natural gas is also a major input for heating, power generation, plastics, and synthetic rubber. From this it is seen that recent developments have not only increased agriculture's dependence on the nonagricultural economy but have placed it in the position of competing for resources used for entirely different and essentially more luxury-oriented purposes. Exhaustion of these resources is, therefore, a threat to affluence and to basic subsistence levels.

Although industrialization has done little to raise the global standard of living measured in calories on the average, it has involved a greatly accelerated trend in the urbanization of the world's population. The dependence of the city on agriculture should be clear; although agriculture may decline in political importance, the inverted pyramid of people in cities who depend on it grows larger and larger. McC. Adams tells us that urbanization closely followed the introduction of agriculture and that changes in agricultural productivity were directly related to the size and sophistication of cities.[9] As noted earlier in this section, traditional agriculture alone made possible a thirty-to-fortyfold increase in population. We also know, through the work for example, of Lynn White, that the development of horse mechanization (made possible by the horse collar), the three-field rotation system, and the introduction of the potato had a great deal to do with the rise of the city in Northern Europe. This laid the foundation for the extension of the Renaissance to England, France, and Germany, which in turn paved the way for the Industrial Revolution and the growth that followed.[10] Even if we measure

---

[8] Revelle (1974).
[9] McC. Adams (1968).
[10] White (1962).

urbanization by counting cities of over 100,000 population, the trend of urbanization is pronounced.[11] Evidently, rapidly increasing numbers of the world's poor and undernourished are located in highly concentrated urban environments.

Pollution has always been a major problem for humankind. On the one hand, we are reminded that much improvement had taken place within the nineteenth century in developing waste disposal systems – an improvement that may have had as much influence on declining death rates as medical advances.[12] On the other hand, sources of pollution entirely overlooked before have now been discovered. The effect of pesticides and mercury on animal life was dramatized by Carson. The feedback to humans about which she warned has now been experienced prominently in several parts of the world. Greatly complicating the picture is the fact that some new "advanced" technologies with great potential for reducing shortages add to rather than subtract from the problem. For example, nuclear wastes are growing at a rapid rate and could pose problems millennia hence.[13]

Two additional trends in environmental pollution have been observed and represent real and potential economic threats that are serious. These are the accumulated quantities of carbon dioxide and particulate matter in the air. The former is thought to cause general heating of the atmosphere. A possible consequence is recession of the polar ice cap and flooding of major coastal cities throughout the world.[14] Particulate matter is thought to cause atmospheric cooling and thus a possible return of Ice Age conditions in the temperate zones and extensive drought in subtropical regions.[15] Evidence that global warming is winning out over the cooling effects of particulate matter appears to be growing. Although highly controversial, these hypotheses must be taken seriously and the possible implications for world agriculture and industry studied.

The global trends in population, production, resource utilization, urbanization, agricultural industrialization, pollution, and climate lead to a far different view of future development than is obtained by a single-minded projection of the last century's trends. It is comforting but probably misleading to look at past technological advance as a harbinger of future panaceas

---

[11] Davis (1971, p. 270).

[12] Sampedro (1967).

[13] AEC (1971). (Although some of the planned expansion of atomic power was abandoned, it remains nonetheless one of the major environmental problems.)

[14] Plass (1971).

[15] Bryson (1974).

for accumulating economic ills. The magnitude of the problem is greater than ever before, and the rate of technological discovery can scarcely be guaranteed to come in time – especially without consummate effort now and in the coming years. Great civilizations have declined and disappeared before. The extent to which these events were due to problems like those we face is unknown, but this factor is probably not trivial.[16] In any case, it is virtually certain that we face a protracted period of rapidly changing economic, social, and political structures throughout the world as accommodation is made – for better or for worse – to the past trends in global development summarized here.

2.2 The World Modeling Controversy

Malthus observed the trend toward geometric growth in population, postulated eventually decreasing returns, and deduced an eventual decline in real wages and the approach of a stationary state. His argument dominated decades of thinking about long-run development. But it appeared to be discredited by events of the nineteenth and twentieth centuries – so much so that "disparagement of the Malthusian doctrine [became] as common as praise had been before."[17]

At various times a concern with the deleterious effects of growth did command attention. The conservation movement established national parks and forests in an effort to preserve a part of the natural environment. In the post–World War II period, development economists concerned with underdeveloped countries focused on overpopulation and the "Malthusian trap."[18] As the Green Revolution became established in some of the most impoverished countries, however, interest in the neo-Malthusian literature faded. Economists, especially economic theorists, resumed their preoccupation with balanced, essentially endless growth.[19]

The new Cassandras – the "Ecossandras" – with their ecological point of view did achieve a widespread impact on public thinking, although many (if not most) economists continued to ignore their warnings. Carson's *Silent Spring*, Ehrlich's *Population Bomb*, Commoner's *Closing Circle*, and a host of others appeared. But when the National Bureau of Economic Research

---

[16] Marsh (1965).
[17] Blaug (1963).
[18] Leibenstein (1954), Buttrick (1960), Neidhans (1963).
[19] This work stems first from von Neuman (1937); the exegesis by Dorfman, Samuelson, and Solow (1958); and even more from the extremely simple model of Solow (1956). The standard text is Burmeister and Dobell (1970).

celebrated its fiftieth anniversary by commissioning a work titled *Economic Growth* by James Tobin and William Nordhaus, the result was an excellent study based on mainstream growth theory and econometrics that found "no reason to limit growth" and no need to modify the orthodox economist's "unlimited growth" paradigm.[20]

Then, Forrester's *World Dynamics* (1971) appeared and *The Limits to Growth* by the Meadows, J. Randers, and W. Behrens III (1972). These works, written by members of MIT's system dynamics group, returned to the classical practice of treating population as an endogenous variable and, in addition, incorporated exhaustible resources and pollution feedbacks. The "world models" use nonlinear difference equations to represent the dynamic development process but express them in the unique system dynamics language developed by Forrester in his earlier works. The results are not unlike those of classical economic development theory. They are even more dramatic because the new models incorporate exhaustible resources and pollution explicitly together with highly nonlinear functions rarely found in orthodox economic models. In their standard mode, intended to represent behavioral patterns of the nineteenth century, the models display a continued rise in population and material growth for about fifty years, then peak and begin a decline, returning, after a hundred years or so, to their early twentieth-century levels.

Experiments with the models indicate that a concerted policy that would yield zero population growth, zero net-capital formation, increased use-life and recycling of commodities, increased resource productivity, and reduced pollution emissions would allow a slowly diminishing growth for a century or more converging to a more or less sustainable stationary state.

These publications raised a storm of controversy – first in the popular press and then in the general intellectual and specialized professional journals. Critics attacked the methodology, the assumptions. and the conclusions of the work. This is not the place to review this literature, for this has been done elsewhere.[21] What is worth noting is the uniform response by prestigious economists who reviewed the work. That response was universally negative.

Criticisms were not groundless. There are various shortcomings in the model. But because the model is essentially an elaboration of classical growth theory and yields similar, if more dramatic, results leads one to ask why the

[20] Tobin and Nordhaus (1972).
[21] Day and Koeing (1974a) and Day and Koeing (1974b).

reaction should be so strong. My own conclusion is that, although some of the assumptions may be suspect, when classical (or neoclassical) economic growth models are modified to accommodate the additional variables considered by Forrester and Meadows et al., similar results will flow from them: namely, that only under optimistic assumptions about technological change, population control, pollution abatement, and resource conservation can long-run economic decline be averted.

From a methodological point of view, Forrester et al.'s models are multiadaptor systems based on switches and rules in which purposive behavior is servomechanistic.[22] The functioning of markets, prices, and financial intermediation and the modeling of explicit economizing (or suboptimizing) on the part of agents received little explicit consideration. Economists will therefore find copious opportunities to produce model improvements that will lead to a more realistic representation of the world economy in this way enhancing the credibility of long-run projections.

Until we economists do these things, we must admit that the world modeling studies are – with the exception of a small underground neo-Malthusian cadre[23] – the first serious attempts to study the classical problems of economic growth and decline with population endogenous for a very long time. They created a new "magnificent dynamics" (Baumol 1951) probably more "classical" and certainly more relevant by far than most economists are now willing to admit.

2.3 Problems of Adaptation

The first concern of living systems is homeostasis: the maintenance of critical variables within the boundaries that define existence or survival. Humanity in its economic activity can be no exception. Yet humans, like other species, may fail. Individuals who fail to adapt effectively to changing circumstances die or live unpleasant lives. The same is true of populations or of entire species. The behavioral problems faced by an individual are complicated not only by the complex set of interdependencies among his or her kind but also by the accumulated effects, transmitted through the environment, of predecessors' past activities. For example, overpopulation leading to overgrazing may destroy the environment of a ruminant species to such an extent

---

[22] See Day (1975) for definitions of multiadaptive systems of switches and rules.
[23] See note 17.

that effective adaptation is eventually foreclosed.[24] Humanity, however, is armed with an instrument that vastly extends its ability to cope with its impoverished inheritance. It is the synthetic faculty of mind that enables us to discover and to invent new activities that expand the inventory of resources we can exploit.

Some students of ecology argue that the behavior of many animal species serves to limit population so that an optimum relationship is maintained between the population and the resources that sustain it. The average product per individual is at a maximum. In this way the chance of maintaining homeostasis is maximized. Wynne-Edwards asserts that the cultural patterns of primitive human groups evolved that way, but the effect of civilization and its rapid cultural evolution broke down the primitive barriers that limited population growth and resulted in runaway human expansion.[25] If that is so, then runaway expansion has been sustained by runaway economic growth. During the course of this explosive development, specific resources in specific localities have been exhausted. The resulting scarcities probably contributed to a temporary abatement of economic expansion or even to the demise or decline of the resource-dependent populations. But inventive activity has in effect created new resources to replace those used up, and the process of expansion has been renewed, often in the hands of a new, formerly less fortunately endowed group. Consequently, homeostasis for the species as a whole has been maintained, not through the control of numbers as in more primitive beings but through the evolution of technology. Humanity has, in short, become dependent on inventive genius and on the socioeconomic infrastructures within which inventive activity flourishes.

The conception of economic growth provided by orthodox theory is quite different. Resource exhaustion and the corresponding great waves or epochs of economic activity are not accommodated within its borders. Instead, balanced, intertemporally efficient growth of capital stocks, accumulating in harmony with an exponentially growing population, sustained by perfectly competitive prices, and maximizing a utility function defined over an infinite horizon is the picture presented in the economic growth theory.[26]

---

[24] Hardin (1968).
[25] Wynne-Edwards (1962).
[26] See note 19.

These theories may in fact effectively describe economic growth in societies well endowed with resources, for there appears to be a pervasive tendency for societies to grow and exploit resources as fast as possible. When, however, resource exhaustion is close enough to affect perception, a more general model is required – one that includes the foresight of resource exhaustion, the control of population, and limitations on affluence.

A model based on discounting future values but incorporating exhaustible resources will generate trajectories that have the initial appearance of exponential growth at a maximal rate.[27] But they must eventually pass into minimal exponential decay. The path as a whole must look much like the typical bell-shaped exploitation curve for a single resource.[28] The only way our strategic choices can then be prevented from leading to the impoverishment of unborn generations is through inventive activity. That alone makes possible indefinite or renewed expansion. Then, if we also discount the past, as we do the future, we and our descendants will be happy with the results. That is, the destruction of past ways of life that comes to pass as old technology gives way to new will be looked upon by most people not with regret but with satisfaction.

If, however, technological advance should diminish so much that contraction eventually sets in, then the benign feelings of the living generation for the past may give way to bitter regret. Previous growth, looked upon as optimal by the living generation's predecessors, will be thought of as nonoptimal or pessimal just as unfortunate heirs may regret the plundering of their inheritance by profligate parents or relatives. So it seems that the optimizing individual may be deceived in believing that what he or she does now is in the best interest of future generations. To put the matter another way, what we call optimal growth may better be called *deceptively optimal growth*.

The beauty of the market mechanism, at least in theory, is that it appears to support optimal growth without centralized direction. Some equilibrium economists and free market enthusiasts argue that the market brings about a state of economic efficiency with no social control behind it. When inefficiencies arise, or resources appear to be exploited too fast, their remedy is to create new markets with the appropriate mechanisms to cause externalities

---

[27] The type of utility function used in such strategic planning methods assumes a discounting of future values that biases choices toward the satisfaction of present or near future generations.

[28] Hubbert (1969).

to be internalized and social efficiency restored – again without direct social control.[29]

However, if there is a tendency for private purpose to follow deceptively optimal adaptation, it may be necessary to overlay private purpose and the market system with institutions through which a public purpose is formed that will regulate present economic activity in the interest of generations yet unborn. Indeed that is exactly what has been done. Technological inventiveness has been sponsored. At the same time, exploitation of existing resources has been restrained and population expansion discouraged. These institutions must be insulated from the rationality of those who guide their actions by deceptively optimal strategies and who oppose policies aimed at very-long-run goals on grounds that such policies are irrational or suboptimal.

That public purpose can be established within a society dedicated to individual freedom is demonstrated in our own. In America great domains of grasslands, forests, and minerals have been placed under public control. Pressures to release them from the public domain and allow their exploitation for present enterprise illustrate the inevitable tension between future-oriented and present-oriented deceptively optimal strategies.

The resolution of this inherent conflict by the establishment of socialism is no guarantee that future-oriented strategies will be pursued. Indeed, many socialist planning models incorporate time preferences in just the way Bohm-Bawerk said characterized impatience and Ramsey said characterized immorality in man. Evidently, a socialist state – like a capitalist one – must develop special institutions whose primary function is to protect the future from the present. Ironically, the Democratic, capitalist countries' records in this regard are significantly better than are those of the socialist or formerly socialist ones.

In any event the problems of global development no longer appear to be local. In former times the exhaustion of forests may have led to the decline of maritime civilizations. But later, those who were able to employ appropriate technology for the exploitation of coal and iron could send great navies to every corner of the earth. Great powers have come and gone; the flow of economic activity has waxed and waned. Nonetheless, until now, the general trend of populations and economic development has been ever accelerating expansion.

---

[29] For example, see Goldman (1972).

Now the great economic powers draw on the global supply of resources. The interdependencies among nations have led to the rapid, worldwide diffusion of technology, crowding out primitive peoples who fail to adapt and establishing industry and industrialized agriculture everywhere. Accompanying these trends is the growing dependence on, and competition for, nonrenewable resources. The developed nations, seeing their own resources decline, urge others to conserve. Those others, throwing off the constraining customs of traditional culture rapidly assume the goals of resource-intensive development.

Can the world, in its uneven state of advancement, with its conflict of local interests, evolve a world purpose to stand as guardian of the world's future given the desire for economic expansion? Can nations recognize and effectively pursue long-run well-being for the species as a whole without massively destructive conflict that would destroy all semblance of well-being in the short run? These are the fundamental problems of what we may call *whole-earth economics*.

If these problems are to be solved, the way people really adapt and the way economies really work must be better understood. Adaptive economics and simulation concepts may help in building that understanding. It may be that the modes of behavior presently pursued are not optimal but deceptively optimal and maladaptive. If that is the case, as current world modelers already argue, we must find this out in a convincing enough fashion to motivate a successful search for new strategies more suited to benefit our heirs.

References

AEC. 1971. U.S. Atomic Energy Commission. *Forecast of Growth of Nuclear Power.* Washington, DC: U.S. Government Printing Office.

Baumol, W. J. 1951. *Economic Dynamics.* New York: The Macmillan Co.

Blaug, M. 1963. "Introduction" in Irwin Paperback Classics in Economics, edition of Malthus. *An Essay in the Principles of Population.* Homewood, IL: Richard D. Irwin, Inc.

Bryson, R. 1974. "World Climate and World Food Systems III: The Lessons of Climatic History." IES Report 27. Madison, WI: University of Wisconsin, November.

Burmeister, E., and R. Dobell. 1970. *Mathematical Theories of Economic Growth.* London: The Macmillan Co.

Buttrick, J. 1960. "A Note on Growth Theory." *Economic Development and Cultural Change* 9:75–82.

Cipolla, C. 1975. *Economic History of World Population.* Penguin Paperback Co.

Daly, K. (ed.) 1973. *Toward a Steady-State Economy.* San Francisco: W. H. Freeman and Co.

Davis, K. 1971. "The Urbanization of the Human Population." *Scientific American* September 1965. Collected in P. Ehrlich, J. Holdren, and R. Holm (eds.) *Man and the Ecosphere.* San Francisco: W. H. Freeman and Co.

Day, R. H. 1975. "Adaptive Processes and Economic Theory," Chapter 1 in Day, R. H. and T. Groves, *Adaptive Economic Models,* New York: Academic Press.

Day, R., and E. Koenig. 1974a. "Malthusia: Population and Economic Growth in the Preindustrial State." Social Systems Research Institute. Workshop Paper. Madison, WI: University of Wisconsin.

Day, R., and E. Koenig, 1974b. "Population Growth and Capital Accumulation in a Malthusian Economy." Social Systems Research Institute. Workshop Paper No. 7415. Madison, WI: University of Wisconsin.

Deevey, E. S., Jr. 1971. "The Human Population." *Scientific American* September. Collected in P. Ehrlich, J. Holdren, and R. Holm (eds.) *Man and the Ecosphere.* San Francisco: W. H. Freeman and Co.

Dorfman, R., P. Samuelson, and R. Solow. 1958. *Linear Programming and Economic Analysis.* New York: McGraw-Hill.

Forrester, J. 1971. *World Dynamics.* Cambridge: Wright-Allen Press.

Goldman, M. 1972. *Ecology and Economics: Controlling Pollution in the 70s.* Englewood Cliffs, NJ: Prentice-Hall.

Hardin, G. 1968. "The Tragedy of the Commons." *Science* 162:1243–48.

Hubbert, M. 1969. "Energy Resources," in *National Academy of Sciences, Resources and Man.* San Francisco: W. H. Freeman and Co.

Jastrow, R. 1967. *Red Giants and White Dwarfs: Man's Descent from the Stars.* Chicago: The New American Library.

Kaysen, K. 1972. "The Computer that Printed Out W*O*L*f'." *Foreign Affairs* July: 660–68.

Leibenstein, H. 1954. *A Theory of Economic–Demographic Development.* Princeton: Princeton University Press.

Malthus, T. R. 1817. *An Essay on the Principles of Population.* Homewood: Richard D. Irwin, Inc., 1963.

Marsh, G. P. 1965. *Man and Nature* (originally published in 1864). Cambridge: The Belknap Press of Harvard University Press.

McC. Adams, R. 1968. "The Natural History of Urbanism." In *Fitness of Man's Environment.* New York: Smithsonian Institute.

Meadows, A. J. 1967. *Stellar Evolution.* London: Pergamon Press, Ltd.

Meadows, D. L., D. H. Meadows, J. Randers, and W. Behman III. 1972. *The Limits to Growth.* New York: Universe Books.

Neidhans, J. 1963. "Economic Growth with Two Endogenous Factors." *Quarterly Journal of Economics* 77:359–71.

Plass, G. N. 1971. "Carbon Dioxide and Climate." *Scientific American* July 1959. Collected in P. Ehrlich, J. Holdren, and R. Holm (eds.) *Man and the Ecosphere.* San Francisco: W. H. Freeman and Co.

Pratt, G. N. 1971. "Chemical Fertilizers." *Scientific American* June 1964. Collected in P. Ehrlich, J. Holdren, and R. Holm (eds.) *Man and the Ecosphere.* San Francisco: W. H. Freeman and Co.

Revelle, R. 1974. "Food and Population," *Scientific American* September:161–70.

Sampedro, J. 1967. *Decisive Forces in World Economics*. Translated by S. E. Nodder. New York: McGraw-Hill.

Solow, R. M. 1973. "Is the End of the World at Hand?" *Challenge*. March–April: 39–50.

Tobin, J., and W. Nordhaus. 1972. *Economic Growth*. New York: Columbia University Press.

White, L. 1962. *Medieval Technology and Social Change*. Oxford: Oxford University Press.

Wynne-Edwards, V. C. 1962. *Animal Dispersion in Relation to Social Behavior*. New York: Hafner Publishing Co., Inc.

THREE

Adaptive Economic Theory and Modeling

The current controversy over energy policy and the apparent suddenness with which abundant supplies turn to scarcity and back again to (at least temporary) gluts – not to mention a host of other pressing economic problems like stagflation – have brought to the fore a need to improve our understanding of how the present economy works and how it can and should be controlled or modified. This chapter outlines the essential features of a diversely developing but more or less coherent approach to this task, which may be called *adaptive economics*, and illustrates some salient insights it affords. I begin by describing some facts of economic life that must be dealt with by a credible economic theory: typical trajectories that must be explained and characteristics of economic structure that must be accommodated. Before turning to a discussion of the theory itself, I pause to explain what adaptive economics is, not to contrast its content with some erroneous interpretations, and to establish its place in the development of economic thought. I then outline basic concepts of adaptation and evolution and summarize the primary ingredients that must be a part of an adaptive economic theory. This is followed by a brief discussion of one class of models incorporating adaptive features and generating the types of trajectories it is a part of our purpose to explain. The chapter concludes with some general

This chapter is based on R. H. Day, "Adaptive Theory and Modeling: A Review," in E. Castle (ed.), Contemporary Issues in Natural Resource Economics, Copyright 1978, with permission from Resources for the Future. It contains ideas that have arisen in diverse scientific contexts and that have been expressed by many authors in one way or another. I have not tried to track down their origins, but many of them must inevitably arise more or less spontaneously in the development of dynamic economic models – at least that has been my experience. I hope their appearance here constitutes for the reader a new and useful synthesis. I have incorporated material published elsewhere in Day (1975), Day and Singh (1977), and Day and Cigno (1978). The support of the Electric Power Research Institute is also acknowledged.

observations about the nature of economic change and policy that the point of view advocated here seems to suggest.

3.1 Facts of Economic Life: Trajectories and Structures

Over time, economic trajectories exhibit one or more of several characteristic patterns of change such as growth, decay, or oscillation. As we know, world population and certain aggregate indexes of economic activity, such as energy use, have displayed a generally increasing growth mode for millennia. Within this broad pattern, constituent variables have exhibited cycles or fluctuations of varying amplitudes and durations. Perhaps after themselves exhibiting periods of growth or oscillation, other variables have decayed. Examples are textile production in New England, food production using animal draft power, and the supply of energy from windmills. Many formerly important economic activities have disappeared altogether. Such decay and demise have, from archeological evidence, characterized various long-vanished economies – indeed, entire cultures and civilizations. The pre-Colombian societies provide one class of examples (Culbert 1973).

Complicating the empirical picture are the overlapping waves of activity: sequences of growth, decay, and demise that occur beneath the surface of aggregate growth as new technology is introduced, competes with already established technology, rises to dominance, and is replaced gradually by still newer modes of production or consumption. An example of such a wavelike pattern is provided by the components of energy supply.

Originally, in food collecting and primitive agricultural societies, human muscle furnished most of the energy for production and consumption. Next, animal draft power, wind, and wood-fueled fire were dominant sources of power – all directly or indirectly based on renewable solar energy sources. In the course of the Industrial Revolution, coal and water power began to take over. Then petroleum emerged as a dominant source of energy. Now atomic energy is slowly expanding, and we are witnessing a switch back to coal and to renewable solar energy sources.

The point is that economic change rarely exhibits balanced growth – except in highly aggregated variables and when important declining variables are omitted. Instead, it is characterized by advances, declines, and counterpoints of growth and decay. Economic historians have emphasized an aspect of economic change closely related to these waves of activity and with very broad significance for an understanding of economic change over long periods. These are epochs characterized by specific types of activity and dominated by specific types of constraints called development stages, which switch from time to time, leading to a succession of distinctly different regimes that vary in structure and behavior.

Thus the various historical theories of growth in which economies were held to pass through a unique, small number of stages in an immutable order are refuted, but the grain of truth they recognize is the existence of periods of development distinctly different from others with more or less abrupt switches among them. To distinguish them from the notion of immutably sequenced stages and to follow conventional mathematical parlance, we call these periods *phases*.

Econometricians acknowledge the existence of phase switching by selecting data for certain historical periods that exclude specific years or subperiods for estimating model parameters. The idea is that the model equations do not represent the economy being studied during these subperiods, which may be war years, years of hyperinflation or depression, or periods of exceedingly rapid technological change. It is usually thought that using data for these "exceptional" periods will bias estimates of the "normal structure." Clearly, the idea implicit in this practice is that the structural equations which govern the behavior of the economy in these "exceptional" periods are different than those that govern in the "normal" periods.

The demands to be made of adaptive economic theory are accordingly that it incorporate multiphase behavior and generate phase switching endogenously, thus making it possible to explain rich patterns of development that involve changes in underlying dynamic structure.

3.2 What Adaptive Economics Is Not and What It Is

Before considering the ingredients of adaptive economics it may be a good idea to put down any attempts to resurrect social Darwinism – a philosophy based on the idea that evolutionary forces of competition and selection bring about "best fitness" to the environment in the biological world and that these forces, if properly reproduced, can bring about an optimal state of adaptiveness in the human sphere.

That evolution can achieve truly astonishing feats is readily apparent to the most casual observation and is a fact beautifully summarized in Jacques Monod's observation that evolution is blind yet has produced vision! But evolution has also produced and discarded more species than now exist. Proceeding as it does in the biological world by varying trials and errors, evolution produces local, temporary adaptedness at best – more or less improving fitness sometimes – and frequent monstrosities, anachronisms, and extinctions much of the time. Our interest in adaptive economics, therefore, must surely not be motivated by a desire to mimic in human affairs the blind, profligate, and callous mechanism that governs other species but rather to understand better and to make possible the more effective participation of human intellect in the evolutionary process that governs life in general and conditions human affairs in particular.

Moreover, our interest in extending economic theory and modeling methodology should not be construed as an iconoclastic attack on traditional economics. Indeed, concepts of adaptation, evolution, and economy have been intertwined throughout their development. Adam Smith's concept of a market within which agents pursue their self-interest to their mutual benefit, perhaps *the* central theme of economics, is in its classical form a dynamic concept involving some of the essential features of adaptive processes. Even Walras's formalization of the theory, which focuses on competitive equilibrium (in our terms, on a state of adaptedness), retains, in the concept of *tâtonnement* (a groping adjustment process), an explicitly adaptive character. Marshall's treatment of the market economy also incorporates several adaptive features. Replete with biological analogies, it describes the process by which low-cost firms drive out high-cost competitors, how firms adapt to the market environment by adjusting investment to prevailing quasi rents, and how marginal changes carried out in disequilibrium converge to long-run equilibrium through a series of temporary, short-run adjustments. Marshall's conception of market dynamics is a direct descendent of Malthus's "struggle for existence" that inspired Darwin at precisely the time the neoclassical school was formalizing the classical concept of market economy.

But, in fact, the adaptive and evolutionary character of economic dynamics has in this century received much less attention than statics. Both Walras and Marshall are remembered primarily for their contributions to static equilibrium theory. In modern terms, equilibrium theory begins with axioms of rationality and focuses on the existence and welfare characteristics of equilibria. As a model of the real world, equilibrium theory underplays the complexity of technology, overplays the rationality and knowledge of households and firms, and exaggerates the efficiency of markets. It is designed for comparative statics – the study of how equilibria vary with parametric changes in the data of the problem. It is essentially a theory of economic processes in a state of adaptiveness. Adaptive economics, on the other hand, begins not with structures of rationality and equilibrium but with an assumption that change evolves from current conditions. It focuses on the economizing of partially informed agents whose transactions are imperfectly coordinated; who use various adaptive procedures such as servomechanisms, behavioral learning rules, suboptimization with feedback, and the like; and whose numbers, activities, rules of behavior, and organization evolve. Adaptive economics is primarily the study of how economies adapt when the actions of individuals and institutions are not perfectly coordinated and, secondarily, whether or not, and if so how, equilibria or states of adaptiveness are achieved.

Lotka (1924) regarded economics as a branch of biology, which is a view that should be followed to the point of recognizing in human activity the forces of adaptation and evolution that apply universally to living things: the reaction to changing environmental states without the benefit of clairvoyance or omniscience, the finite lives and changing numbers of players in the game, and the mechanisms of competition and selection to which all biological activity is subject. Yet the way these forces work themselves out in human activity in general, and economic activity in particular, is in many important respects unique. Biological analogies may be suggestive, and in some cases biological models will be directly applicable (see for example, Lloyd, Rapport, and Turner 1975), but economic models must go well beyond biological analogies and indeed may subsume many aspects of human nature shared by other species to focus on those aspects of development characteristic of humankind. In this endeavor models of rational economizing and exchange must be expected to play a continuing central role.

We would be equally mistaken, however, if we were to turn Lotka's order around in an attempt to explain biological facts solely by means of orthodox equilibrium economics. For example, an attempt has been made to augment the sociobiological explanation of the emergence of altruism with economic utilitarianism (Becker 1976), but this is tantamount to explaining one evolutionary artifact by another, when indeed the problem is to explain how both emerged, how they are related (if at all), and what competitive advantage each lends its possessor. To summarize, what is needed and what we propose is not an entirely new field but a new synthesis of biological and economic concepts and an extension and reinterpretation of existing economic theory.

3.3 Adaptation and Evolution

3.3.1 Adaptation as an Agent–Environment Interaction

Beginning with the observation that economic events exhibit change and development, adaptive economics takes as its first axiom that economic experience is determined by a system of cause and effect in which the change in the system at any time is governed by its state at that time. Adaptive economics proceeds by decomposing the system into two parts: one representing the behavior of a part of the process of special interest, which we may call – quite arbitrarily – the *agent*, and the other representing all other parts of reality, which we call – equally arbitrarily – the *environment*. Adaptation may then be defined as the agent's adjustment to the environment or, more generally, as the interaction of agent and environment. The agent may be a person, a household, a firm, a group of firms, or even an entire economy as determined by the purpose at hand. The agent, therefore, must be understood here to be a purely formal entity. The output of the agent is called an act. It is based on the current output of the environment and the agent's past act. The mechanism that connects inputs and outputs may be called an *adaptor*. Likewise, the environment generates an output we may call an *environmental state*. This is derived from an input consisting of the previous state and the agent's act through a mechanism, which we may call a transitor or *environmental operator*. We arrive in this way at the concept of an *adapting system* consisting of an interacting adaptor and transitor (agent and environment).

3.3.2 Systems of Adaptors

The environment of a given economic agent includes other agents, and the agent may be thought of – insofar as its actual mode of behavior is concerned – as a collection of coordinated adaptive functions. In this way one arrives at the concept of a system of adaptors. There are three distinct but closely related types of such systems. These are (1) the adapting economy, (2) the adapting organization, and (3) the adapting algorithm.

The adaptive economy is a collection of agents who adapt to each other and to the "outside" environment. It includes cases in which the number of agents is so large that direct adaptation to other agents, even through feedback, would require so many linkages that effective action would be unthinkable. In such systems, adaptation to other agents occurs, in part, indirectly through the environment. For example, the "market," by means of prices, communicates information about the entire system to each agent without its having to monitor any but its own economic activity. In this way markets economize interagent linkages. Of course, direct (lagged) linkages in the form of "conjectural variations" are also included in the notion of an adapting economy and have been studied in well-known theories of oligopoly that go back to Cournot.

The adaptive organization is a collection of agents who adaptively coordinate their activity, pursue some common purpose, and share some benefits. A hierarchy or multilevel structure may exist among these linkages in which agents play differentiated roles and thus coordinate activity to take advantage of specialization. The adapting economy includes, of course, the notion of a collection of adapting agents and organizations.

When the internal structure of adaptation is the focal point of interest, concern is with the adapting algorithm – a collection of adaptors coordinated for the purpose of solving specific problems. The notion of the adapting algorithm is quite general, for individual agents, organizations, and economies solve problems: they consume, produce, and coordinate supply and demand. However, the explicit use of the adapting algorithm may entail too much detail for the purpose at hand. The economist may prefer to treat the agent or organization as a kind of black box and focus on the "external" interactions.

From a purely formal point of view these systems are composed of two basic structures, parallel and hierarchical, that may be combined to give many different structures of interaction. Thus, we can conceive of parallel adaptors representing individual, independent firms or adaptive functions, each member or function of which may be further decomposed into a hierarchical subsystem of managerial units or computation steps.

3.3.3 Meta-Adaptation

Adaptation as defined so far involves the interaction of agent and environment according to fixed rules of behavior for a fixed agent or population of agents. If we are able to consider how a given process comes into being or if we are to inquire how a system changes (or may be changed) from one structure to another, then we come to a more complex type of adaptation, which may be called *meta-adaptation*, in which rules of behavior or the population of agents, or both, are variables.

Three forms of meta-adaptation may be distinguished: evolution, cultural adaptation, and cultural evolution. In *evolution*, the population of agents is a variable determined at any given time by the previously existing population interacting with its environment through forces of competition, cooperation, and selection. This concept was, of course, developed to explain the progress of biological populations, but its application to socioeconomic organizations is of obvious relevance.

Humans, at least, possess the ability to create new rules of adaptation in their behavior, which may or may not be passed on to future generations.

This selection or modification of adaptors for a given agent or population of agents through conscious effort may be called *cultural adaptation*, which is a type of meta-adaptation so important that society as a whole and many of its institutions set aside resources for the use of specialists in this function. These specialists include, for example, engineers, management scientists, and economists. Individuals, too, set aside resources, time, and money for learning new modes of behavior through education and training. Cultural adaptation enables agents to survive in the face of evolutionary forces that would spell their demise if they did not acquire new modes of behavior. It also enables them to improve their performance in the sense of some criterion or outcome measure.

When both evolution and cultural adaptations are present, we have *cultural evolution* (Childe 1951), which allows for the response of agents to their environment, the modification of strategies or modes of behavior by given agents, and the modification of the population of agents itself.

3.4 Modeling Adaptation

3.4.1 Adaptive Functions

The elemental decomposition of an adaptive agent is into two constituent parts: that of sensor, which filters and processes information about the environment, and that of effector, which responds in terms of behavior to the informational cues. Very simple combinations of these two elements can have great survival power, as effectively illustrated by Lotka's example of the mechanical mouse (Lotka 1924). To model behavior completely, however, a decomposition of these two constituents must be recognized. The sensor function may be divided into observation, memory (or information storage), and information processing, which results in planning data (Marschak 1968). The effector function may be divided into planning and implementing activities. The latter distinction recognizes that plans are not always realized and that an individual or organization must react to an unfolding situation according to a procedure quite different from that characteristic of rational decision making or planning. Individuals embody the distinction in separate reflecting and effecting capacities. Many organizations institutionalize it in separate staff and command systems. Many mechanisms have been or might be used for representing the working of these several functions. We summarize here (1) rules and switches, (2) homeostasia, (3) learning algorithms, (4) behavioral learning and (5) economizing with feedback or recursive programming, and (6) adaptive programming or dual control.

3.4.2 Rules and Switches

A function is a set of ordered pairs; the first member is the input (argument) and the second is the output (image) of the adaptor. When the function is represented by a closed-form expression or formula, it is an *operator* or *rule* that associates an image to each possible argument. Rules may be derived from economizing theory by a statistical analysis of inputs and outputs when the agent is regarded as a black box, or they may be identified by direct observation in the case of persons and organizations. In the latter case, one speaks of behavioral rules.

Not all functions used in mathematics can be computed exactly. For example, equilibria for a given economic system – if they exist in a mathematical sense – are functions of the parameters of the equations making up the system. In general they can only be approximated. A procedure for computing an image of a function for a given argument is an algorithm. To be operational, all models of economic behavior must be computable in this sense. To make the full structure of algorithmic computation explicit, one must appeal to the class of simplest functions or rules from which algorithms must ultimately be constructed. Thus, not only models of adaptive behavior but all operational models, including equilibrium models designed to work on computers, are founded on the existence of such rules.

Among the simplest rules is the switch, which changes action from one mode to another on the basis of the environmental state and modifies the paths or loops through which the system flow occurs. Numerical algorithms for computing functions consist of systems of switches and simple arithmetical rules. Computer simulation models of directly observable behavior in economic organizations all ultimately boil down to systems of switches and rules. Examples of the latter are the behavioral economic models of Cyert and March (1963), the system dynamics models of Forrester (1966), and the general systems simulation models of Manetsch et al. (1971).

3.4.3 Homeostasis

All living systems, including humanity in its economic activity, possess critical variables that must be maintained within the boundaries of certain critical sets if they are to survive. In general, these critical sets depend on the current situation as determined by an admissibility operator. The agent must possess an adaptor that leads to an action within the admissible region determined by this operator. The agent survives so long as the admissible set is nonempty and its action belongs to this set. In this case the agent exhibits *homeostasis in the general sense* (Ashby 1967, Day 1975). If either of these conditions fails, then the agent goes out of existence and the system collapses to a transitor that maps a given environmental state into a succeeding environmental state.

A mechanism for achieving homeostasis is the negative feedback control device or servomechanism that adjusts actions on the basis of an observed discrepancy between a desired or target value of the critical variables and their experienced values. Extensively developed by Canon (1939) in the context of human physiology, the idea was first applied to economic behavior by Cooper (1951), Simon (1952), March and Simon (1958), Boulding (1962), and Forrester (1966) and is the basis of the flexible accelerator (Goodwin 1948). Systems that behave according to such rules exhibit *homeostasis in the specific sense*. Note that homeostasis in the specific sense is an algorithm for minimizing the distance between target and observed critical outcomes and implies a preference for outcomes closer to the target than others. This distance can clearly be thought of as a "disutility." We thus see in this widely observed form of adaptation an implicit optimizing algorithm.

3.4.4 Behavioral Learning

Economizing behavior as described, for example, by the marginalist Marshall involves incremental, economically improving adjustments. Optimality of full equilibrium only occurrs – if at all – through a converging sequence of marginal changes in behavior. Marshall's focus, however, like many of his contemporaries, was on the characteristics of the state of equilibrium – if it was brought about. But to understand the adaptive mechanism that underlies economizing, one must study the process of marginal adjustment itself. Under what conditions will it bring about optimality and at what speed? And, because explicit optimizing takes time, involves the consumption of other resources, and is far from easy, the process of optimizing itself is a part of the economizing problem. When investigating such issues, learning algorithms must be constructed that describe economizing as an adapting process.

The canonical form for learning algorithms is a system of rules and switches in which the rule governing behavior at any time is determined when the performance measure belongs to the rule's associated switching set. A change in the performance measure sufficient to bring its value to a different set of such values causes a change in the rule governing behavior.

Simple examples can readily be constructed using four elemental principles of learning: (1) successful behavior is repeated, (2) unsuccessful behavior is avoided, (3) unsuccessful behavior is followed by a search for alternative modes of behavior, and (4) behavior becomes more cautious in response to failure. Well founded in psychological theory and experimentation, models incorporating the first three of these four principles have been the basis of the behavioral theory of the firm developed by Cyert and March (1963). Day (1967a, b) and Day and Tinney (1968) have shown that behavioral learning models, augmented by failure response, the fourth principle, can converge to the economist's traditional economic equilibria for individual agents or two-agent teams with stationary environments. Recently, empirical evidence has been assembled that indicates businesses are actually governed by such learning rules (Crain and Tollison 1984).

3.4.5 Optimizing with Feedback or Recursive Programming

The essence of the behavioral learning model is an exceedingly simple local or approximate optimizing of marginal variations in action based on an extremely limited knowledge of past results. This characteristic is shared by mathematical algorithms for computing optima of complex unconstrained or constrained optimization problems. Optima for such problems cannot usually be intuited but must be approximated through a process of trial and error based on local, approximate suboptimization with feedback. Gradient methods are transparent examples of such algorithms in which search is directed along the locally steepest path of ascent (or descent). The locally steepest path is the gradient (or constrained gradient) that solves a local maximization problem. Increasing caution is represented by shortening step lengths as marginal payoffs decrease or local optima are overshot.

The analogy between elemental learning behavior and optimizing algorithms exposes a fundamental duality between optimizing and learning. The solutions of complex optimizing problems must be learned by what are in effect elemental adaptive processes, and elemental adaptive processes that exhibit learning involve optimization in a simple way. This duality motivates a consideration of the class of all processes that represent behavior or planning computations by sequences of recursively connected, local, approximate, or behaviorally conditioned suboptimizations with feedback or *recursive programming models*.

Such models appear in a great variety of special forms that share a common mathematical structure. From a purely formal point of view, they are three component systems involving data, optimizing, and feedback operators. The *data operator*, which subsumes observation, storage, and processing functions, defines how the "parameters" or data entering objective and constraint functions depend on the current state of the system as a whole. The *optimizing operator* describes the dependence of certain decision or choice variables on objective and constraint functions that in turn depend on the various parameters or data. The *feedback operator*, which subsumes implementation and environmental transition functions, specifies how the succeeding state of the system depends on the current optimal decision variables, the data, and the current state. Given an initial state for the system, the data for an optimization can be generated, the optimization problem formed and solved, and the next state of the system evolved through feedback. In this way a sequence of optimization is generated in which parameters or data upon which any one optimization is based depend on past optimizations and parameters or data in the sequence.

It is essential to note that, although each solution in the sequence of recursively generated optimizations satisfies certain optimality properties, the sequence as a whole need not and in general will not. Indeed some models of this structure can be constructed that will generate pessimal performance, just as other examples can be shown to generate optimal performance. We emphasize that the behavioral learning model and gradient algorithms are simple examples of this general approach. In recursive programming models of economic behavior, constrained maximizing is used to describe the plans or intended behavior of an economizing agent or group of agents but with the added assumption that actual performance is determined by additional forces unaccounted for in the individual optimizations. These additional forces may act on the agent through environmental and behavioral feedback in the form of physical and financial accumulations (and decumulations), through information incorporated in estimates of current states and forecasts of anticipated states, and through behavioral rules that make allowances for future decision making, that modify objectives on the basis of past behavior, and that limit change from established behavior as a tactic for avoiding uncertainty.

The description of a decision maker who proceeds according to a succession of behaviorally conditioned, suboptimizing, more or less myopic decisions corresponds reasonably well to behavior observed in many business firms and government agencies. Nonetheless, strategic considerations can also be incorporated into a recursive programming model by using optimal control or dynamic programming for the optimizing operator in which the payoff (or expected payoff) of an anticipated sequence of future actions is maximized subject to a feedback operator that represents the perceived environmental feedback operator. A plan consisting of optimal intended future behavior is derived or, more generally, an optimal strategy is derived that specifies how current behavior should be controlled given current information. When such a "strategic" optimizing (dynamic programming) operator is embedded in a "true" or "complete" feedback structure, the model as a whole now becomes a recursive programming model that represents an agent or several agents who are forward looking and whose plans have strategic quality but whose actual behavior is conditioned by forces whose exact structure is not incorporated in the optimizing calculations. The "true" optimal strategy cannot be used unless the true, complete feedback structure is perceived by the agents and represented by the modeler. Then the recursive programming and dynamic programming representations will coincide.

As we have already observed, the paradigm of a behaviorally conditioned, suboptimizing economic decision maker is also a good description of certain algorithms for computing solutions to complicated planning models. These algorithms are developed by decomposing the original problem into a simpler one or set of simpler problems and a feedback rule that describes how the simple problems should be modified on the basis of past solutions so that, when they are solved by a known, convenient, economical method, the solution will be closer than before to the optimum of the original complicated problem. One may think of the original complicated problem as an "environment," the simplified optimization problem as a decision maker's suboptimizing tactic, and the feedback rule as a means of using past decisions and feedback from the environment to obtain a new approximate decision problem. The sequence of suboptima may converge to the desired overall optimum, but in general one can only approximate the desired solution in this way. The degree of approximation depends on the planner's computing budget and how efficient the algorithm is. The parallel with the gradient and behavioral learning algorithms to which we referred in the preceding section should be evident. For a review of recursive programming models and their precedents, see Day and Cigno (1978).

3.4.6 Adaptive Programming or Dual Control

When applying strategic considerations to the problem of adaptation and to achieve global optimality, the agent must account for all the decision functions: observation, storage, processing, planning, and implementation. The advantage to be gained by allocating present resources to learning about the system through conscious experimentation must be compared with their allocation for maximizing current performance given the current level of knowledge of the system's operation. Formal models that embody these considerations are called adaptive control or adaptive programming models and seem to have been originated by Fel'dbaum (1965) in a generalization of Bellman's dynamic programming. Extensively studied by control engineers, alternative models of this general type have been described in several recent surveys and need not be elaborated here (Aoki 1977).

Imagine now a process in which aspects of the "true" environmental feedback structure are newly learned with the passage of time. Then the adaptive control model to be optimized depends recursively on the "true" external environment. A model of this complete system is a recursive programming model involving suboptimization with feedback, as before, but in it intended behavior at each stage is influenced by an attempt to learn as well as to control optimally.

The more inclusive the range of decision-making considerations explicitly incorporated within the adaptive control framework, the more complex, costly, and time-consuming the implied algorithm for obtaining "optimal" decisions. Such costs indeed rise more or less exponentially with the level of detail accommodated, and thus the model must become an extreme simplification of actual operating decisions.

The implication is that an adaptive programming strategy is simply one way of planning in a state of partial knowledge. In practice, it must involve substituting a complex and extremely costly computational algorithm for "real-time" behavioral learning, servomechanistic procedures, or simple tactical optimizing. And, if there is something to learn about the structure of the environment (and not just its parameters), then the decision maker cannot be sure that sophisticated strategies will, in fact, perform better than the simpler ones they replace. Whether or not, and under what conditions, very sophisticated strategies will perform better than less sophisticated strategies depends on how stable the "true" environment is when plans roll and knowledge evolves in interaction with it. These questions, indeed, pose a host of theoretical problems of deep significance and wide relevance.

Evidently a universal form of explicit optimizing cannot govern evolution! Instead, the form of optimizing is itself a product of learning (that is, of adaptation) and, as experience adds to the store of knowledge, the conception of what exists, what is possible, what is desirable, and how to plan evolves. In adaptive economics, then, adaptive control models form merely one among several fundamental classes of techniques for describing the adaptive procedures by which humans and organizations solve their economic problems.

3.5 Disequilibrium

3.5.1 Meta-Adaptation

In cultural adaptation, in which rules of behavior (adaptors) are modified, one has a process more or less analogous to elemental adaptation except that change occurs in a function (adaptor) space as well as in the agent's action space. The subsystem governing the selection (or modification) of adaptors or behavioral rules is based on an orchestration of activities in which the memory, data processing, and observation functions are called investigation; the planning function that involves synthesizing new rules is called theorizing or model building; and the implementation function involves practice, education, training, or indoctrination.

The ways people respond to unfolding events change as they mature. The seeking of immediate pleasure, the direct avoidance of pain, and the dominance of curiosity become less apparent. Reflective activity emerges, and rational choice gradually plays an increasing role in some domains of activity. Analogously, as organizations mature, rules of thumb make way for scientific management. In either case, however, rational modes of operation are limited in scope and contend with habit, tradition, impulse, and imitation. Emerging behavior probably follows a weighting of rational and nonrational rules in which the emphasis on one or the other evolves on the basis of experimentation and the knowledge of past results and the superiority and eventual dominance of rational behavior cannot be assumed or taken for granted.

Agents must exhibit homeostasis in the general sense (as defined in Section 3.4.3) if they are to survive. Evolutionary adaptation – as contrasted with the cultural adaptation just considered – occurs when actions carry critical variables outside their critical sets of values. Of course, humans are subject to ordinary biological selection mechanisms, and these are thought by some extreme advocates of evolutionary theory to exert a powerful influence on human development even within the historical epoch (Darlington 1969). But economic organizations add wholly new human modes of competition and selection that transcend the callous profligacy of the biological world. Bankruptcy, for example, allows for the demise of firms and households while preserving the human participants. It is this kind of organizational evolution that is the special province of economics and whose formal study has been launched impressively by Winter (1964, 1971).

3.5.2 Disequilibrium Mechanisms

So it is that considerations of adaptation and evolution lead inevitably to an emphasis on disequilibrium phenomena in adapting – as opposed to adapted – systems: the disappointment of expectations, imperfect coordination of separately managed enterprises, the inequation of supply and demand, inefficiencies in the allocation of resources, and declining as well as improving fortunes of some participants in the system. The extent of these phenomena may be greater at one time than at another. At all times they pose threats to survival. They virtually always bring about the demise of individual firms, the number of bankruptcies in the United States running in the thousands per month even in good times! They occasionally conspire to drive industries, regions, even entire nations to ruin. The primary concern of the firm then must be for its survival, whereas the institutional development of society must be guided to a considerable degree by the need to maintain viability in the face of imperfect coordination.

For the individual, as well as for the organization, caution is an element strongly influencing adaptive behavior, and a part of cautious behavior is the maintenance of stocks of unused resources and the existence of organization slack to absorb unpredictable divergences between plans and realization. In addition, organizations evolve whose functions are to mediate disequilibrium transactions and to sustain critical variables within homeostatic bounds. Stores, for example, function as inventories on display mediating the flow of supplied and demanded commodities without the intervention of centralized coordination or of complicated and time-consuming market *tâtonnement* procedures. Banks and other financial intermediaries regulate the flow of purchasing power among uncoordinated savers and investors and mediate the flow of credits and debts that facilitate intertemporal exchanges without simultaneous bartering of goods. Ordering mechanisms with accompanying backlogs and variable delivery delays together with inventory fluctuations provide a flow of information that facilitates adjustment to disequilibria in commodity supplies and demands.

To these mechanisms must be added insurance and other transfer schemes such as unemployment compensation that place resources in the hands of agents who would possess no admissible action without them.

Models of adapting economies will contain elements representing these and other devices for maintaining economic viability. The preservation of such institutions is always threatened when a system is working relatively well, for they create unused stocks and apparent inefficiencies. Frequently, they are instituted after a disaster for which they had been needed and are later abandoned if they go unused for long only to be reinstated after the next crisis, in this way ineffectually reacting to experience. It is, of course, their existence when not needed that makes possible their effective contribution when disequilibrium conditions are running strong. In any case, their emergence is a central feature of the adapting economy.

3.6 The Nature of Economic Change

3.6.1 Rapid Change

Equilibrium thinking often leads the economist to view the economic system as changing slowly and sluggishly toward optimum conditions and to recommend policies to accelerate adjustment. Adaptive models incorporating behavioral rules, such as cautious optimizing, information lags, and adjustment delays, explicitly describe the inertia governing the economic system. They explain how changes in any one short time interval are limited. Nonetheless, study after study shows that, with the passage of time, quite drastic changes are brought about even though short-run movements are modest.

For example, Cyert and March's (1963) behavioral duopoly model explains how an exmonopolist's market share fell from 80 to 45 percent in about a quarter century. Other recursive programming examples explain the transition of backward regions or countries to a developed status with a massive migration of rural peoples to urban areas within a few decades (Day 1967a, Fan and Day 1978).

Explicit attention to dynamic processes consequently leads to a different perspective than obtained in static analysis. Instead of comparing the economy at one point in time to an equilibrium state, one focuses on the accumulation of short-run, inertia-bound changes out of equilibrium. The impression derived from this point of view is one of great and often rapid change after only a few years. Certainly, a generation, and often a decade, is adequate for producing pronounced alterations in commodity patterns and production technology.

Such change produces many "externalities." People are required to accommodate themselves to changing occupations, changing locations, and often to changing life styles. Such adaptation is achieved more readily by some than by others. Moreover, various new imbalances are created even when old "uneconomic" activities are dying out. This phenomenon is seen in wide and varied agricultural settings. Uneconomic commodities and traditional techniques give way to new farm organization, technologies, and cropping patterns. Very often, growth in the industrial sector is not adequate to absorb the released rural workers. The consequence is severe short-run employment problems. It may well be that much less attention should be paid by policy makers to accelerating adjustment and much more attention paid to controlling its speed and diminishing its costs.

3.6.2 Phases of Economic Change

The adaptive models considered here, especially those based on recursive programming, have the capacity to display drastically changing "modes," "stages," or "phases" of behavior. Indeed, the picture of economic activity these models give is of a sequence of more or less distinct periods of development characterized by discrete sets of resource scarcities and productive activities and distinct qualitative characteristics of change (growth, cycles, stationariness, etc.). Such discrete periods do not come in some fixed or immutable order as proposed by the stage-making theories of economic history. Rather they come in a great variety of orders and types that depend on the initial technological and behavioral conditions of the economy in question. They also depend on the economy's peculiar parameters of geography, technology, and culture.

A consequence of these multimode, multiphase, overlapping wave solutions is that trajectories often exhibit trends that reverse themselves and have the character of moving away from the path they were traversing. If this is also a characteristic of real economic systems – as I think it is – then information about the past behavior of such systems available at any given point may be inadequate as a guide to future system performance. In this case, econometric methods based primarily on fitting single-phase systems of equations to time series data would provide extremely misleading forecasts of future directions of change in the system.

3.6.3 Surprise and Survival

In summary, adaptive models lead us to expect surprises in the evolution of economic activity whose exact timing and magnitude defy prediction – for otherwise they would not be surprises. Instead of, or in addition to, focusing on economic efficiency and forecasting, policy should perhaps be aimed at preparing for surprises – not predicting, which is a contradiction in terms. The way this is done in individual living organisms (Canon 1939), in animal and primitive human societies (Wynne-Edwards, 1972), or in complex business firms (Cyert and March 1963) is to allow for slack, which in essence means surplus resources, redundancies, less than maximal growth, and so forth.

An approach used in the last century was the maintenance of surplus stocks for stabilizing agricultural prices. The cost in terms of reduced efficiency led to attacks on, and indeed a reduction in the use of, this mechanism. But the absence of stocks may lead to severe hardships in the future just as overproduction in the Sahel has led to the exhaustion of surplus grazing resources with catastrophic implications for the dependent populations.

Another way surprises are prepared for is through knowledge: the accumulation of facts, theories, and operational methods that may be used to generate new rules of behavior, new forms of organization, new chemical and biological processes, and new physical mechanisms for controlling the environment when and if they are needed or desired. Certainly the attempt to discover and apply new knowledge can be induced. The knowledge to be accumulated as a defense against surprise, however, surely cannot be induced by surprising events – another contradiction in terms. Instead, that kind of knowledge must be pursued without a goal, without identifiable economic motive just as, according to biological evolution theory, the planning mind itself has been generated without a plan.

References

Aoki, M. 1977. "Adaptive Control Theory: Survey and Potential Application to Decision Processes." Paper presented to Stochastic Control Workshop, AIDS National Meeting, Chicago, October 1977.

Ashby, W. R. 1967. "The Set Theory of Mechanisms and Homeostatis." In *Automation Theory and Learning Systems.* D. J. Stewart (ed.) Washington, DC: Thompson Book Co.

Becker, G. S. 1976. "Altruism, Egoism, and Genetic Fitness." *Journal of Economic Literature* 14:817–26.

Boulding, K. E. 1962. *A Reconstruction of Economics.* New York: Science Editions, Inc.

Canon, W. B. 1939. *The Wisdoms of the Body.* Revised and enlarged edition. New York: W. W. Norton and Co., Inc.

Childe, V. G. 1951. *Social Evolution.* London: Watts and Co.

Cooper, W. W. 1951. "A Proposal for Extending the Theory of the Firm." *Quarterly Journal of Economics* 65:87–109.

Crain, W., and R. D. Tollison. 1984. "The Convergence of Satisficing to Marginalism: An Empirical Test." *Journal of Economic Behavior and Organization* 5:375–86.

Culbert, T. P. (ed.) 1973. *The Classic Maya Collapse.* Albuquerque, NM: University of New Mexico Press.

Cyert, R., and J. G. March. 1963. *The Behavioral Theory of the Firm.* Englewood Cliffs, NJ: Prentice-Hall.

Darlington, C. D. 1969. *The Evolution of Man and Society.* New York: Simon and Schuster.

Day, R. H. 1967a. "The Economics of Technological Change and the Demise of the Sharecropper," *American Economic Review* 57(3):427–50.

Day, R. H. 1975. "Adaptive Processes and Economic Theory." In *Adaptive Economic Models.* R. H. Day and T. Groves (eds.) New York: Academic Press.

Day, R. H., and A. Cigno (eds.) 1978. *Modelling Economic Change: The Recursive Programming Approach.* Amsterdam: North-Holland Publishing Co.

Day, R. H., and T. J. Singh. 1977. *Economic Development as an Adaptive Process.* New York: Cambridge University Press.

Day, R. H., and E. H. Tinney. 1968. "How to Cooperate in Business without Really Trying: A Learning Model of Decentralized Decision Making." *Journal of Business Economics* 76:583–600.

Fan, Y. K., and R. H. Day. 1978. "An Adaptive, Multi-Sector Model of Economic Development and Migration." In *Modelling Economic Change: The Recursive Programming Approach.* R. H. Day and A. Cigno (eds.) Amsterdam: North-Holland Publishing Co.

Fel'dbaum, A. A. 1965. *Optimal Control Systems.* New York: Academic Press.

Forrester, J. W. 1966. "Modelling the Dynamic Processes of Corporate Growth." Proceedings of the IBM Scientific Computing Symposium on Simulation Models and Gaming. White Plains, NY: IBM Data Processing Division.

Goodwin, R. 1948. "Secular and Cyclical Aspects of the Multiplier and Accelerator." *Income, Employment and Public Policy.* Essays in honor of Alvin Hansen. New York: W. W. Norton and Co.

Lloyd, C., D. Rapport, and J. E. Turner. 1975. *Adaptive Economics Models.* New York: Academic Press, Inc.

Lotka, A. J. 1924. *Elements of Mathematical Biology.* New York: Dover Publications, Inc., Dover Edition.

Manetsch, T. S., and coauthors. 1971. "A Generalized Simulation Application to Agricultural Sector Analysis with Special Reference to Nigeria." East Lansing, MI: Michigan State University.

March, J. G., and H. A. Simon. 1958. *Organizations.* New York: John Wiley and Sons, Inc., pp. 47–52.

Marschak, J. 1968. "The Economics of Inquiring, Communicating and Deciding." *American Economic Review* 58:1–18.

Simon, H. A. 1952. "Application of Servomechanism Theory of Production Control." *Econometrica* 20.

Winter, S. G. 1964. "Economic Natural Selection and the Theory of the Firm." *Yale Economic Essays* 4:225–72.

Winter, S. G. 1971. "Satisficing, Selection and the Innovating Remnant." *Quarterly Journal of Economics* 85:237–61.

Wynne-Edwards, V. C. 1972. *Animal Dispersion in Relation to Social Behavior.* New York: Hafner Publishing Co., Inc.

PART TWO

TECHNOLOGICAL CHANGE IN AGRICULTURE AND INDUSTRY

FOUR

The Economics of Technological Change and the Demise of the Sharecropper

Ten years ago, at the University of Oxford, a lecturer on political economy laid it down as axiomatic that science and invention, the division of labor, the law of diminishing returns, could do little to save human labor on the farm.

Ellis and Rumely, Power and the Plow (1911)

The economic history of a region is determined by a complicated interaction among geological, biological, technological, social, and economic forces. A vivid portrayal of this process is found in the recent history of the rural American South; the resulting interplay of economic and social movements has been displayed there with irony and violence. Beginning gradually in the late 1930s, the adoption of labor-saving technology increased rapidly through the late 1940s and early 1950s. In some cases, the diffusion of a

Reprinted from Richard H. Day, "The Economics of Change and the Demise of the Share-cropper," *American Economic Review* 57:427–49, Copyright 1967, with permission from the American Economic Association. The writing of the paper reprinted here with minor modifications was financed by a grant from the National Science Foundation. The research on which it is based was initiated in the Farm Production Economics Division, Economic Research in Stockholm, U.S. Department of Agriculture. It owes much to the encouragement and expert consultation of Glen T. Barton, Grady B. Crowe, Robert V. Glasgow, and E. L. Langsford from that organization. The study was enhanced by the support of the National Cotton Council while the author was on leave from the U.S. Department of Agriculture. It is a pleasure to thank George Townsend and Claude Welch for making that arrangement possible. James Hand, Jr., former special assistant to the President, of Rolling Fork, Mississippi, offered advice and insights indispensable in tailoring the model to local realities. Criticisms of my colleagues in the economics department at the University of Wisconsin (Ralph Andreano, Glen Cain, Theodor Heidhues, and Jeffrey Williamson) are keenly appreciated. I am also indebted to the referee, Karl Fox, of Iowa State University, whose cogent criticisms have, I hope, led to a very considerable improvement in the text.

new technique grew by more than 100 percent per annum.[1] Greatly lowered physical labor coefficients of new techniques created relatively profitable investment opportunities by substituting capital-intensive, low-variable-cost methods for labor-intensive, high-variable-cost methods of production. A similar process was also at work in other parts of the United States. From 1940 to 1960, the index of man-hours of farm work dropped from 191 to 92 for the United States as a whole and in the Delta States of Alabama, Louisiana, and Mississippi from 247 to 93. On the other hand, output per man hour in the production of cotton alone increased more than threefold from an index of 36 to one of 127 (Durost 1960, Loomis and Barton 1961; Schaller and Dean 1965, p. 46).

The human counterpart of these technical facts was an exodus of 17 million people from U.S. farms. In Mississippi, where the concentration of population in agriculture was much higher than for the nation as a whole, almost a million people left agriculture – a decline of 62 per cent in two decades. In the ten counties of the Mississippi Delta, the decline in the rural farm population was also 62 percent – a drop of 54 percent occurring from 1950 to 1960 alone.[2]

During these years, agricultural economists focused on problems of agricultural surplus and policies of control. At a time when the rest of the economy sluggishly ignored the growing influx of displaced agricultural workers, economists and popular commentators ironically suggested policies that would move resources out of agriculture even faster.

In accordance with the policy concerns of that time I attempted to estimate the influence of technology on supplies of agricultural commodities. A "recursive programming model" was developed and applied to a small but more or less representative Southern area. But it is evident that this dynamic model of production and technology is equally a dynamic model of resource utilization and labor demand. Moreover, in the shadow of the labor requirements generated by the model moves the history of changing farm organization and emigration. This side of the story received little attention in my initial report.[3] Because of its current relevance, it seems worth telling now (Wood 1951, Roberts 1965).

In the next section, the dynamic model of field crop production is briefly described in nontechnical terms. The results of its application to the Mississippi Delta are presented in the following two sections. The first

---

[1] Examples were the adoption of highly mechanized rice cultivation methods and self-propelled combines. See Day (1963b, p. 92).

[2] See Tables 4.3 and 4.4.

[3] Day (1963b, Part III, "A Dynamic Production Model, Production Response of Cotton, and Alternative Field Crops in the Mississippi Delta, 1940–1957.")

of these displays the derived trends in output, technology, and productivity; the second focuses on the demand for labor and the central hypothesis of the chapter – the two-stage push off the farm. These are followed by a brief section on population effects in which collateral census data are given. The interested reader will find a mathematical description of the model in the original paper.

It is important to recognize that the economic model presented here can generate no data beyond those inherent in already known facts. Instead, it explains well-known events in terms of basic economic principles. Still it is possible, if the model's explanatory power is affirmed, to estimate variables for which little quantitative information is available. Here we do have excellent quantitative data on production. These data are used to test the model. The evidence suggests that the model is correct in essentials if not in every detail. On this inference are based my new estimates of the derived demand for labor and of labor productivity.

Recursive programming provides a general method for studying processes of economic development. It describes how development at once creates new opportunities and generates binding limitations and how it presents a counterpoint of growth and decay. Suitably modified for special properties of time and place, models similar to the one described here should be equally useful for investigating production, investment, and technological change and their consequences in almost any industry.[4]

4.1 A Dynamic Model of Production

4.1.1 The Region and Its Technologies

My initial study dealt with a small, relatively homogeneous and highly productive part of the South, the alluvial plains of the Mississippi River, or, as it is commonly known, the Mississippi Delta.[5] In the 1930s the area was

---

[4] Subsequent applications to agriculture are Schaller and Dean (1965) and Heidhues (1965). A model of urban land development has been proposed by Schlager (1966), and one of the U.S. iron and steel industry is described by Tsao (1965). A model that comes closest to the one described here in those aspects that deal with the regional impact of technology on labor demand is being developed in the Social Systems Research Institute by William Tabb and the author. It deals with the U.S. coal mining industry.

[5] The area to which the quantitative model was applied includes the Mississippi State counties of Bolivar, Coahoma, Humphreys, Issoqueno, Leflore, Quitinan, Sharkey, Sunflower, Tallahatchie, Tunica, and Washington. This small area is similar to the entire Delta region, which includes, in addition, State Economics Areas 7a, 7b, 8a, and 8b of Arkansas; Areas 1, 2, and 3 of Louisiana; and Areas 9a and 9b of Missouri. See *State Economic Areas*, U.S. Department of Commerce, Bureau of the Census, 1954.

dominated by sharecroppers with mule-powered, small-unit production. Mechanization was introduced in stages, first affecting land preparation and cultivation as tractor power displaced mules, then handweeding as flame throwers and herbicides were applied, and finally harvesting as mechanical cotton pickers replaced the sharecropper and his family. To summarize this picture, four representative technologies were constructed. They were as follows.

Stage I: Sharecropper unit. Mule-powered cultivation, hand picking of cotton and corn.

Stage II: Partial mechanization of preharvest operations on the operator's share of the plantation. Tractor-powered land preparations; mule-powered cultivation; handpicking of cotton and corn; small-scale combines for harvesting soybeans, oats; three-man hay balers for hay crops.

Stage III: Complete mechanization of preharvest operations except some handweeding of cotton and corn. Handpicking of cotton. Complete mechanization of corn. Self-propelled combines for oats and soybeans; one-man hay balers for hay crops.

Stage IV: Complete mechanization, introduction of rice, a very small amount of handweeding of cotton remaining.

These classifications omit some detail in the variety of technologies actually employed. However, a detailed analysis of costs indicates that the main differences likely to have had any economic importance have been included.

4.1.2 Inputs and Outputs

Decisions involving the application of each technology to three different soil groupings at up to four levels of fertilization were included. In all, about 100 alternative production processes were used to describe the region's basic set of agricultural opportunities. The process outputs included the production of cotton lint and cotton seed, corn, soybeans, oats, rice, soybean hay alfalfa, and lespedeza hay and the utilization of 36 variable inputs including labor, power, machinery, materials, and custom operations. The labor inputs included unskilled labor for chopping weeds, handpicking labor for cotton, tractor drivers, and special machine operators. The first two were almost always provided by sharecroppers or by displaced sharecroppers in the form of resident or nonresident day laborers. Special machine operators received a wage premium above tractor drivers and represent a special skill level because of their requirement to make timely repairs in the field in addition to routine operations.

4.1.3 Net Returns, Expectations, and the Profit Objective

Price series for outputs and inputs developed from a variety of sources made it possible to compute "per acre net returns" for each year, 1939–1958. Of course, returns are not known at the time the crop is planted and must be guessed by the farmer when he makes his decisions. Farmers' guesses of future prices are based on a variety of sources. The one most amenable to quantitative analysis is the immediate past. For this reason the previous year's prices were used as a first approximation, and this appears to be good enough for useful results.

Because farmers do not know what prices will be, it is useless to assume that they actually maximize profits. On the other hand, it is not useless to suppose that they try to improve profits given their information about the past and their uncertain guesses about the future. Accordingly, the model includes an objective function that represents the farmer's effort to decide process levels (i.e., the acreage devoted to each product, technology, soil class, fertilizer combination) that will increase total profits.

4.1.4 Constraints on Choice

The choice among production opportunities is constrained by land availability, machine capacities, supplies of off-farm inputs, uncertainty, and the acreage allotments of federal farm policies. These forces are represented by a set of 35 dynamic inequalities that relate the magnitude of these factors to production decisions the preceding year. A brief description of them will complete the resume of the dynamic production model.

Land availability for the region as a whole is a more or less fixed factor. Some land clearing and draining are still taking place, but their effects within the time period considered here are negligible. Land can, of course, be bought and sold on the regional land market, but this real estate activity was not included. Rather, my study focused on the growth and decline of specific technologies. This was not because changes in farm size are uninteresting or unimportant but because they are essentially derived from investment in capital-intensive production. Three land constraints representing the regional availabilities of the three major soil groupings were included. To avoid the complexities of full-blown capital theories and at the same time to emphasize the role of technological change, a simple scheme of representing investment in machine capacities was adopted. I have called it the "maximal potential growth principle," which is based on the empirical observation that "production can be expanded in a geometric ratio... during a given unit time period."[6] Behind it lies the basic logic of production in time that governs the growth of industries generally and the principles of learning that influence the adoption of new techniques. The former limits the supply of machinery from the manufacturing sector, and the latter limits the demand for machinery at any one time by farmers. These two forces conspire to produce an upper bound on the utilization of a given technique during a given year.

Consequently, investment in the new technique is limited in the model to not more than a given proportional increase over the preceding period's utilized capacity. Whether or not investment proceeds to this limit is determined in the model by farmers' efforts to improve profits. Investment is pushed to the limit only if it accords with the objective of increasing production in a direction that increases profits as they can be judged from past experience. Otherwise, investment falls short of the limit by a determinate amount or is zero. The amount of investment is determined by the model, but its limit is predetermined as a behavioral characteristic of the region. This treatment is not a necessary part of the method of analysis employed. Rather, it is a practical expedient for building a model in a reasonably short time that includes investment and emphasizes technological change.[7]

Variable factors are those inputs that – to the individual firm – appear to be available in unlimited supplies at going prices. But what is true as an appearance for the firm is categorically false as a reality for the industry or the region of which it is a part. Though each firm may ignore its negligible effects on variable input markets, their markets must strike a balance between available supplies and existing demands for the groups as a whole. This commonplace principle of standard economic theory is unfortunately difficult to accommodate quantitatively because of the rich structure of marketing activities in the "real world." Yet it is not difficult to allow for the fact that the total amount of a given variable factor in a region is limited at a given time to display its effects on production activities.

In the present study the limited supplies of unskilled labor and of commercially produced nutrients were treated as fixed at the time of the

---

[6] M. K. Wood (1951) observed this "law" in the aircraft industry. For an exegesis of the concept in terms of agriculture, see Day (1963b, pp. 89–92) or Day (1962).

[7] For a much more elaborate approach to investment, see Heidhues (1965). His concern is with agricultural adjustment in Germany to EEC policy. His methodology is quite similar.

production decision. They were assumed to follow "exogenously" determined trends over the history of the period considered. We thus focused attention on the *effects* of the emigration of labor and the explosive increase in the use of commercial nitrogen, leaving an *explanation* of those two diverse movements to more general studies. The "pull" of labor from the farm to the village and from the farm and village to industrial centers in the South and North was not explained by the model either. Yet, as will be seen, our results indicate something quite significant about that pull all the same.

Attention has already been called to the uncertain guesses about the future that direct farmers' decisions. This uncertainty restrains the change in acreage of a given crop in any one year. In the model this restraint is represented by behavioral bounds that are determined as proportional increases or decreases over the preceding year's acreages. They circumscribe the flexibility with which the farmer – and therefore the region – responds to changing economic conditions.[8]

During the 1940–58 period, the primary instrumental variables controlled by federal farm policy were commodity price supports and acreage allotments. Price supports are easily included in the model by replacing price expectations by the support values whenever the latter were above the former. Allotments simply introduce an added constraint on the acreage totaled for all technologies, soils, and fertilizer levels for a given crop. Cotton had such restrictions in 1940–3, 1951, and 1954-7, whereas rice had allotments in 1955–7.

4.1.5 Review of the Recursive Programming Model and How It Works

The model that emerges from the constituents just described is applied to the Mississippi Delta. The objective criterion and the set of constraints are computed for the region as a whole and form a sequence of recursively dependent

---

[8] This approach was first used by J. M. Henderson (Henderson 1959). For a further elaboration, see Day (1963b, pp. 86–9) or Day (1962). I would have preferred to accommodate uncertainty in a much different, theoretically more meaningful way by representing its effects through a stochastic "risk programming" model, thus treating the crop selection problem much like the "portfolio selection" problem to which it is so closely similar. But the difficulty of developing such a model without sacrificing detail in what I thought were the more important technological aspects of the study deterred us from that line of development. This behavioral approach has the virtue of operationality given current model-solving capabilities. It also appears to come very close to the kind of considerations that are really made by the farmer and has an empirical justification on that account alone.

linear programming problems. The solution of each problem in the sequence approximates the aggregate choice of a large number of similar firms.[9]

The solution procedure begins with an initial set of capacities and expected net returns. The corresponding linear programming problem generates a solution that estimates the acreage of each process, the expected output of each crop, the utilization of each input, and the increase – or decrease – in the capacity of each quasi-fixed factor. These are then used to estimate the availabilities of capacities and the magnitude of the uncertainty constraints for the succeeding period, which together with the exogenously determined supplies of labor and nitrogen, the fixed supply of land, and the actual prices of the given period yield the programming problem for the succeeding year. This chain of constrained maximizing problems is thus solved step by step for each period under consideration. The procedure was applied to data for the Mississippi Delta for the period 1939–57, generating estimates of production, investment, land, and labor utilization for the years 1940–58 (Day 1963, pp. 193–220).

4.2 Trends in Output, Technology, and Productivity

The Crop Reporting Board (CRB) and the Agricultural Census data on harvested acres were used to test the model. The comparisons are shown in Figure 4.1 for the major field crops. They are reasonably good for all except oats. In the latter case, the evaluation is based on a shorter period because of missing CRB data. The census data indicate that, even for this crop, the model estimates are not far removed from the trend, at least for the 1940–50 decade.[10]

These graphical comparisons indicate that the model is essentially correct even though it is incapable of estimating acreage changes with exact precision. On this evidence I indeed accept the model's general validity[11]

---

[9] For a discussion of the aggregation problem and the justification for this microeconomic interpretation, see Day (1963a).

[10] The proportion of variation in the CRB data "explained" were for cotton, 0.91; corn, 0.72; soybeans, 0.89; oats, −0.05; and rice, 0.83. Unlike regression models, in which the method of estimation guarantees coefficients of determination between zero and one, recursive programming gives coefficients that may be large negative numbers; however, like their regression counterparts, they can never exceed one. This explains the negative figure for oats.

[11] For a more complete presentation and critique of the model tests, see Day (1963b, pp. 117–41). A statistical theory of hypothesis testing is not available for recursive programs. Still, a systematic comparison of model estimates with data has been performed.

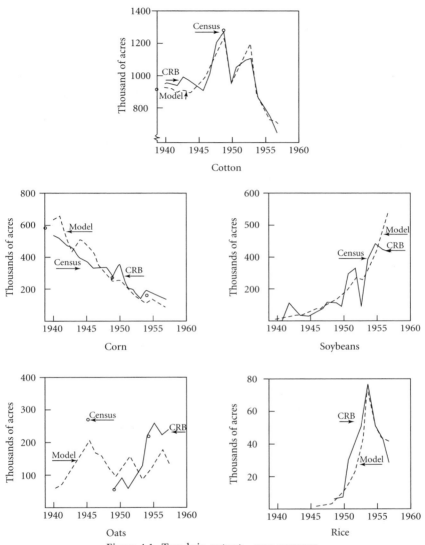

Figure 4.1. Trends in output – crop acreages.

and in this and the next section turn to an exploration of its implications. Some of the latter relate to population movements. For this reason census data can add indirect information about the model's veracity. This is done in a section on population effects.

The top panel of Figure 4.1 shows the effect of allotments during the years 1940–3, 1950, and after 1954 on cotton acreages. The rapid buildup of cotton acreage during 1944–9 and again during 1951–4 contrasts sharply with the allotment years.

These trends illustrate the powerful brake of production controls when they are in effect and the growth potential of the crop when unrestricted by government controls. The steady abandonment of corn and the explosive increase in soybeans and in rice acreages display significant shifts in cropping patterns. The decline in corn accompanies the abandonment of the mule technology and the shift of land to the profitable cash crop, soybeans. The sharp break in the explosive adoption of rice is associated with the imposition of federal controls in 1955.

The pattern of technological change *derived from the model* is shown for cotton and corn in Figure 4.2. Because Stage III technology was introduced in the model in 1945, whereas in fact it was started in the 1930s, the pattern for Stage II cotton production shows a discontinuity at 1946 that could be eliminated by correcting the initial conditions. The model also exaggerates the Stage IV adoption of cotton after 1954. This is due to an oversimplification of the investment process. But these are errors of detail that do not modify the story of rapid adoption of new techniques and rapid abandonment of the old.

Stage I is the most labor- and mule-intensive set of techniques and is associated with the sharecropper tenure system. Roughly speaking, one sharecropper family and one or two mules provided the power for a 15-acre unit of a larger farm or plantation (Langsford and Thibodeaux 1939, Glasgow 1954). The abandonment of the Stage I technology in favor of Stage II and Stage III indicates a decline, therefore, in the sharecropper system and a shift to wage labor supplied by resident, former sharecropper families or by workers transported to the farm from neighboring villages.

Productivity is measured in various ways, but because we are concerned here with the effect of technological change on the derived demand for labor, it is particularly useful to show productivity in terms of labor input per unit of physical output. Actual input–output ratios change randomly from year to year as yields respond to the capricious movements of weather. To eliminate these deviations we have used the "average" yield coefficients of the model.[12] Also, the contribution of each alternative way of producing cotton is included, weighted by its corresponding process level as estimated by the model. The ratios thus derived for cotton and corn are illustrated in Figure 4.3. Separate indexes for skilled and unskilled labor and the numerical counterpart of Figure 4.3 are presented in Table 4.1.

[12] For the estimation of average yields, see Day (1963b, pp. 75–80, 175–84).

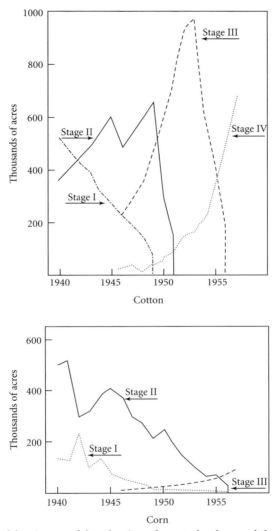

Figure 4.2. Model estimates of the adoption of new technology and the abandonment of old technology.

They display declining ratios for unskilled labor and rising ratios for skilled labor. But the average effect, due to the vastly higher productivity of the skilled labor, is a sharply declining overall trend in the input–output ratios, as shown in the figure. It incorporates both shifts to labor-saving technology and to higher levels of fertilization.

Table 4.1. *Average labor input per unit of output estimated by the model*

Year	Cotton (hr/cwt)			Corn (hr/bu)		
	Unskilled labor	Skilled labor	Total	Unskilled labor	Skilled labor	Total
1940	33.5	0.32	33.82	1.2	0.20	1.40
1941	33.0	0.36	33.36	1.1	0.20	1.30
1942	32.5	0.40	32.90	1.4	0.17	1.57
1943	32.5	0.44	32.94	1.2	0.20	1.40
1944	32.4	0.51	32.91	1.2	0.20	1.40
1945	32.6	0.61	33.21	1.1	0.21	1.31
1946	23.5	1.07	24.57	1.0	0.21	1.21
1947	22.4	1.13	23.53	1.0	0.21	1.21
1948	21.3	1.16	22.46	1.0	0.21	1.21
1949	19.4	1.30	20.70	1.0	0.23	1.23
1950	11.5	1.45	12.95	1.0	0.34	1.34
1951	8.4	1.64	10.04	1.0	0.37	1.37
1952	3.0	1.82	4.82	1.3	0.10	1.40
1953	5.2	1.91	7.11	0.8	0.30	1.10
1954	4.5	1.89	6.39	0.7	0.33	1.03
1955	4.0	2.02	6.02	0.7	0.10	0.80
1956	3.1	2.29	5.39	0.4	0.23	0.63
1957	2.4	2.50	4.90	0.3	0.20	0.50

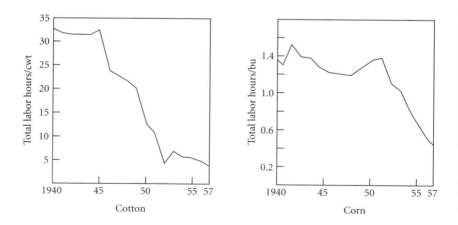

Total labor requirements in manhours per unit of output

Figure 4.3. Trends in average labor requirements derived from the model.

4.3 The Derived Demand for Labor and the Two-Stage Push off the Farm

The flow of investment into new production techniques implies a changing composition of labor demand. The trends in regional farm labor requirements, estimated by the model, are presented in Table 4.2. They include the utilization of "unskilled" labor, the use of "skilled" labor (tractor drivers plus special machine operators), and the trend in total utilization of labor of both kinds. These show the combined effects of changes in machine technology, in fertilizer usage, and in cropping patterns. The effects of the first and last of these items are to reduce labor requirements, the first by substituting capital-intensive for labor-intensive techniques and the last by substituting labor-saving for labor-intensive crops – primarily soybeans for cotton and corn.

The second item, increased fertilizer usage, tends to cancel some of the downward spiral in labor demand by raising cotton and corn yields per acre and thus increasing per-acre labor requirements for cotton and corn picking. But as hand labor is replaced by mechanical harvesting techniques this effect also declines in importance. The implications of these patterns for farm organization may best be viewed by considering the contrast with

Table 4.2. *Farm labor requirements in the Mississippi Delta estimated by the model (millions of man hours)*

Year	Unskilled labor	Skilled labor	Total labor
1940	170.2385	0.6908	170.929
1941	168.0305	0.7330	168.764
1942	166.6669	0.5615	167.228
1943	162.6678	0.6418	163.310
1944	161.9752	0.7588	162.734
1945	161.0240	0.8685	161.893
1946	130.1204	1.0672	131.188
1947	133.0420	1.1261	134.168
1948	141.2348	1.1899	142.425
1949	137.6645	1.3185	138.983
1950	76.0648	1.4504	77.515
1951	59.3976	1.6621	61.060
1952	38.6422	1.6477	40.290
1953	39.7715	1.8218	41.593
1954	28.4525	1.6837	30.136
1955	25.0885	1.6628	26.751
1956	17.5346	1.8570	19.392
1957	13.6818	1.9334	15.615

agriculture outside the South. Labor demand in midwestern agriculture is predominantly satisfied by the "farm operator." That is, management and labor are combined. But the tenure pattern in the deep South at the beginning of our period displayed a quite different arrangement. Here the farm operator participated, if at all, only in the mechanized phases of the work. He reserved the remainder of his time for supervising the plantation's portion of the sharecropper's work and attending to the financial aspects of the plantation as a whole.

As a result of technological change, this pattern changed radically. The operator himself increasingly participated in the work of his now predominantly mechanized enterprise. His decision to invest in machinery also meant a decision to change the status of the sharecropper. The full effect of this pressure cannot fully be appreciated, however, without a look at still another aspect of the region's farm technology: seasonal distribution of labor requirements.

During the early parts of the 1939–57 period, the shift to labor-saving technology did not drastically reduce peak season labor demands. Rather it began a radical shift in its seasonal distribution. Stage II technology, for example, eliminated the mule-powered land preparation and cultivation activities. Stage III further reduced hand labor requirements and also mechanized labor requirements – the latter through adoption of larger scale equipment, the former through advancements in the use of flame throwers and herbicide applicators. But only after considerable investment in Stage IV technology took place did the labor demand during the cotton harvesting season decline for technological reasons.[13] The basis for this seasonal effect is found by examining the average unskilled labor–time distribution functions shown in Figure 4.4. One can see that the consequence of adopting Stages II and III was to eliminate virtually all hand labor except for the summer weeding and fall harvesting seasons. This meant that maintaining sharecroppers the year round became uneconomic. Instead, a combination of resident wage labor and labor hired from nearby villages was favored. The implications for changing social structure are clear.[14]

But before we describe the implied two-stage push of labor off the farm we must take up one further technicality that was not included in the basic

---

[13] The labor demand did fall during the 1950, 1954–7 years because of cotton production allotments.

[14] A similar phenomenon will surely be encountered in other developing areas and industries having quite asymmetric seasonal labor requirements. Seasonal unemployment – or in the aggregate, disguised unemployment – may very well be aggravated by technological advances that increase both output and peak season employment in the region or industry.

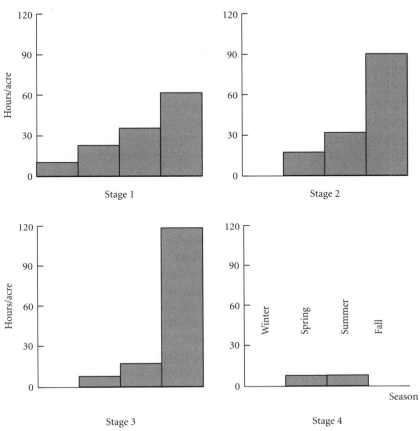

Figure 4.4. Seasonal distribution of unskilled labor demand in cotton production by stage of technology.

model description. This item is a peculiarity of the model structure that identifies bottleneck and surplus resources. If one of the various constraints of the model is "equated" or "tight," this implies that more of the corresponding resource could profitably be used at current expected prices. If the constraint is "slack" or "loose," the opposite condition is implied. The implications of this feature in the present analysis are that a declining resource that is tight is not being replaced at a rate sufficient to meet demand or, alternatively, it is being "pulled out" of the sector altogether.

On the other hand, if the resource is loose, it is a surplus item and, if there is some cost to maintaining the surplus, it is likely to be "pushed out" of the sector. During the recent history investigated here, the unskilled harvest

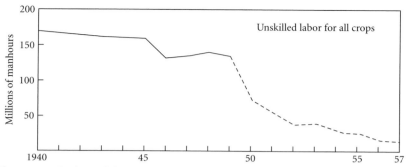

Figure 4.5. The derived demand for unskilled labor in Delta agriculture. Solid lines show year of labor shortage. Dotted lines show year of labor surplus.

period (September–December) labor exhibited both categories (Day 1963b, p. 215). This is shown in Figure 4.5.

During the War and immediate post-War era, labor shortages were felt everywhere. After the War, the increase in cotton acreage raised the derived demand for labor faster than the adoption of labor-saving techniques lowered it. During this period, the model shows that labor was a tight resource. But very soon, as the adoption of Stage III and IV methods accelerated, labor lost this status, so that from 1941 to 1949 was a bottleneck, but after that date it became a surplus commodity – even at the pitifully low wage rates in existence at the time.[15]

Consequently, without looking at migration data at all, it is possible to infer from the dynamic production model that, during the first half of our period, the labor released by mechanization was at least partially absorbed by the burgeoning economy in the industrial centers of the South and North. After that time, external growth in demands for displaced sharecroppers was too sluggish, and one may infer that such migration as may have occurred was induced more by a push than by a pull effect.

It is here that the consideration of seasonal labor distribution is important. The early stages of technological changes were not associated with a push of sharecroppers out of the region (because of the remaining harvest season peak labor demands) so much as they were associated with a push of sharecroppers off the farm itself (where they had to be maintained year

[15] Wage rates in 1949 were roughly 32 cents per hour. They hit a 1940–58 peak in 1951 of about 40 cents per hour (Day 1963b, p. 210). Data are not included here to show the annual income of wage earners in the class we are considering, but $500 per year would not be at the lower end of the wage earner's income range. It seems to me unlikely that still lower wages would have moved the surplus faster than its already rapid rate of exodus.

round) to the village (where they provided a conveniently located labor pool that could be inexpensively transported to surrounding plantations and farms).

In summary, the peak harvesting season handwork load declined only with the adoption of Stage IV technology. It was this peak season load that formerly kept the agricultural worker in relatively short supply – even as he or she became increasingly urbanized. With this last vestige of economic livelihood rapidly dwindling, the second-stage push of labor out of the agricultural sector altogether and out of the region in search of some other way of life took place.

4.4 Population Effects

If the two-stage push is a correct inference from the model, its effects should be reflected in population movements. We should observe a shift of people from a rural farm to a rural nonfarm status as a result of the first-stage push off the farm. Sharecroppers formerly classified as farmers become rural nonfarm workers as they move from a share–tenure arrangement to a wage–labor status either on the farm or in the villages and small towns. As a result of the second-stage push, we should observe a movement of population from the rural to the urban sector, and this should be reflected in a population increase in the cities or by a decrease in population in the region as a whole.

Although a related ecological study cannot be pursued here in any great depth, a brief consideration of census data should provide a useful check on the analysis. Tables 4.3 and 4.4 present decile census data for the Mississippi Delta area, the State of Mississippi, and the United States as a whole – the former in absolute numbers of people and the latter in percentage changes 1940–50, 1950–60, and 1940–60.

Table 4.3. *Decile population data*

	Delta			Mississippi			United States		
Population	1940	1950	1960	1940	1950	1960	1940	1950	1960
	(thousands)			(thousands)			(millions)		
Rural farm	316	257	119	1400	1097	543	30	23	13
Rural nonfarm	51	66	128	351	475	814	27	31	40
Urban	63	87	121	433	607	821	74	96	125
Total	430	410	368	2184	2179	2178	131	150	178

Table 4.4. *Relative population changes*

Population	Delta			Mississippi			United States		
	1940–50	1950–60	1940–60	1940–50	1950–60	1940–60	1940–50	1950–60	1940–60
Rural farm	−19	−54	−62	−22	−50	−62	−23	−43	−56
Rural nonfarm (Cities 2500 or less)	+30	+93	+151	+35	+71	+132	+14	+29	+48
Urban (Cities over 2500)	+38	+39	+90	+40	+35	+89	+30	+30	+67
Total	−5	−10	−12	0	0	0	+14	+19	+34

It seems to me there can be little doubt that the two-stage push occurred more or less as the model described it, though it is worth remembering that both push effects took place to some extent at the same time. That is, some farms were in the second-stage push (caused by the adoption of Stage IV technology), whereas others were still in the first (caused by the shift to Stage II and III technology from the Stage I sharecropper unit).

It is also important to remember that the census data only measure numbers of people in a given year. Because intervening births and deaths are not reflected in the figures, they only indicate a lower limit on the net flow of people from one sector to another. No doubt the migration was considerably more intense.

References

Day, R. H. 1962. "An Approach to Production Response." *Agricultural Economic Research* 14:134–48. Also Reprint No. 35. Madison, WI: Social Systems Research Institute.

Day, R. H. 1963a. "On Aggregating Linear Programming Models of Production." *Journal Farm Economic* 45:797–813. Also Reprint No. 57. Madison, WI: Social Systems Research Institute.

Day, R. H. 1963b. *Recursive Programming and Production Response*. Amsterdam: North-Holland Publishing Co.

Durost, D. D. 1960. "Index Numbers of Agricultural Production by Regions, 1939–1958." Agricultural Research Service Station Bulletin No. 273. Washington, DC: USDA.

Glasgow, R. V. 1954. "Cotton Producers and Cotton Production." *1954 Census of Agriculture*, Volume III, Part 9, Chapter 11. Washington, DC: USDA.

Heidhues, T. 1965. "A Model of Farm Growth with a Comparative Dynamic Analysis of EEC Policy." Research on the Firm and Market, Workshop Paper 6508. Madison, WI: Social Systems Research Institute.

Henderson, J. M. 1959. "The Utilization of Agricultural Land: A Theoretical and Empirical Inquiry." *Review Economic Statistics* 41:242–60.

Langsford, E. L., and B. H. Thibodeaux. 1939. "Plantation Organization and Operation in the Yazoo–Mississippi Delta Area." USDA Technical Bulletin 682. Washington, DC: USDA.

Loomis, R. A., and G. T. Barton. 1961. "Productivity of Agriculture, United States 1870 to 1958." Washington, DC: USDA.

Roberts, G. 1965. "Sharecropping Doomed." *New York Times*: July 16, 1965.

Schaller, W. N., and G. W. Dean. 1965. "Predicting Regional Crop Production." Technical Bulletin 1329. Washington, DC: USDA.

Schlager, K. J. 1966. "A Recursive Programming Theory of the Residential Land Development Process." Land Use Evaluation Committee. Washington, DC: Highway Research Board.

Tsao, C. 1965. "The Dynamics of Industrial Performance: A Recursive Programming Study of the U.S. Steel Industry." Annual Meeting of the Econometric Society. December 1965.

Wood, M. K. 1951. "Representation in a Linear Model of Nonlinear Growth Curves in the Aircraft Industry." In T. C. Koopmans (ed.) *Activity Analysis of Production and Allocation.* New York.

U.S. Department of Agriculture. 1962. "Changes in Farm Production and Efficiency." Statistical Bulletin No. 233. Washington, DC: USDA.

FIVE

Economic Development as an Adaptive Process

A Green Revolution Case Study

With Inderjit Singh

5.1 Introduction

Only a short while ago it was commonplace for the most distinguished social scientists to regard peasants in the less developed agricultures as bound by culture to traditional agricultural practices, unable or unwilling to respond to commercial development.[1] During the past decade a quite different view has all but replaced this position: A series of econometric investigations has confirmed T. W. Schultz's contention that traditional patterns are maintained because peasant farmers are economic people in the same sense as their Western counterparts and, faced with economic incentives, will respond in a manner predicted by economic theory.[2]

Our own work on agricultural development in the less developed countries began with a case study of the Indian Punjab. We commenced this study with an extensive tour through the region, tramping through villages and farms, interviewing farmers, and discussing agriculture with experts at

[1] The most prominent recent representative of this school is G. Myrdal, *Asian Drama: An Inquiry into the Poverty of Nations* (New York: Twentieth Century Fund, 1968).

[2] T. W. Schultz, *Transforming Traditional Agriculture* (New Haven, CT: Yale University Press, 1964). P. T. Bauer and B.S. Yamey, "A Case Study of Response to Price in an Underdeveloped Country," *Economic Journal* 69 (1959): 300–5, was among the first of the studies that obtained this finding. This chapter draws on material published in R. H. Day and I. Singh, *Economic Development as an Adaptive Process: A Green Revolution Case Study* (Cambridge: Cambridge University Press, 1975) and is included here with permission of the publisher.

The research upon which this essay is based was initiated under a grant from the Agricultural Development Council and continued with the support of the National Science Foundation; the Graduate Research Committee and the Department of Agricultural Economics, University of Wisconsin; and the Departments of Economics and Agricultural Economics, Ohio State University. We gratefully acknowledge the help and encouragement of Professor S. S. Johl of the Punjab Agricultural University, Ludhiana, India.

Punjab Agricultural University and in the state and federal governments. These direct observations and in-depth interviews, augmented by a survey of secondary statistics, revealed a state in rapid transition from age-old production methods to modern technology, a rapid growth in farm output, and a drastic change in the seasonal work pattern of farmers. The transformation has clearly involved extensive investments and the substitution of capital for labor as various individual tasks were being mechanized and as wholly new methods and materials were being adopted.

Confronted with these empirical facts and encouraged by the findings that economic analysis might aid in understanding them, we set out to construct a simulation model that would describe the process of agriculture in transition and make useful projections of the sector's likely future course possible under various economic policies designed to promote its future development. The model structure was to incorporate the microeconomic details that appeared to be a strategic part of the revolution we had seen in our travels as well as strategic details of farm decision making, of technology, and of market structure.

The model "predictions" were then compared with the available data. These comparisons are shown in Section 5.3. Our conclusion is that the model "works," that is, it is indeed capable of approximating past developments. From this we inferred that it could be used to augment our understanding of the process of change by presenting a detailed, quantitative chronicle of the farm activities as they must have occurred – including those for which no independent data other than our direct observations were available. Section 5.4 presents this chronicle traced by the model for the period 1952–65, focusing on productivity, capital utilization, employment, technological change, factor substitution, commercialization, and mechanization. We conclude with our inferences about the nature of development and some speculation about its future course.

5.2 The Theory[3]

5.2.1 Adaptive Microsystems

The agricultural sector in most countries is a decentralized decision-making system made up of numerous farms, each of which receives market

---

[3] For a detailed description of the model components and the theory on which they are based, see Inderjit Singh, "A Recursive Programming Model of Traditional Agriculture in Transition: A Case Study of Punjab, India" (Ph.D. dissertation, University of Wisconsin, 1971), and Day and Singh (1975; see note 2).

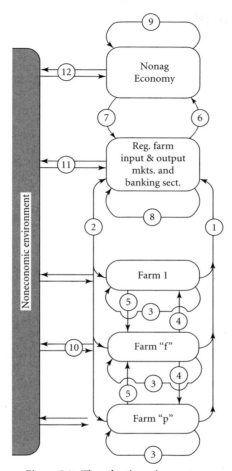

Figure 5.1. The adaptive microsystem.

information and is constrained or stimulated by direct government controls. The market and government sectors thus form an environment that is not controlled or well understood by farmers but to which the farmers adapt by responding to various variables such as prices, revenues, quotas, and price supports that are exogenous from their point of view. The farmer's rules of adaptation link current actions to past behavior and performance. From the formal point of view, these facts mean that the decentralized decision process within the sector is recursive and based on limited information. It is one in which the various farmers' actions depend on one another through the feedback effects of the market and their own past behavior.

The structure of a complex, decentralized decision system of farms and markets is illustrated in Figure 5.1. The feedback loops connect a given agent in the present period to its experience (loop 3) and its "environment" (loops 1, 2, 10–12). Loops 4 and 5 show interagent linkages that exist because of imitation and direct exchanges of goods and services between neighboring agents. Loops 1 and 2 show the indirect feedback that comes through the market, which is something that affects financial feasibilities, profit, and commercial consumption goals. Loops 6 and 7 indirectly connect each farm to the outside economy. We refer to the system illustrated in Figure 5.1 as an *adaptive microsystem.*

5.2.2 Adaptive Macrosystems

Obviously, it is impossible in quantitative work to develop an empirical microsystems model for an entire economic sector. In agriculture, thousands upon thousands of individual microcomponents would be required. To overcome this problem, individual agent interactions may be suppressed and agents represented by a few types or by a single model for the sector as a whole. We call this greatly simplified structure of decision and feedback an *adaptive macrosystem.* It is illustrated in Figure 5.2. In simulation studies, it is often of interest to model a given sector somewhat "finely" and the outside economy somewhat coarsely. In many applied studies, the outside economy is treated entirely exogenously, in which case the analysis focuses entirely on the internal structure of the sector and on its adaptive response to outside influences. In the remainder of this work, we follow this operational expedient and concentrate on how adaptive decisions within a given sector may be modeled and simulated. However, the specific hypotheses exploited cannot be justified unless we have in mind the complex system of which the sector is a part and the agent imperfectly perceives.

When one treats the noneconomic environment and the outside economy as exogenous linkages and suppresses interagent interactions, an *open adaptive macrosystem* is obtained that represents the behavior of an aggregate of adaptive decision makers who adjust their behavior in response to outside influences that are themselves not a part of the model. We thus arrive at the subsystem within the dotted lines in Figure 5.2. Notice that the experience-dependent feedback loop is still present.

The question that must be raised in this connection is this: Under what conditions of technology and behavior will such a model, constructed as an open adaptive macrosystem, behave in a manner analogous and quantitatively similar to the real part of the world for which it is the supposed analog? Two approaches have been suggested for answering this question. The first

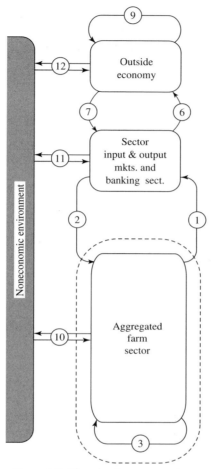

Figure 5.2. The adaptive macrosystem.

is to discover how much alike firms must be in order that a single model applied to the aggregate of their resources will predict the same aggregate allocation as one would obtain by solving a model for each individual firm and then adding up the results to obtain the sector aggregate. If the technology is linear, we find that farms need not be identical, but they must be similar in the same sense that we say triangular or geometric figures that are not the same size are similar. This approach leads to a representative firm approach in which similar, or almost similar, farms are grouped together.

A second approach suggests that, even though farmers may not be technically similar, they behave as if they were because of managerial leadership and imitation. The theory of such an approach involves explaining why decision makers who are not skilled in the optimal selection of complex choices might prefer to imitate the choices of "leaders" they consider to be more rational than themselves. For such followers, imitation may be the optimal course even though leaders would, in their followers' shoes, do something quite different in their own situation. Either or both of the two lines of thought support the use of an adaptive macrosystem whose structure is determined by a theory of behavior at the microlevel but is empirically estimated and simulated for the sector as a whole.[4]

5.2.3 The Adaptive Economizing Model

The core of the present approach is a model of adaptive economizing that represents the efforts of decision makers to respond rationally to current opportunities but within limits imposed by their immediate resource situation, by their sense of caution, and by their limited knowledge and cognitive abilities. We suppose that the regional variables are the result of the actions taken by these adaptively rational individuals whose aggregate behavior at the macrolevel can be approximated by one or more representative agents.

The model as a whole is made up of seven basic components:

1. A set of farm activities representing decision variables for farms within the region;
2. An annual objective function measuring the expected revenues from crop sales, the costs of purchased inputs, and annual investment charges for resource-augmenting investments;
3. A technology matrix representing the traditional and modern input–output structure of home and cash consumption, farm production, investment, sales, purchase, and financial activities;
4. Technical constraints representing regional resource and financial limitations;
5. Behavioral constraints representing adaptive limitations for protection against mistakes of cropping and investment choices as well as drags on investment due to learning and unwillingness to change;
6. Feedback functions that relate the availability of machine capacities and working capital to previous investment, savings, and borrowing decisions; and

---

[4] The central five districts of Amritsar, Kapurthala, Ludhiana, Jullunder, and Patiala were used for regional analysis to ensure a regional aggregate that is fairly homogeneous with respect to soils, climate, topography, farm size, tenure conditions, and resource distribution.

7. Exogenously given input and output prices, regional supplies of land and labor resources, and exogenously estimated subsistence and cash consumption requirements.

These components represent the following hypotheses:

1. Farmers first determine subsistence needs.
2. They then determine cash consumption and savings based on current cash income and predicted return on savings.
3. Their investment in off-farm production inputs and machinery is constrained by working capital and borrowing restrictions.
4. They attempt to distribute marketing risk by choosing a "portfolio" of crops and capital goods within an adaptive zone of flexible response.
5. Their willingness to adopt new practices is related to previous exposure represented by the amount of production already involving the new practice.
6. Anticipated prices are based on recent market experience.
7. Given these considerations, farmers allocate their available resources so as to maximize anticipated net cash returns from farming.

From a formal point of view the model is a sequence of recursive programs. The decision strategies represented by the recursive programs do not satisfy Bellman's principle of optimality. Rather, they satisfy an adaptive economizing principle stating that behavior is determined by local optimization in a neighborhood of the immediate past experience that evolves in response to feedback.

5.3 Testing the Theory

The Indian Punjab is one of the fastest growing agricultural regions in the world and affords an excellent laboratory for a detailed case study using the adaptive economic theory outlined in the previous section. Economic development in the Punjab has involved rapid accumulation of capital, a transition from traditional to modern agricultural practices, and an extreme change in the structure of labor utilization. These features are of interest to the study of development anywhere.

Farms in the Punjab engage mainly in the production of field crops for home consumption and commercial sale. The farms are fairly homogeneous with respect to soil, climate, topography, farm size, resource distribution, and tenure conditions. Field crops are sown in both winter (rabi) and summer (kharif). Rabi crops include wheat, gram, barley, and green winter fodders – mainly Egyptian and Indian clovers. Kharif crops include cotton, maize, rice, groundnut, and bajra or spiked millets. Along with sugarcane, whose culture extends through both seasons, these crops accounted for over 96 percent of the total cropped area in the state. The production of these crops is represented for both traditional and modern farm practices, under irrigated and nonirrigated conditions, with traditional varieties and – for wheat, cotton, maize, rice, and bajra – with new and improved varieties of seed.

The model was used to simulate regional agricultural history of the central districts in the Indian Punjab for the period 1952–65. The results can be aggregated to yield a set of variables for which comparable regional data exist. In this set are the acreages sown to various crops over the 14-year period. They also include variables for which no comparable data are available such as predicted levels of resource use for family labor, hired labor, animal draft

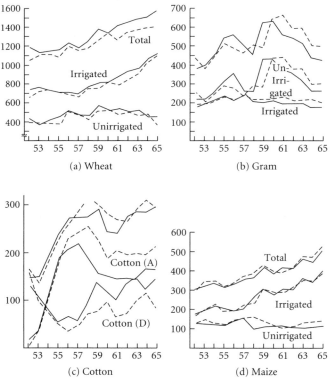

Figure 5.3. Observed and model explanations of field crop acreage in the Central Punjab, 1952–65 (thousands of acres).

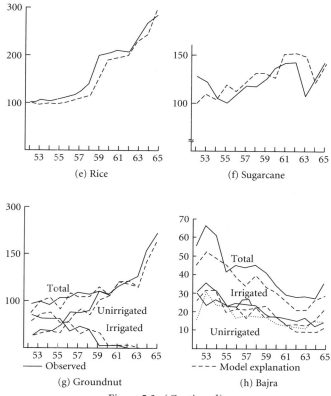

Figure 5.3. (*Continued*)

and various machine capacities, levels of investments and capacity used of new power sources, levels of production, sales (marketed surplus) and retained consumption of various farm outputs, use of chemical fertilizers by crop and predicted levels of grain sales, working capital used, and borrowings at various rates of interest and savings – all on a regional basis. The first set provides the basis for our model evaluation. The second set provides the basis for our chronicle of the Green Revolution in Section 5.4.

The easiest way to get an idea of how well the model mimics the development process is to look at the comparison displayed in Figure 5.3. This visual comparison has been augmented with a battery of statistical tests by Day and Singh (1973). On the basis of these tests the model explains acreages and directions of change and of cropping patterns rather well. Turning points and year-to-year changes are only modestly well explained. Nonetheless, the model presents an overall qualitative picture of development in close accord with descriptive characterizations of the region's recent history, as verified by regional experts (Singh and Day 1975; see note 2).

5.4 A Microeconomic Chronicle of the Green Revolution

The model estimates are not selected to produce a best fit, as is done in normal econometric practice. Instead, the model "chooses" cropping levels over a range of possible levels. It is therefore quite capable of estimating patterns very different from reality and such errors could accumulate over time to give a totally different history than that observed. From this point of view the results seem to be particularly impressive.

Given this finding, we felt justified in using the model to derive a detailed quantitative picture of the economic history of Punjab agriculture – a picture that can otherwise only be sketched in vague, imprecise terms on the basis of piecemeal data. This quantitative chronicle of the green revolution is described in terms of various indexes of outputs, inputs, and productivity.

Figures 5.4–5.7 display the model-estimated history in terms of index numbers of total farm output, marketed surplus, average factor productivities, aggregate input uses, and the growth in the use of new power sources. These indexes outline in broad terms the green revolution as it occurred in the Punjab: the rapid rise in output, factor productivity, the growing marketed surplus, and the explosive adoption of nonfarm inputs. Figure 5.4

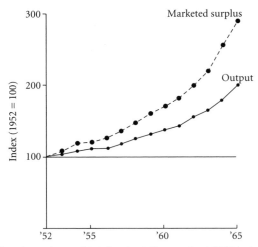

Figure 5.4. Marketed surplus and total output (in constant 1952 prices; base: 1952 = 100).

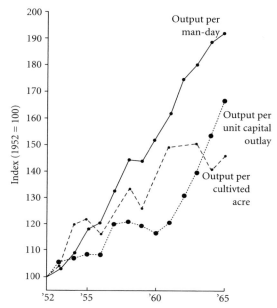

Figure 5.5. Average factor productivities (base: 1952 = 100).

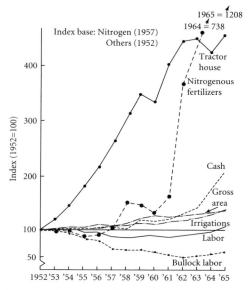

Figure 5.6. Annual use of various inputs (base: 1952 = 100; nitrogenous fertilizers' base: 1957 = 100).

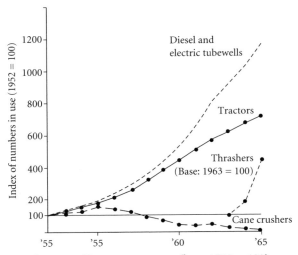

Figure 5.7. New power sources (base: 1952 = 100).

shows that aggregate output doubled during the period, which is a result achieved at a 7.8-percent average annual growth rate, and that marketed surplus tripled for the period with an average annual growth rate of
15 percent. As shown in Figure 5.5, these trends were accompanied by a
67-percent increase in output per cultivated acre, a 46-percent increase in
output per unit of capital outlay, and a 45-percent increase in output per
cultivated acre.

5.4.1 Input Utilization

Underlying these astonishing trends in output and productivity are equally
dramatic changes in input utilization. The most important of these are
shown in Figures 5.6 and 5.7. The greatest increases are evident in non-
farm-produced, nontraditional inputs, tractors, and nitrogenous fertilizer.
The introduction and adoption of new high-yielding varieties in the Punjab was less than a decade old when this study was commenced. These
varietal changes were closely associated with changes in total acreage fertilized for various crops. According to the model's estimates, total nitrogen use increased over twelvefold; the total acreage of all crops fertilized
increased fourfold. On the basis of this evidence it seems clear that new
crop varieties were so profitable under fertilization that, once they were

introduced and planted, the area planted was rapidly converted to artificial fertilization.[5]

Rapid mechanization accompanied the adoption of hybrid seeds and commercial fertilizers. According to model estimates (Figure 5.4) the number of tractors in use increased over sevenfold, the number of tube wells nearly twelvefold, and the number of power threshers over fourfold. These results appear to be very close to the actual number of these new power sources in use except in the case of cane-crushing equipment for which the model substantially underpredicts investments and consequently the number in use.[6]

An important feature of this rapid mechanization brought into sharp focus by the model results is its task specificity. The choice with regard to technique is made task by task. During the period studied, investments in non-farm-produced capital goods have been concentrated on tractors for land preparation, sowing, and transportation; tube wells for irrigation; and power threshers for threshing winter crops. As a corollary, the traditional bullock and labor-intensive practices are rapidly replaced for these tasks, whereas other tasks continue to be performed in the traditional manner.[7]

In these concrete terms the model describes the increasing commercialization of the farm sector in the Punjab by explaining the growing demand for non-farm-produced capital and variable inputs and by tracking its

---

[5] There is ample corroborating evidence on the trends in the use of nontraditional inputs, on the decline in the use of bullock labor (*The Dynamics of Punjab Agriculture*, Ludhiana: Department of Economics and Sociology, Punjab Agricultural University, 1966; W. E. Hendrix and R. Giri, "Approaches to Agricultural Development in India, 1944 to 1965: Progress, Regional Differences, and Associated Factors," New Delhi: USDA Economic Research Service and the Directorate of Economics and Statistics, Ministry of Food, Agriculture, Community Development and Cooperation, Government of India, 1969), and on increased land and water use (see Economic and Statistical Organization, *Statistical Abstract of the Punjab, 1965, 1966, 1967, 1968, 1969*, Chandigarh: Government of Punjab, 1965–9) but less agreement about what has happened to total employment. We elaborate on this issue later. For further information, see also Hendrix and Giri, p. 175.

[6] One of the reasons for this discrepancy may be that recorded investments in diesel cane crushers were carried out by few individual farmers who then performed this processing task as a separate enterprise. The model does not capture this because it concentrates on the investment behavior of cultivating households. For them, given that their family labor is a fixed resource, traditional bullock cane crushers became relatively unprofitable only when labor was seasonally scarce.

[7] Thus, for example, one observes fairly labor-intensive tasks like hoeing, weeding, cutting and stripping of sugarcane as well as cotton picking still being performed by manual methods alongside other labor-intensive tasks like irrigation and land preparation being performed by mechanical means on the same farm.

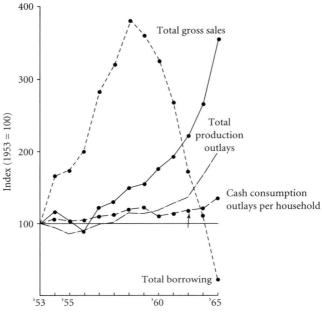

Figure 5.8. Indexes of financial flows (in constant 1952 prices; base: 1952 = 100).

increasing commercial orientation on the supply side: the increasing disposal of food off the farm instead of in the home. The increasing forward linkage is shown in Figure 5.8, which charts the trajectory of total farm sales. The increasing backward linkages are also shown in Figure 5.8. The demand for nonfarm inputs is evident in the growth of cash outlays for various non-farm-produced goods, both in absolute terms and as a percentage of total cash outlays. It is especially noteworthy that income from market sales allowed the farmers to reduce their borrowing. By the end of the period, only about 3 percent of the total cash requirements were met through borrowings (as compared with 53 percent at the beginning). Indeed, in less than a decade after the modernization process got underway, increases in output and sales were large enough to make further growth almost entirely self-financed.

The model explains labor utilization as the result of two conflicting forces: a reduction in demand due to the adoption of task-specific labor-saving technologies and, at the same time, an increase in demand due to the increase in yields and total output. The composite impact on total annual labor use was an initial decline, a leveling off, and then a sharp increase coinciding with the rapid rise in output. At the end of the period, total labor use was 5 percent higher than at the beginning despite the rapid mechanization described

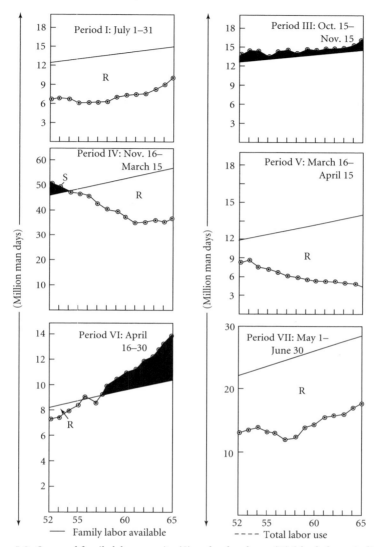

Figure 5.9. Seasonal family labor scarcity (S) and redundancy (R) (shaded area indicates labor scarcity).

earlier. This is shown in Figure 5.6. Nonetheless, from 36 to 52 percent of the total labor force and 17 to 37 percent of the family labor force were estimated by the model to be "surplus" or "redundant." But this observation fails to account for the seasonal distribution of labor use. This aspect of structural change is graphed in Figure 5.9. It contrasts markedly with the annual data.

Labor use increased in Period I, when summer crops are planted; Period III, when land is prepared for winter planting; Period VI, when winter crops are harvested and threshed; and Period VII, when winter crops are transported and land has to be prepared for summer planting. But labor use declined substantially in Period IV, when summer crops are harvested and sugarcane processed, and in Period V, when winter crops receive most of their irrigation. In summary, the model reflects a drastic structural shift in the seasonal demand for labor, one that has increased demand in some periods and lowered it in others.

Instead of a chronic labor surplus one finds a picture of seasonal scarcity. The model shows family labor is "very scarce" in Periods III and VI but "slack" in others. In Periods III and VI, when labor is very scarce and family labor is exhausted, labor has to be hired in order to perform all the tasks. The seasonal scarcity is explained in part by the nature of technological change.

5.5 Implications and Conclusions

The Green Revolution is one of rapid growth of food production accompanied and caused by the increased use of hybrid seeds, artificial nutrients, and mechanical power. Its corollaries have been the commercialization of agriculture: growth in off-farm sales of food, the increased purchase of industrially produced inputs, and the decline of subsistence farming and animal-powered technologies. The model has explained these trends in terms of an economic adaptation to the opportunities created by available supplies of industrially produced inputs and available supplies of credit in the early years of the transition.

Mechanization in a labor surplus economy has often been viewed as a paradox. But market forces, once unleashed, made it extremely cost effective. New power sources are so efficient in the performance of specific tasks that they overcome higher costs per hour of power use. Although the operating costs per tractor-hour were 10–13 times greater than the cash costs per bullock hour (Table 5.1), they were offset by the fact that it requires 10–30 times as many hours to perform the task by human and animal draft as it does by mechanical power sources. In addition, animals have to be fed even when not in use and require additional fodder when worked. If we consider the variable fodder requirements when animals are worked in terms of the opportunity cost of the land required to grow the fodder, we see the overwhelming cost advantage of mechanical technologies over traditional technologies. The cost effectiveness of mechanical technology is further

Table 5.1. *Wage rates and operating costs for bullocks and tractors (rupees/day)*

Year	Labor I III[a]	Labor IV[b]	Labor II VII[c]	Labor V VI[d]	Bullock labor[e]	25 hp-tractor (rupees/hour)[f]	Ratio of hourly tractor/bullock cash costs
1951	1.70	2.42	1.30	2.12	1.62	2.15	10.62
1952	1.78	2.42	1.42	2.26	1.57	2.12	10.80
1953	1.86	2.45	1.52	2.40	1.54	2.08	10.81
1954	2.01	2.37	1.69	2.56	1.40	2.07	11.83
1955	1.98	2.50	1.69	2.69	1.28	2.02	12.62
1956	1.98	2.50	1.75	2.62	1.41	1.98	11.23
1957	2.16	2.37	2.02	3.13	1.61	2.17	10.79
1958	2.29	2.51	2.03	2.51	1.52	2.36	12.42
1959	2.35	2.36	2.12	2.30	1.82	2.40	10.55
1960	2.45	2.20	2.37	2.40	1.63	2.41	11.83
1961	2.50	2.28	2.39	2.48	1.60	2.50	12.50
1962	2.59	2.61	2.60	2.80	1.60	2.54	12.70
1963	2.82	2.52	2.59	2.88	1.57	2.59	13.2
1964	2.89	2.91	2.93	3.61	1.83	2.90	12.68
1965	3.19	2.84	3.02	3.62	1.86	3.01	12.94

[a] Plowing and showing task.   [b] Other tasks.   [c] Cultivation tasks.
[d] Harvesting task.   [e] Includes only the costs of purchased concentrates; excludes fodder.
[f] Costs of fuel, oil, maintenance, and repaires.
Source: *Statistical Abstract of the Punjab*, 1965, and I. J. Singh (1971a), pp. 319–20.

reflected in the shadow prices on quasi rents of various machine capacities estimated by the model. They demonstrate the high-marginal-value productivity associated with investment in labor-saving technology.

In the wake of these developments are a seasonal redistribution of labor demand with drastic declines in labor utilization in the seasons in which mechanical power has replaced labor- and animal-intensive tasks and a drastic increase in seasons, especially those when harvesting takes place, where labor-reducing technology has not yet been implemented, as in the case of cotton harvesting, or where it is being introduced more slowly. The resultant of these divergent trends is the continued scarcity of labor in some (if different) seasons of the year even though the supply of labor in most seasons exceeds by far the work force available.

The adaptive economizing model has tracked the agricultural development in the Punjab through a transition from traditional to modern technology in a way that shares many common characteristics with the process as it has occurred elsewhere. The model has displayed how, in spite of vast institutional differences distinguishing them from their counterparts elsewhere, peasant farmers are amenable to incentives and respond economically once appropriate account is taken of their decision milieus. The model has also shown that, in spite of continued belief to the contrary, traditional agriculture can develop rapidly within a framework of a decentralized market-oriented economy given policies that facilitate appropriate developments outside the farm sector.

Although this study has been concerned with the Green Revolution as it occurred in the Indian Punjab, its insights are more generally applicable. They indicate that the process of development involves the removal of particular strategic constraints as seen by the individual decision maker. Not only is his or her ability to respond to market incentives limited by these constraints, but their existence leads to a path of development perhaps dramatically different from the one that would have been predicted by more aggregate analyses. Which constraints turn out to be crucial depends on the particular case under consideration, but the Green Revolution package of water, chemical nutrients, and new varieties would appear to offer hope of raising biological production functions in other regions with dramatic results. However, the concomitant effects on resource use, market linkages, technology, and employment depend on the local situation, the specifics of which must be quantitatively pinpointed and incorporated into the analysis.

We have used the Punjab model to project the possible future development of the region; we describe the results elsewhere. Briefly, the model predicts that the trends displayed here will continue and that within two decades more it will have reached a state of "maturity"—of more or less complete commercialization and modernization.[8] An important implication is the projected eventual decline in labor demand for crop production. With continued population growth this could have serious implications for rural–urban migration. In this regard the development process in the Punjab seems to be reproducing some of the events of a similar transformation that occurred in the American South two decades earlier.[9] The social and economic consequences will no doubt be just as dramatic.

---

[8] See I. Singh and R. H. Day, "Factor Utilization and Substitution in Economic Development: A Green Revolution Case Study," *Journal of Development Studies*, April 1975.

[9] See R. H. Day, "The Economics of Technological Change and the Demise of the Sharecropper," *American Economic Review* 57 (1967): 427–49.

SIX

Industrial Development and
Technological Change

With Masatoshi Abe, Jon Nelson, William K. Tabb, Che Tsao

This study summarizes four models that track production, investment, technological change, and resource utilization in the U.S. coal industry and the steel industries of the United States and Japan.[1] The post–World War II history of these industries is one of rapid technological change accompanied by large investments and capacity accumulation. Consequently, we focus on the technological structure of each industry and on the economic rules determining production and investment plans. Although the behavioral and technological structures of the three industries vary in many significant details, they share several common features that make possible the application of logically similar modeling techniques. Our goal has been to derive a positive understanding of the development process in particular industries based on microeconomic realities, in a manner that might guide government agencies whose concern is not so much with the internal performance of the industries in question as with the external macroeconomic effects of their production, investment, and resource utilization behavior.

After a brief description of the industries, we present a nontechnical description of our work. Important properties of the models are summarized, and their implications for explaining chronic excess capacity are outlined. We then review our estimation and testing methods, describe a few preliminary empirical results, and comment on their policy implications.

[1] The research reported in this chapter was supported by grants from the National Science Foundation, the Graduate Research Committee of the University of Wisconsin, and the Institute for Research on Poverty. All computations were performed at the University of Wisconsin Computing Center. The critical assistance of Dr. E. Herbert Tinney in all phases of the computational work is gratefully acknowledged.

6.1 The Industrial Settings

In all three cases under consideration, rapid changes in technology have occurred. In coal mining three basic types of production are practiced: underground, strip, and auger mining. As techniques have been improved and costs reduced, production and investment have shifted from one to another of several new methods for performing various tasks. The consequence has been a major improvement in the competitive position of coal as a major supplier of fuel inputs and a general boom in the coal industry.

Ironically, however, economic advantage within the industry is shared by fewer and fewer participants as new technology rapidly reduces labor requirements. The process – like that of U.S. agriculture – has proceeded so rapidly that pools of displaced laborers remain in those regions dominated by the industry long after the need for them has been eliminated. In the meantime, the growth in the labor supply generally and the insufficient growth in demand for unskilled labor in other industries within and outside the coal-producing regions have created major policy problems for the United States. They concern not only the allocation of resources among industries but also income distribution and employment policies for regional poverty pockets. Through the rapid displacement of labor, the process of development has created a pressing need for still more development, but of some wholly different kind, either for the development of new industries within the coal-dominated regions or more rapid growth outside.

The iron and steel industries have also invested rapidly in new techniques. The process has been quite similar to that in coal, tracing out a shift from one major method to another, as newer cost-reducing techniques are adopted. The use of oxygen and electric furnace processes has increased labor productivity both in Japan and the United States, although because of different postwar conditions and resource bases, the structure of the process has been dissimilar in several essential regards. Consequently, these two industries afford a good laboratory for a comparative study of industrial development.

The external effects of developments in the steel industry have been as important as those of the coal industry. Japan has become the third largest producer of steel, having developed a modern industry after World War II literally from the ground up. Changes in technology in the United States have, since 1955, been equally rapid, causing geographical relocation of much of the industry and major structural change in the labor market.

6.2 Modeling Technology and Economizing Behavior

The starting point for the type of analysis we have in mind is the representation of production as a process.

6.2.1 Activity Analysis of Production and Derived Supplies and Demands

Production is a controlled conversion of materials using energy governed by laws – the state of the arts – that define how inputs are transformed into outputs. The path from "primary" inputs to "final" product usually involves a sequence of conversions constituting a *production process*, a series of discrete steps during each of which a given task is performed. A *task* performed by a specific transformer or machine is an *operation*. The transformers use various inputs such as labor, fuel, lubricants, and so forth. The output of the operation is an intermediate good ready for the next task or a final good ready for storage or sale and shipment. The use of an operation in a given time period is an *activity* – Koopmans' "elemental atom of technology." Its intensity is the *activity level*, which is the fundamental decision variable of an economic unit. A collection of alternative activities for producing a given intermediate product or final good is a *stage* of production. Most industries involve sequences of such production stages.[2]

Each production stage may involve several capital goods. Because alternative activities in a given stage may use different primary input combinations, they constitute a kind of *technological portfolio* that enables substitution among alternative inputs in response to short-run price and demand variations. For this reason, industrial planners may desire to hold capacity in several competing technologies such as the electric and oxygen furnaces for steel refining that use quite different charges of scrap, ore, and pig iron. Each activity is represented by a vector of input–output coefficients and the complete set of activities by a technology matrix. Although individual activities possess fixed technical coefficients, alternative activities for given tasks allow for substitution and complementarity in the use of industry resources.

Innovations in production technology are accommodated by introducing new production and investment activities. New investment activities may represent construction of capacity for the new technology or conversion of existing capital equipment. Diffusion of a given technique is described endogenously, and thus the entire model explains its dominance or lack of

---

[2] On activity or input–output analysis, see Koopmans (1951) and Leontief (1951, 1953).

dominance over competing techniques.[3] A given production activity uses "primary" inputs – that is, inputs not produced within the sector being modeled – or intermediate products produced earlier in the sequence of activities, or both. It also utilizes the services of one or more transformers, machines, or capital stocks. It produces one or more intermediate goods or final products (i.e., products shipped to external consuming industries).

Because each model is applied at an industry level it is not possible to treat supplies as infinitely elastic for those inputs whose markets are dominated by the industry in question, such as iron ore in the case of the steel industry. In such cases, the derived demand for primary inputs may be constrained by available supplies. The derived demand for intermediate inputs like that of primary inputs must not exceed the supply; hence, we have the intermediate good balance constraints. The derived demand for capital services must be constrained by inherited capacities and by new capacity-augmenting investment.

For each capital good there is a corresponding investment activity. Certain investment activities involve the conversion of capacity to a technologically superior form. Inherited capacity of each capital good is determined by the usual equation of capital accumulation, that is, last period's capacity, plus investment, less depreciation.

6.2.2 Production and Investment Costs

Associated with each production activity are unit costs that include charges for labor, power, and materials purchased from outside the industry. Each investment activity is given an investment cost based on the common business practice of estimating the marginal cost of investment using "the cash-flow, payoff" concept (Smith 1961, ch. 9). According to this principle, an investment project will be undertaken if its payoff period does not exceed the previously fixed target established on grounds of liquidity, uncertainty, and capital rationing. The target payoff period can be used to compute the marginal cost of investment; thus, if long-run equilibrium were to occur, all projects would show marginal payoffs equal to the cost of capital, and the discounted value of an infinite series of equilibrium quasi rents would exactly equal the cost of the capital good.[4]

---

[3] Both new and converted capacities involve capital-embodied technological change. Disembodied technological change, which leads to a gradual modification of technical coefficients, requires periodic updating of the input–output matrix.

[4] On the payback concept, see Gordon (1955), Hallston (1966), Smith (1961), Spencer and Siegelman (1959), and White (1962).

The profitability of an individual capital input generally cannot be established independently of alternative or complementary technologies. For example, the use of underground continuous coal mining machines depends on the cost of alternative strip mining and auger mining machinery. Similarly, the use of the basic oxygen furnace for steel making depends on the cost of using alternative steel making furnaces and possible required additions to supporting facilities (blast furnaces, coke ovens, sinter plant). The choice among investment alternatives is determined by comparing the marginal returns of cost-reducing technologies with investment costs.

6.2.3 Sales Forecasts and Production Goals

Sales forecasts enter the models at two points: first in establishing production goals and second in determining desired capacities for capital goods. Sales forecasting may be an elaborate process – as is generally the case in steel firms – incorporating forecasts for the general economy, the industry, principal customer industries, and so forth, or it may consist of less formal estimates or hunches, as is typical of small-scale coal mining establishments. For a given industry a sales forecast equation is specified for each final commodity, which includes lagged values of some or all of the following independent variables: production and inventories, various indexes of economic activity in the general economy and in customer industries (such as indexes of electric power, construction, automobiles, etc.), and two exogenous "shock" variables that represent temporary effects of strikes, wars, and other discrete events that influence the industry's demand. Production is based on sales forecasts adjusted to maintain desired inventory levels.[5]

6.2.4 Behavioral Restraints on Investments: The Maximum Behavioral Growth Principle

Investment bounds are in reality an important and pervasive part of the firm's internal planning process, whether the constraints are externally imposed by the capital market (Freimer and Gordon 1965, Jaffee and Modigliani 1969) or imposed by management's preference for using internally generated funds only (Weingartner 1963, 1966; Scherer 1970). In our models behavioral bounds are based on two specific considerations. The first is a version of

---

[5] On the role of sales forecasting in firm behavior, see Spencer, Clark, and Hognet (1965), Kavesk (1966), Higgins (1968), Abromovitz (1950), Crawford (1955), Broude (1963), Bratt (1958), Rich (1956), and Woodward (1966).

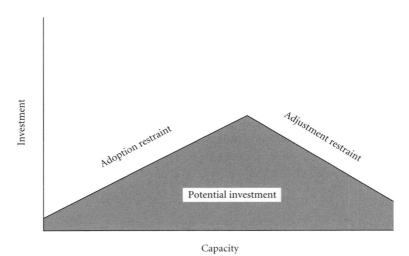

Figure 6.1. The maximum behavioral growth hypothesis. Investment in constrained to occur within the shaded area.

the flexible accelerator, which we call an *adjustment constraint*. It is based on the unwillingness of firms to expand capacity in any one year purely on considerations of capitalized values and cost differentials because of doubts about future capacity requirements and the possibility of future, superior innovations. The adjustment constraint places an upper bound on investment in an individual capital good based on a maximum willing adjustment of current capacity toward the current conception of desired capacity.[6]

The second restraint on investment is an *adoption restraint* that represents resistance of investing in a new technology until confidence in its feasibility and economic advantage can be determined either by internal research or by observing its results in other firms that have already adopted it. The idea is that learning is proportional to exposure, and exposure is measured by existing capacity.

Investing is then bounded above by the lesser of the adoption and adjustment constraints. This hypothesis might be called the *maximum behavioral growth principle*. Other influences, such as product demand or input supplies, could force investment below this potential. Thus, investment will belong to the shaded area shown in Figure 6.1.

---

[6] The capital adjustment, adoption, and abandonment constraints all represent an application of the *principle of cautious suboptimizing* (Day 1976). See Day et al. (1969) for the form used here and Day (1970). For closely related ideas, see Griliches (1957), Schmookler (1964), and Mansfield (1968).

6.2.5 Summary and Properties of the Model

Production planning is viewed as passing through four stages. First, data concerning input–output structures, production goals, input supplies, behavioral rules, production costs, and annual investment charges are formulated. Second, feasible production goals are determined. Third, production-investment activity levels are planned that minimize production and investment costs, which are determined by a cash-flow, payback criterion. Investment is motivated by two distinct considerations: (i) capacity expansion to meet anticipated sales and (ii) replacement of existing plant and equipment by technologically superior alternative capital goods to lower production costs. This implies that excess capacity can be generated even in the face of stable or declining demand for final production, for, as long as an investment will "pay for itself" by reducing production costs to pay back the sacrificed capital in a sufficient period of time (the payback period), investment will occur.

The fate of a particular production technique depends on relative production costs of associated processes, on capitalized values of investment goods, on sales forecasts, and on the "maximum potential behavioral growth" constraints. During one period, one set of these forces may be critical in limiting the expansion of capacity; during another period, quite a different set may be critical. In this way our models incorporate a view held by many institutionally oriented students of economic development that, during its history, an economy passes through distinct stages in which the dominant economic forces are different. Our approach, however, places no prior order on the possible historical "stages" or phases but rather determines their order as a resultant of all the forces contending to explain the time path of the system.[7] The dynamic process resulting from this "recursive programming structure" is illustrated schematically in Figure 6.2.[8]

If investment in a given capacity is proceeding at its maximum rate, it might be thought of as "modern." If it proceeds at less than this rate (within

---

[7] Like most econometric models, our models can be used to forecast the progress of endogenous variables on the basis of forecasts of the exogenous variables. They are conditional forecasting tools. But the exogenous variables are points of linkage with the "outside" economy, and one can think of coupling detailed models of many industrial and agricultural sectors. Consequently, recursive programming models of individual sectors could be used as building blocks in a dynamic input–output model of a complete economy. In this way many, if not all, of the variables exogenous to a given sector can be made endogenous in a broader model in which they are embedded.

[8] For the econometric estimates and model evaluation techniques, see Day and Nelson (1973).

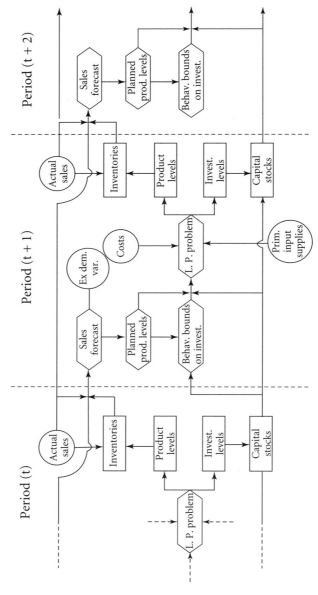

Figure 6.2. Schematic representation of model structure. (Decision rules or forecast equations are represented by hexagonal boxes, endogenous variables by rectangular boxes, and exogenous variables by circles).

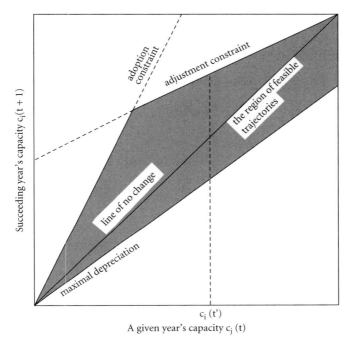

Figure 6.3. Phase diagram for an individual capital good with a constraint sales forecast. The trajectory of capacity must lie within the convex shaded region. Source: Day and Nelson (1970).

the interior of the shaded area of Figure 6.3) but investment takes place at the maximum potential rate in competing capacity, then the good is "obsolescent." If no investment takes place at all in a given good, whereas it still occurs in competitors, the good is "obsolete." In the latter case, capacity decumulates at a maximal rate. These four distinct phases may be summarized as follows:

1. *Adoption.*   Early diffusion is constrained by learning (the adoption constraint), which is contingent on the previous experience within the industry.
2. *Adjustment.*   At some point the rate of growth of capacity declines. The upper bound of investment during this phase is determined by expected demand and the desire to avoid the risks of excessive specialization. These considerations are represented by a *flexible accelerator with relaxation*: the adjustment constraints.
3. *Obsolescence.*   If some investment in an older technique still occurs, though not at its maximal potential rate, while a newer, competing

technique is growing at a maximum rate, the good is obsolescent. An example is the continued investment in open hearth capacity several years after the introduction of basic oxygen furnaces. In this phase, when the adjustment constraint is relaxed, investment is essentially a residual filling-out capacity needed to meet projected demand when learning and adjustment strategies limit investment in superior techniques.

4. *Obsoleteness.*   Eventually, an obsolescent capacity becomes obsolete and is allowed to decay or run down at a maximum rate determined by physical depreciation or by production abandonment constraints.

Our models thus simulate the wavelike patterns of diffusion, the superimposed waves of "creative destruction" so characteristic of industrial development. Indeed, such patterns have been observed so often that they have been called "the Law of Industrial Growth," for example, by Schmookler (1965). An idealized history generated by one of our models is shown in Figure 6.4, which approximates the path of U.S. open hearth steel capacity since the turn of the century.

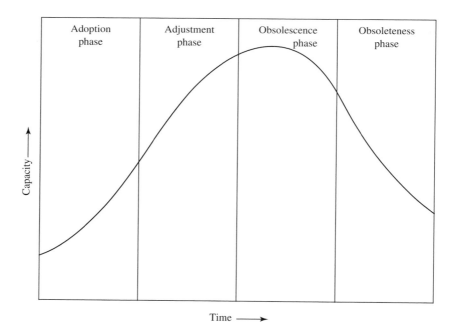

Figure 6.4. A typical capital good trajectory generated by one of the recursive programming models. Source: Day and Nelson (1970).

6.3 Technological Change

In contrast to the production function approach used in most econometric studies, each of our models incorporated a very detailed representation of technology with dozens of individual activities, constraints, and parameters. This level of detail enables us to identify the specific changes in embodied technology that transform resource utilization in these industries.

6.3.1 The Coal Industry Model

The effect of investment in the technology of advanced continuous mining machines in underground mining illustrates the substitution of new production processes for older ones. This is shown in Figure 6.5, which compares the amount of output by individual task cutting and drilling machines produced by hand labor, by the cutting machines and machine loading, and by continuous mining machines that, in effect, integrate all of these activities by a single continuous process. Along with the introduction of larger size trucks, immense power shovels in strip mines, and huge augers in specialized exposed seam mines, this technology is a major example of the substitution of capital for labor. The result was a reduction in the number of production workers employed from 369,000 to 129,000. During the same period, production per man day almost tripled.

6.3.2 National Steel Models for the United States and Japan

The steel sector affords an especially clear example of the waves in industrial activity caused by the introduction and accumulation of a succession of cost-reducing technologies. Like the coal industry, iron and steel making can be divided into more or less distinct stages: (1) producing coke using a beehive or byproduct oven; (2) producing iron using the blast furnace; (3) refining steel using the Bessemer converter, open-hearth furnace, open-hearth furnace with oxygen lancing, electric furnace, or basic oxygen furnace; and (4) producing finished steel shapes and forms in rolling mills and finishing plants. In between are ancillary stages involving power generating, ore benificating and ferro-alloy making. Most of these stages allow a considerable range of input substitution, such as, for example, the relative amounts and kinds of ores and scraps in steel refining. Moreover, by using several entirely different processes with different plants or furnaces, still further substitution is possible. For example, the electric furnace can accept a charge almost entirely of ore. By combining both operations at varying intensities, an almost

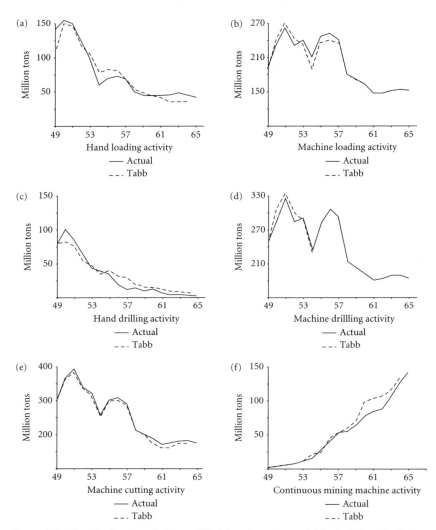

Figure 6.5. The substitution of advanced for labor-intensive activities in U.S. coal mining. (Notice that the vertical scales differ from chart to chart.)

continuous range of ore-scrap input combinations is possible. Labor requirements also vary with the type of transformer and alternative inputs used. Oxygen lancing, which uses large amounts of oxygen, reduces labor costs by about 20 percent compared with the open hearth without oxygen lancing. A still greater labor economy is attained using the basic oxygen process, which cuts the labor cost more than half with, of course, a consequent increase in oxygen use. These substitution possibilities are represented by including in each stage activities for which different input combinations are defined. The results of the model simulation for the U.S. industry is shown in Figure 6.6. Those for Japan are shown in Figure 6.7.

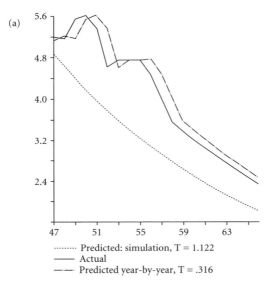

(a) Bessmer converter capacity: U.S.

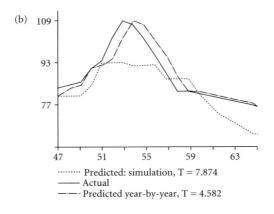

(b) Open hearth without oxygen-lancing capacity: U.S.

Figure 6.6. Simulations of the U.S. steel model.

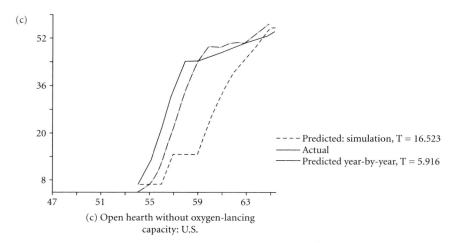

(c) Open hearth without oxygen-lancing
capacity: U.S.

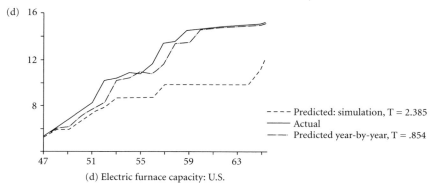

(d) Electric furnace capacity: U.S.

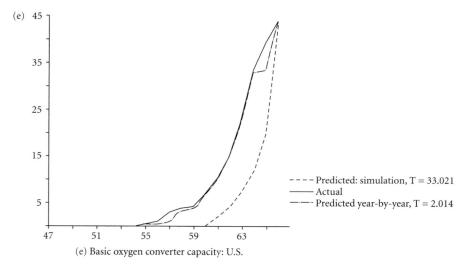

(e) Basic oxygen converter capacity: U.S.

Figure 6.6. (*Continued*)

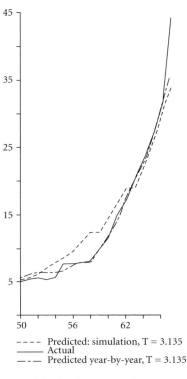

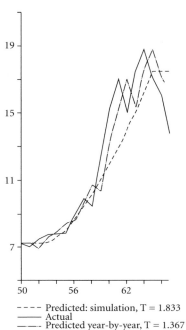

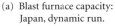

---- Predicted: simulation, T = 3.135
—— Actual
—·— Predicted year-by-year, T = 3.135

(a) Blast furnace capacity:
   Japan, dynamic run.

---- Predicted: simulation, T = 1.833
—— Actual
—·— Predicted year-by-year, T = 1.367

(b) Open hearth furnace:
   Japan, dynamic run.

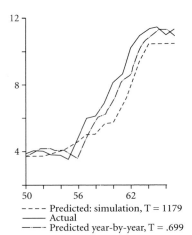

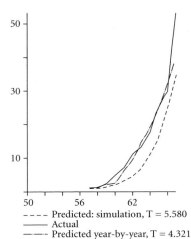

---- Predicted: simulation, T = 1179
—— Actual
—·— Predicted year-by-year, T = .699

(c) Electic furnace capacity:
   Japan, dynamic run.

---- Predicted: simulation, T = 5.580
—— Actual
—·— Predicted year-by-year, T = 4.321

(d) Basic oxygen converter capacity:
   Japan, dynamic run.

Figure 6.7. Simulations: Japanese Steel Industry.

For the United States the model generated the decline of the Bessemer and open-hearth processes as they became obsolete after the expansion of the more efficient oxygen and electric furnace capacities. After the introduction of the open-hearth processes with oxygen lancing and the oxygen furnaces, these capacities expanded rapidly. However, the onset of that expansion occurred sooner than the model predicts. The model also demonstrates that the conversion of the open hearths to oxygen lancing was more economical than scrapping the old open hearths and replacing them with the basic oxygen converters. The expansion of the open-hearth capacity even after the introduction of the more efficient basic oxygen process is thus apparently explained by this low-cost conversion process compared with the construction of the pure oxygen converters.

The results for Japan present a different picture: one of growth in all of the basic technologies except Bessemer, for which no initial capacity was recorded. Japanese industry was still recovering from World War II and invested heavily in the three more advanced technologies. The oxygen converter grew even faster than the model estimated and began to take over the use of open-hearth capacity only toward the end of the period, when it became obsolescent in the sense described in Section 6.2.2. In the United States the open hearth with oxygen lancing also became obsolescent according to the model.

It is interesting to note that the growth of the advanced technologies was about the same in both countries, but the United States, unlike Japan, possessed a huge open-hearth capacity when the Japanese takeoff began. Nonetheless, the oxygen process was introduced in both countries at about the same time. Thus, Japan's surge was not due to a more rapid adoption and investment in advanced technology, nor did the United States lag behind. The United States with its much greater domestic market simply utilized its high cost capacity to absorb the difference between demand and output with the new cost-effective technology.

6.4 Policy Implications

Evidently, our models are able to describe the sweeping changes in technology within specific industries that have been occurring, more or less continuously during the past several decades, in the United States and Japan. They show that those changes were due to relative cost efficiencies, conditioned by frictions in adoption, and adjustment of new capacity toward subjectively conceived capacity goals. We emphasize that our picture of industrial development is quite different from that depicted by macroeconomic growth models. In contrast to "neutral" advances in productivity of something like

1 to 5 percent per annum, our models describe rates of adoption of individual techniques implying productivity advances as high as 75 percent per annum and seldom lower than 5 percent. The consequent downward spiral in the utilization of unskilled labor and the ability of our models to relate this process to well-defined economic, technological, and behavioral variables predicts rapid – indeed revolutionary – changes in the *structure* of labor markets. To the unskilled laborers affected by technical progress, the discussion about structural versus nonstructural unemployment would – if it were translated for their benefit – seem fatuous indeed.

A further corollary of our models is that increases in aggregate demand for an industry's final products will accelerate the diffusion of new techniques by raising the investment potential in new methods, thus increasing the upper bound on investment determined by the adjustment hypothesis. If excess capacity in old techniques already exists, as in the U.S. coal and steel industries, the net result may still be a decline – possibly even a faster decline than before – in demand for labor. Employment in Japan's steel industry has so far not declined because a large part of its expansion in capacity did not involve replacement of one technology by another. But if Japan's remarkable growth in steel production tapers off (as it eventually must) and if still newer, more efficient, steel-making techniques are perfected (as they surely will be), then our model suggests that technical progress will decrease employment opportunities in that Japanese industry.

In summary, in sectors motivated by cost efficiency and experiencing innovations in labor-reducing technique, our models predict continuous, irreversible, and rapid changes in the composition and the level of demand for labor. With proper response the situation is salutary. Japanese and U.S. industries appear willing and able to effect increases in productivity and to adapt quickly to new economic opportunities. As a consequence, backbreaking or otherwise debilitating labor is progressively – even radically – reduced. The problem for policy makers is to provide an environment counteractive to the decline in employment opportunity that will accompany the process of change. Our work has not suggested a solution, but if it clearly states and explains the problem, perhaps it will be found useful to industry decision makers and architects of economic policy.

References

Abe, M. A., R. H. Day, J. P. Nelson, W. K. Tabb. 1978. "Behavioral, Suboptimizing Models of Industrial Production, Investment and Technological Change." Chapter 4 in R. Day and A. Cigno, eds. *Modelling Economic Change: The Recursive Programming Approach.* Amsterdam: North-Holland Publishing Company.

Abromovitz, M. 1950. *Inventories and Business Cycles, With Special Reference to Manufacturers' Inventories.* New York: National Bureau of Economic Research.

Bratt, E. C. 1958. *Business Forecasting.* New York.

Broude, H. W. 1963. *Steel Decisions and the National Economy.* New Haven: Princeton University Press.

Crawford, C. M. 1955. *Sales Forecasting: Methods of Selected Firms.* Urbana.

Day, R. H. 1978. "The Structure of Recursive Programming Models." Chapter 2 in R. Day and A. Cigno, eds. *Modelling Economic Change: The Recursive Programming Approach.* Amsterdam: North-Holland Publishing Company.

Day, R. H., and Cigno. 1978. "Modelling Economic Change: The Recursive Programming Approach." Chapter 1 in R. Day and A. Cigno, eds. *Modelling Economic Change: The Recursive Programming Approach.* Amsterdam: North-Holland Publishing Company.

Day, R. H., and J. R. Nelson. 1973. "A Class of Dynamic Models for Describing and Projecting Industrial Development." *Journal of Econometrics* 1:155–190.

Gordon, M. 1955. "The Pay-Off Period and the Rate Profit." *Journal of Business* 28:253–260.

Hallsten, B. 1966. *Investment and Financing Decisions.* Stockholm: Economic Research Institute.

Higgins, C. 1968. "An Econometric Description of the U.S. Iron and Steel Industry." Ph.D. Dissertation. University of Pannsylvania.

Kavesk, R. A. 1966. *How Business Economists Forecast.* New Jersey: Prentice-Hall.

Koopmans, T. C. 1951. *Activity Analysis of Production and Allocation.* New York: John Wiley and Sons.

Leontief, W. W. 1951. *The Structure of the American Economy, 1919–1939.* Second Edition. New York: Oxford University Press.

Leontief, W. W. 1953. *Studies in the Structure of the American Economy.* New York: Oxford University Press.

Rich, J. L. 1956. "Techniques and Uses of Forecasts of General Business in U.S. Steel." *Proceedings of the Business and Economic Section.* American Statistical Association. 161–164.

Smith, V. 1961. *Investment and Production.* Cambridge: Harvard University Press.

Spencer, M. H., and C. G. Clark, and P. W. Hoguet. 1965. *Business and Economic Forecasting.* Homewood: Irwin Press.

Spencer, M. H., and L. Siegelman. 1959. *Managerial Economics.* Homewood: Irwin Press.

White, W. H. 1962. "The Changing Criteria in Investment Planning." In *Variability of Private Investment in Plant and Equipment.* Part 2. Joint Economic Committee. 87th Congress. 2nd Session. Washington: U.S. Government Office.

SEVEN

An Adaptive Economizing Analysis of Chinese Enterprises Under Alternative Reform Regimes

With Zhigang Wang and Gang Zou

7.1 Introduction

This chapter develops a dynamic analysis of the industrial firm that can be used to simulate enterprise behavior over time under alternative policy environments. The objective is to provide a tool for evaluating and projecting the response of key variables, such as output, employment, productivity, and profitability, to specific instrumental changes in economies that are undergoing major transitions in technology and to changes in the relationship between government and individual enterprises. In particular, we use it to consider China's economy during a period of evolving reforms that began in 1980. The Chinese example is, of course, of tremendous contemporary importance given the sheer size of the country, the dramatic progress that has occurred, and its unique process of introducing market mechanisms gradually within a Communist political system. Our model will be useful for understanding some aspects of this process and, we hope, for understanding similar processes in many different settings.

Aside from differences in the level of technology, the underlying engineering conditions of production and capital accumulation are more or less common to any economic system. The managerial conditions, however, depend on the political environment and the precise manner in which the government's plans and policies impinge on the constraints, costs, and benefits associated with enterprise opportunities. As policies change, these several components of the managerial problem also change. Thus, to explain previous performance, and to estimate the future repercussions of possible policy developments, one must incorporate at the level of the

The research upon which this chapter is based was sponsored by the World Bank as part of a project on transition economics, directed by Inderjit Singh.

firm the instrumental variables that embody various policies under specific operating conditions.

Rather than build a separate model for each different policy situation, we work toward a stylized model of a generic business firm that can accommodate a wide class of potential policy instruments. By generic we mean a modeling strategy in which decision variables and constraints are common to various levels of government control. As policies change from central planning based on direct policy instruments to a more or less free market system with decentrally determined prices and indirect policy instruments, the general model structure does not change; only the values of the instrumental variables are modified.

Developmental economists often draw on general equilibrium theory for the purpose of quantitative analysis, especially versions that represent the economy as optimizing a welfare function over time and as generating prices for which supplies and demands are in balance. A classic theoretical treatment is Malinvaud and Bacharach (1967). The implicit assumption underlying applications of this approach is that it yields good approximations of what markets actually generate. We say implicit because the mechanism by which the economy operates is not modeled. Rather, an algorithm designed to compute the outcome of this unspecified process is used.

In reality, however, markets are nothing more than the totality of efforts by enterprises to adapt both their own prices and their own outputs to changing and largely unforeseen imbalances of supplies and demands. Nowhere is this adaptive, disequilibrium character of development more evident than in those economies undergoing or attempting to initiate a transition from centrally planned, hierarchically administered organization to decentrally planned, privately administered, competitive organization. Our approach in this study reflects this fact.

The firm is represented as an adaptive economizing agent that sets its prices and adjusts its outputs more or less cautiously and more or less flexibly to current profit-making opportunities constrained by its inherited resources and production capacities and the limitations imposed on it by the regulatory and planning authorities. The firm's previous investment, production, and sales experience as well as its market signals, quotas, and regulated prices all condition its current situation. The firm adapts its plans as best it can in light of its experience to unfolding information from outside. Businesses in the most advanced market-oriented economies have similar features. There is no reason to believe that the behavior of enterprises in transitional economies comes closer to textbook ideals of market equilibrium than that in highly developed ones.

We begin by reviewing salient features of China's economy during its transition in the 1980s. This institutional and historical background is required for determining the necessary ingredients for the model structure and for providing data for testing the model's ability to track actual economic performance. We then outline the central features of our model. Its ability to track actual development in China's iron and steel industry is given an initial test of total output and market share. After this, the model is used to project key data for the industry: total output, output by technology, market shares, and the productivity of capital and labor. These projections are conducted for three different policy regimes: a moderate regime that assumes changes in instrumental variables along trends followed in the 1980s, a progressive regime that continues policies in place ca. 1990, and a liberal regime that assumes a more extreme market orientation.

7.2 Historical and Institutional Background[1]

7.2.1 Output Growth and Market Share

China's economy grew impressively during the postwar recovery and first 5-year plans from 1949 to 1957. It subsequently entered two decades in which output per person-year increased only modestly in comparison with the substantial capital accumulation that occurred during the same period. The poor performance stimulated wide-ranging reforms after 1978. These included, among other things, decentralizing supervisory responsibility and gradually replacing two-tiered government pricing with market pricing. Of special importance was the implementation of a director responsibility system that allowed enterprises to negotiate quotas, retain profits, reallocate labor and capital within the enterprise, and make discretionary market sales after fulfilling the quotas. Director responsibility introduced flexibility in selecting inputs, choosing product mix, and determining output levels. Managers could now react to market signals and compete for market shares. In these ways, the firm was gradually converted from a centrally directed institution into a regulated, market-oriented, mixed enterprise.

The reforms were followed by a renewal of rapid growth with an average annual real growth rate of nearly 12 percent during the 1990s. For the iron and steel industry we are using as an example in this study, total output more

---

[1] The following articles were useful in preparing this survey: Jiandong, Shaoji, and Shuxin (1991), Naughton (1985), Perry and Wong (1991), Shen (1987), Tian and Chan (1987), Wong (1985), Wu (1987) and World Bank (1983, 1985), Yi (1991).

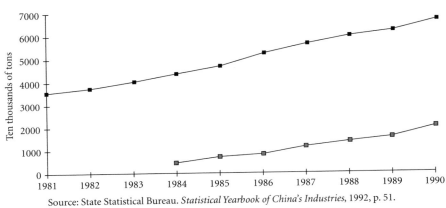

Source: State Statistical Bureau. *Statistical Yearbook of China's Industries*, 1992, p. 51.
Figure 7.1. Output and market sales in the iron and steel industry.

than doubled. Especially impressive is the takeoff of production for market, which reached 30 percent of the total by the end of the decade. These data are displayed in Figures 7.1 and 7.2.

7.2.2 The Need for Further Systemic Changes

Despite the success shown in these data, the broad consensus is that the industrial reform program must be improved. For example, financial shortages and restrictions on reinvestment capital have inhibited market-oriented production, whereas state-owned enterprises have been allowed to continue borrowing despite their profit performances having been so poor that they

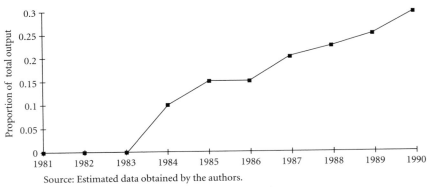

Source: Estimated data obtained by the authors.
Figure 7.2. Market share of total output.

would have gone bankrupt in a market economy. The latter occurrence has been called the *soft* budget constraint phenomenon by Kornai.

At the macroeconomic level, this phenomenon has led to the simultaneous persistence of excess demand with high and growing rates of factor use, declining productivity, and strong inflationary tendencies.

7.2.3 Organizational Forms and the Profit Motive

China's economy embraces a variety of organizational forms: larger state enterprises whose products and inputs were procured primarily by the state government in the pre-reform period, collectively owned enterprises, town and village enterprises, self-employed businesses, and a small number of domestic- and foreign-owned joint ventures. The latter four provided the initial impetus for market-oriented activity, but the giant, state-owned enterprises have joined the ranks of firms that can access the market when they meet the quotas under their plan. However, all enterprises continue to be more or less subject to centrally imposed constraints.

Still, since 1978, enterprises have had greater autonomy in determining their production and marketing activities. Formerly, a firm could hire more labor but could not dismiss any of its labor force. Recently, state-owned enterprises have begun to reallocate excessive labor. To do so, some of them have diversified and developed into multisectoral companies – for example, Capital Steel Corporation in Beijing – by merging with other companies, buying out other firms, and investing in new industries. These options have enabled enterprises to reallocate excessive labor in one industry to another industry in which they can use labor more effectively. Some small state-owned firms also acquired the flexibility of laying off excessive workers. It has been said that many small state-owned enterprises in Shanghai are planning to lay off as much as a third of their labor forces in the next year and another third in the year after.

Early in the reform process, firms were permitted to retain some earnings if they satisfied predetermined targets based on indexes specified by their supervisory agencies. These indexes were based on such determinants as output, product quality, the number of new products, costs, profits, and so forth. But the amount of indexation has gradually been reduced in favor of conventional profits for evaluating firm performance. Recently, a research group under the State Commission of Economic Reform reported that profit seeking had become the major motive for the majority of China's enterprises, including the state enterprises (Research Group of Development and Reform 1992). This development suggests that profit objectives spring up as soon as discretionary market-oriented production is permitted.[2]

7.2.4 Financial and Investment Constraints

One implication is the concern of central planners that profit seeking may have led to the emergence of shortsighted, self-serving behavior. In response to this concern, the government implemented the *director system* to reduce the diversion of profits to bonuses and to ensure that a substantial portion is allocated to investment. Under this program, the retained profit of a firm must be divided into three components: a bonus fund, a working capital fund, and an investment fund. Naturally, the proportion of profit that can be used as bonuses became a contentious issue between the firm and its supervisory agency. As an additional policy thrust, the profit subvention system is gradually being replaced by a tax system. Nonetheless, the distribution among the three components of after-tax profit is still regulated by the government.

For a variety of reasons, including low interest rates,[3] there has been an excess demand for loans. To control the money supply, the central government strictly limits the amount of each type of loan that a bank can issue to firms. The loans must be transacted for a specific purpose before they are granted. A specific loan cannot be transferred to other uses. Although additional money can be borrowed from a non-bank (i.e., private sources), the amount of money available in this market is limited and subject to a much higher interest rate. Furthermore, an equities market has not been fully developed. Although some financial transaction centers have recently been established, few stock-holding corporations have gone public. It is obvious that in the foreseeable future the majority of China's firms will not be able to raise substantial external investment funds. Consequently, a firm's operation is subject to a constrained capital budget based on retained earnings and government allocations.[4]

---

[2] For additional descriptive material on China's reform, see Byrd (1987); Chow (1985); Diao (1987); Jefferson and Xu (1992); Perry and Wong (1985); Zou, Wang, and Yu (1990); and Zou (1992).

[3] China's banks are classified into categories that have different specialized functions. For example, a loan for fixed capital investment must be borrowed from a construction bank, whereas a loan for working capital must be borrowed from an industrial and commercial bank. Such specialization is not unknown in capitalist countries.

[4] In some periods, the real interest rates were negative. In most periods after 1978, the real interest rates were only slightly higher than zero.

7.2.5 Pricing and Output Constraints

A typical firm in China may face three types of prices corresponding to the quota system: a *mandatory* price applying to the portion of product subject to the mandatory quota, an *instructive* (or negotiated) price applying to the portion of product subject to the instructive plan, and a *market* price applying to sales above the mandatory and instructive quotas. Correspondingly, these prices have three distinct production plans: the mandatory, centrally determined quota; the instructive plan, which is not mandatory but can be fulfilled at a higher price than that received for the mandatory quota; and the amount of production above the mandatory quota and the instructive plan targeted for market sales. In general, the instructive price is set above the mandatory price. During the periods when market exchange has been permitted, these discretionary prices have been above the instructive price.

7.3 Modeling the Generic Enterprise

7.3.1 The Generic Modeling Strategy

In a pure, centrally planned economy, the firm is an administrative device for implementing the directives of a central planning authority. Mandatory or instructive quotas bind sales and factor acquisitions because discretionary market exchange is forbidden. Both the amount and specific uses of the capital budget and labor force are centrally determined. The reallocation of capital, financial resources, and labor within the enterprise or among enterprises through voluntary exchanges is not permitted. Various rewards and penalties motivate enterprise managers to pursue these goals. Such systems have typically created material and financial constraints on the firm's systems. Attempts are made to overcome them by relaxing mandatory quotas, relaxing debt repayment schedules, or providing direct subsidies or tax rebates. These administrative strategies for dealing with disequilibrium do not always remove imbalances in supply and demand. Resource reallocation decisions often do not respond to such signals and are based instead on centrally determined political and economic objectives that can be far removed from economic realities. Consequently, imbalances in commodity flows can persist for very long periods without adjustment.

The essence of the problem is the absence of market feedback that signals aggregate commodity imbalances. Such feedback occurs in market economies through prices, interest rates, financial flows, and inventory changes. As we have seen, the economic reforms have introduced some of these market-feedback mechanisms. At the same time, they have influenced resource allocation by gradually reducing the system of quotas and centrally administered prices. But important vestiges of these nonmarket controls still play a major role in many firms. Thus, the mix of centrally planned output quotas, resource use, and prices with decentrally planned, discretionary output targets, resource allocation, and prices has changed over time. Central government direction and decentralized, market-oriented decision making are still mixed.

To capture this variety while limiting our study to a practical level of detail, we endow our generic firm with salient features of both government-directed and market-oriented enterprises so that, with changes in parameters, a single model can represent a great variety of firms in the possible continuum. At any given time, a given mix may broadly represent a relatively important group of enterprises, and thus the economy as a whole can in principle be approximated by a small number of representative types. Over time, the mandatory and instructive quotas and the centrally administered prices and subsidies will be modified. Thus, parameters of the various representative types and their relative importance in the overall economy will also change.

In the sections that follow, the various model components are described in nontechnical terms.

7.3.2 Enterprise Objectives, Performance Constraints, and Targets

The mandatory production quotas represent performance constraints for the enterprise, whose satisfaction is, in principle, the highest-priority objective guiding managerial behavior. Satisfying production quotas permits the firm to satisfy instructive quotas. The added production is rewarded at higher prices than that required for the mandatory quotas, thus giving firms an incentive to perform as well as possible. The allowance for discretionary market sales after the mandatory and instructive quotas are satisfied adds a further incentive to meet the high-order targets. If the firm fails to meet the quotas, central planners may respond by modifying its quotas or by allocating centrally controlled resources to the firm. As we have seen, the energetic pursuit of profit emerged as soon as discretionary market sales were permitted. Thus, together with the system of mandatory and instructive quotas, three distinct objectives have motivated enterprise behavior (in order of importance): (i) to satisfy mandatory quotas to the extent possible, (ii) to satisfy the instructive quota to the extent possible given that the mandatory quota is fulfilled, and (iii) to produce for the market in order to maximize profits given that both mandatory and instructive quotas are fulfilled. The latter objective is usually also constrained in practice by a production target, which represents what firms estimate they can produce at targeted profit rates of return. If the production target can be fulfilled, the firm will allocate excess internal resources to the extent possible to maximize the internal rate of return. In this case, managers may choose to reallocate internal resources to activities outside the enterprise – that is, to invest in financial instruments (bonds and equities) – divest themselves of assets by selling them to other enterprises, and so forth. Thus, the third objective of the firm is to maximize profits, not to produce some target amount.[5]

Cautious behavior induced by uncertain market conditions further constrains discretionary behavior and is as important a consideration as is the role of quotas, production targets, and resource availability. In pure economic theory, uncertainty is treated as an objectively or subjectively estimated probability of the occurrence of possible states of nature. Firms are then assumed to maximize an expected utility or expected profit function. This elegant treatment captures the essence of the decision-making problem but does not reflect the means by which enterprises actually modify their behavior. Actual practice is reflected more directly by the presence of self-imposed restraint in the pursuit of alternative discretionary activities.

Such restraint can be modeled by imposing an adaptive zone of flexibility within which risky decision variables are confined. The more serious the potential loss and the greater the level of uncertainty, the less flexible a decision maker is likely to be in modifying current practices, and vice versa. When a given activity level has been increased over time, it reflects a continuing contribution to enterprise profitability over a corresponding period and, on the basis of experience, a diminished uncertainty. A new practice, or one that has been diminished over time, has a higher level of uncertainty associated with it, which reflects its not having been used much before or an extended period of negative profitability. Firms are more flexible in expanding the former activities and less flexible in expanding the latter ones. Adaptive flexibility constraints that define the zone of flexible response are based on these considerations and add another type of constraint on enterprise behavior. They lead to portfolio-type decisions analogous to the

---

[5] Before economic reform, the financial budget for a firm came primarily from government transfers. Indeed, these transfers were often used to compensate for deficits, creating soft budget constraints. After reform, the share of capital from government declined from more than 80 percent before 1978 to about 20 percent in 1990 (Yi 1991); the share from bank loans has increased, and retained earnings are now a nontrivial component.

production of expected utility or Bayesian decision theory but in a behaviorally operational manner.[6]

In principle, satisfying the flexibility constraints is still another priority goal of the firm that takes precedence over profit maximization at anticipated (expected mean) prices. Thus, our rule is as follows: given that mandatory and instructive quotas are fulfilled, firms will pursue profits but only within their zones of flexible response. Should quotas or resource availability prevent firms from satisfying this goal, then they try to formulate plans that come as close to it as possible. Under these conditions, it is the desire to play it safe that dominates plans, not the pursuit of profit. When sufficiently safe alternatives are available, profit can be pursued within the zone of flexible response.[7]

This essay is concerned primarily with the growing discretionary, market share of production. Thus, in the simulation exercises that follow and given the data used, we assume that the enterprise can satisfy mandatory and instructive quotas. These quotas thus appear as exogenously given levels. However, our generic approach does not require this assumption. Under some quota levels, resource availabilities, or both, market-oriented production would not be possible. In that case, it would be the maximum level of fulfilling the mandatory or instructive quota that would be endogenously determined. Similarly, for the data used in the simulations, the flexibility constraints are satisfied.

7.3.3 Activities and Profits

For production to be profitable within a given firm, prices and interest rates must justify investment inside, as opposed to outside, the firm. If prices are fixed for a given firm and thus do not justify inside investment, then the firm will have an incentive to avoid meeting its production goal and to channel its resources elsewhere. To prevent a given firm from doing so, the government would have to provide various subsidies to the firm or impose various coercive methods of enforcement. In terms of the opportunity cost of capital, investment inside the firm would be uneconomic. If competition were allowed, it would force such a firm out of business, thus reducing

---

[6] The three goals arranged in priority order constitute an ℓ^{**} lexicographic ordering – a representation of planning objectives that is characteristic of many decision problems. See Day (1996).

[7] This behavioral hypothesis of firm behavior under uncertainty was set forth by Day (1971) and tested in various dynamic models of regional agriculture and industrial production. For examples, see Day and Cigno (1978) and Day and Singh (1977).

the supply of the product and allowing the resources to be channeled to enterprises that could earn higher rates.

To accommodate the opportunities and constraints that arise in the mixed enterprises, we must include activities that represent the allocation of output and working capital to alternative uses at alternative prices. We must also incorporate diverse constraints that require various output and input utilization quotas. At the same time, certain investment alternatives that are typical of a growing economy at a relatively early stage of capital accumulation must be incorporated – namely, investment in a *low-tech*, labor-intensive technology; in a *high-tech*, capital-intensive technology; and in the conversion of the low-tech capacity to an intermediate *hybrid* technology. An example in the steel industry has been the open hearth, oxygen, and the hybrid open-hearth with oxygen-lancing technologies. The allocation of working capital to the production and investment budgets must be elaborated to include the division of retained earnings, borrowed funds, and government subsidies.

The profit level associated with any given enterprise plan consists of the sum of the products of the activity levels and their associated costs and return, with cost items given a negative value and return items a positive one.

7.3.4 Resource and Performance Constraints

In addition to the performance constraints described earlier, the firm is limited by its inherited product and input inventories, production capacities, and financial resources. Product inventories are carried over from the past after quotas and sales have been met. Input inventories are carried over after depletion has been accounted for, and production capacities are carried over after depreciation and new investment have been incorporated.

Associated with each constraint is an imputed value, shadow price, or dual variable that represents the marginal change in profits that would be caused by a unit change in profits and that would in turn be caused by a unit change in the associated constraining factor. These dual variables can be interpreted as the opportunity costs of the imposed constraints in terms of expected profits. Thus, for example, the imputed value of material inventory is the cost of adding to it (the price of material inputs weighted by the current rate of return on external investment). For another example, the imputed cost per unit of medium- or high-tech capital stock includes depreciation plus the opportunity cost of invested capital plus the production cost savings of the medium- or high-tech method, or both, also weighted by the external rate of return. This imputed value is the marginal cost to the enterprise of replacing a high-cost method of production with a lower cost one. The imputed value to the mandatory or instructive quota is the increase in profits from market sales that would be possible if resources could be reallocated from quotas to discretionary production. As a final example, the imputed value of a flexibility constraint is the increase in profits valued at the estimated average or anticipated profits that could be achieved if the firm were less cautious. In other words, it is an internally imposed risk premium.

7.3.5 Market Pricing

Competitive equilibrium theory does not describe how market prices are determined. It specifies only the conditions under which equilibrium prices exist. In reality, most large-scale firms (as well as many small enterprises) determine prices themselves according to a cost-markup rule that accounts for a desired rate of return on invested capital. In equilibrium, this markup will be equalized across industries. Out-of-equilibrium rates of return will be higher in some industries than in others, which will induce a market response by government or private banks to supply loans. Accordingly, unless controlled by non-market-oriented rules, the external prices of factors (material, energy, labor, production capacity, and finance charge) will change.

In practice, the desired markup yields only a target price. If sales are less than expected and unwanted inventories are accumulating, the firm's price will be adjusted downward from the target in response to insufficient demand. This adjustment will lower the internal rate of return and prompt the firm to use funds differently than if the prices had been set at the target level. Conversely, if sales are greater than expected and inventories are falling below desired levels, the price will be adjusted upward, increasing the internal rate of return compared with the targeted rate of return. This combination of target pricing with adjustments to market conditions is used in this study.

7.3.6 Enterprise Plans for a Given Period

The enterprise plan consists of production, investment, and allocation levels that meet resource constraints, maximize the fulfillment of mandatory quotas, maximize instructive quotas if mandatory quotas have been met, are sufficiently safe that they lie within the zone of flexible response, maximize profits given the fulfillment of priorities and feasibility requirements (and given the fulfillment of sales targets), and reallocate internal financial resources to external opportunities to the extent permitted by the planning authorities.

This study assumes that these plans can be executed so that they become estimates of what representative firms would do on average, or what the aggregate of firms thus represented would do.

7.3.7 Market Feedback and Adaptive Economizing

Market feedback and accumulated experience coupled with the profit goal connect previous performance with current possibilities, costs, and benefits. Previous market prices determine prior profits and the current financial position of the firm and, hence, its current budget constraint. They provide data for estimating future profits that may accrue from the alternative uses of funds. Many of the variables that enter into the requisite feedback relationship are determined by the central planning agencies and by firms in outside industries. This is true of input supplies, actual market prices and sales, quotas, central and instructive prices, borrowing rates, and external rates of return or funds invested outside the industry. All of these must be treated as exogenous variables in this firm-level study. However, the model does incorporate market feedback by including capacity expansion, adjustments to the zone of flexible response, changes in market production, pricing targets, financial capital, and sales forecasts.

At each period, planning data are updated to account for further feedback and exogenous changes. The firm then calculates its decisions by prioritizing its goals to obtain various production, investment, and resource allocation levels. Previous experience also conditions the extent of the firm's caution in modifying production and investment practices. Continued profitability leads to a buildup of working capital and a willingness to expand activities in profitable areas and investment in profitable capital stocks. Overexpansion leads to falling sales and prices, which reduce profits or increase losses. These automatically reduce working capital, which contracts output and investment. The adjustments that ensue prevent perpetual shortages or gluts, but the implied fluctuations do not necessarily dampen and converge to a competitive equilibrium. Output and prices may continue to fluctuate, perhaps erratically, but gluts or shortages are unlikely to persist indefinitely. The dynamics of this process in terms of models such as those described earlier have been elaborated elsewhere.[8]

---

[8] On the general background of the model in this study, see Day (1971), Day and Singh (1977), and Day (1996). An elaborate example is found in Day, Morley, and Smith (1974).

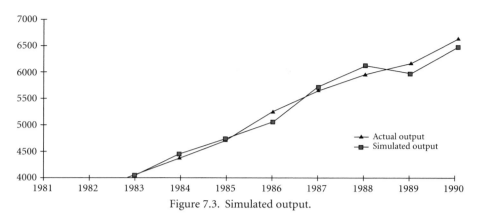

Figure 7.3. Simulated output.

7.4 Simulating a Decade of Change

We now use the model to simulate economic change in China's iron and steel industry. Before the reform, the production technologies of different types of firms varied substantially. Even the giant Capital Steel Corporation in Beijing and the Bao Shan Steel Corporation in Shanghai made technological advances in very different ways. The former developed more hybrid technology, whereas the latter chose to develop high-technology production. Because we are simulating the steel industry as a whole rather than particular firms, our representative firm will mimic average industry performance, not the behavior of any particular enterprise.

Figures 7.3 and 7.4 show the actual and model-generated data for total production and the share of market sales in total output for the 1981–90

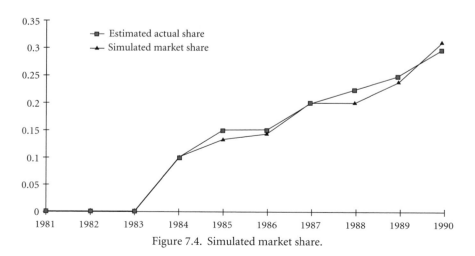

Figure 7.4. Simulated market share.

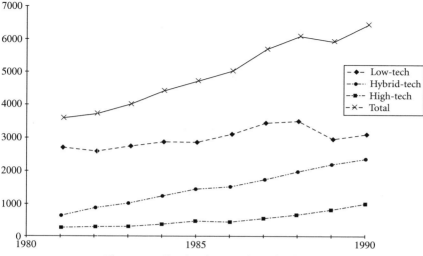

Figure 7.5. Simulated output by technology.

period. The reform started in 1984. Since then, both output and the market share have grown. The model mimics this growth rather well.

Model-generated estimates of output by technology are presented in Figure 7.5. Comparable independent data for the industry were not readily available for testing these estimates but, given the model's performance for total output and market share, the estimates are plausible. They show that both hybrid and high-technology production have increased, and that, by the end of the decade, low-technology production fell. The continued investment in the hybrid technology is explained by the fact that financial resources are constrained and that the hybrid technology is capital-saving. In addition, both hybrid and high-technology methods are relatively new and, thus, the flexibility constraints for their adoption are initially rather small.

7.5 Simulating the Repercussions of Alternative Policy Regimes

To determine how our strategy can be used to project the effect of alternative government policies, we used our model to simulate industry behavior for the 1990s under three alternative sets of instrumental variables. For reference, we have named these the base, moderate, and liberal regimes.

The Base Regime
Under the base regime, the major policy indexes, such as planned prices, the share of quotas in production, the share of quotas in input purchases, the

tax regime, incentive scheme, and so forth, are assumed to be the same in the 1990s as those that prevailed at the end of the 1980s.

The production and input purchases of the representative firm are assumed to be subject to both mandatory quotas and instructive quotas. Production above the quotas is allowed to be sold in the market. Similarly, above-quota inputs can be purchased from the market. The market shares of both input purchases and output sales are subject to change as the reform program goes on. We used survey data to project this change (see Zou 1992). The planned prices are generally lower than market prices. For instance, the ratio of planned price to market price in 1988 was about 0.8 for output and 0.65 for inputs (Jefferson and Xu 1991). The planned price may be even lower than average cost; however, the firm can compensate for the implied loss with profitable market sales.

The Moderate Regime

Under the moderate regime, the major policy indexes are assumed to change according to the trend established in the 1980s. These trends involved rather gradual changes in the various policy instruments.

The Liberal Regime

Under the liberal regime, the instrumental variables are assumed to follow much more rapid trends toward the market economy. In particular, all quotas are eliminated within 3 years.

Differences among the Regimes

The major difference among the policy regimes is the speed at which planned quotas and instructive quotas are reduced. Under the liberal regime, all planned quotas are eliminated by the end of 1992, and all instructive quotas are eliminated by the end of 1993. Under the base regime, the shares of planned quotas and instructive quotas remain roughly the same in the second period as those that prevailed at the end of the first period. Under the moderate regime, the planned quotas gradually decline to trivial ones; the instructive quotas fall at a slower pace but remain a substantial share by the end of the second period.

A gap between planned, instructive, and market prices exists under the liberal and moderate regimes. Under the base regime, the planned relationship between instructive prices and market prices is constant. Under the liberal regime, the firms can lay off workers; under the moderate and base regimes, firms cannot.

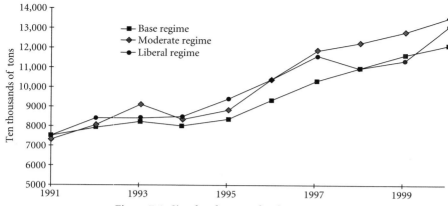

Figure 7.6. Simulated output for three regimes.

All three regimes have the same wage, interest, tax, and depreciation rates. It is obvious that the effects of changes in these variables can be simulated by the model. Nonetheless, our simulations focus on the effects of policies associated with the speed of marketization.

According to an expert in the former State Price Bureau, which was dissolved in 1993, the prices for most final industrial goods had been liberalized by mid-1993. The path of reform has thus been similar to the liberal regime. However, the prices for some major industrial materials and intermediate products, including steel, have been liberalized more gradually. Their paths lie along the price trend assumed for the moderate regime. In particular, the market share of the steel industry is roughly 50 percent of total steel output, which is very close to our simulation for the moderate regime. The prices for some crucial materials and energy, such as oil and refined oil, are still controlled tightly by the government, which is a situation that resembles the base regime.

The results of the simulations are shown in Figures 7.6–7.10. Figures 7.6 and 7.7 show the simulated output and market share for the three policy regimes as projections to the year 2000 from the 1980–90 period. Figure 7.8 shows the corresponding simulated levels of the three types of technology.

Under the base regime, the differentials between planned prices and market prices remain. A demand shock occurred in mid-1993 when the government tightened monetary controls to fight the explosive inflation that had emerged in the first half of 1993. Consequently, the demand for major industrial materials dropped substantially and prices declined sharply. When we add market demand shocks in 1994 and 1998, fewer market sales cause the firm to experience financial troubles because the firm relies heavily

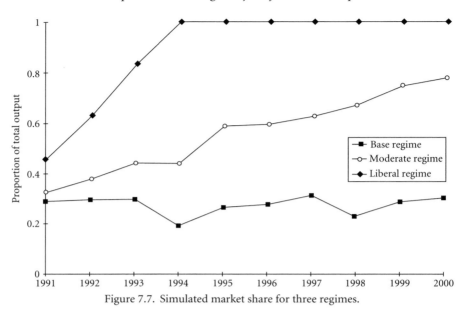

Figure 7.7. Simulated market share for three regimes.

on the more profitable market sales to compensate for its quota production. Thus, the firm must swing away from the capital-intensive investment in the subsequent periods.

Under the moderate regime, the gaps between the planned and market prices narrow gradually. The quotas become a trivial part of production and input purchases at the end of the simulation period. Nevertheless, before quotas are eliminated completely, the market prices for output will generally be greater than the markup prices, since the firm must use the profits from the market sales to compensate for the quota production, but the differentials are moderate. The above-markup prices may be an incentive for the firm to invest in the industry rather than invest outside. Investment in high technology is encouraged because high-technology production saves expensive material and energy. The effects of the market demand shocks are less than those under the base regime.

Under the liberal regime, prices fluctuate widely, especially in the early stage of the second period. Prices rise during the early period of the liberal regime and are then forced down toward the markup prices. At this stage, a shock to the internal return rate caused by external market shocks may prompt the firm to shift investment from internal investment to external investment. Capital-intensive, high-technology production is encouraged because the firm is allowed to lay off excessive labor. The pattern of changes under the liberal regime is similar to the pattern under the moderate regime

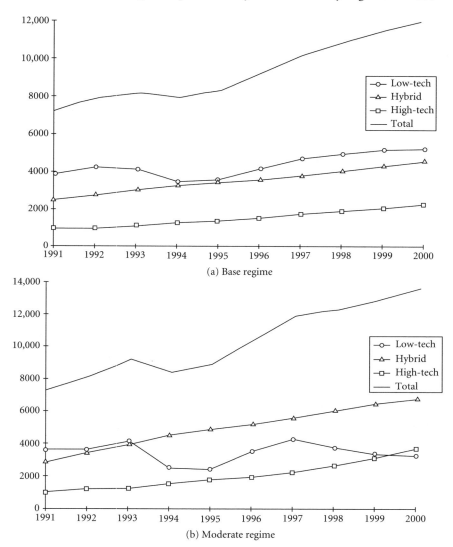

Figure 7.8. Simulated capacities by technology.

except that fluctuations under the liberal regime are larger than those under the moderate regime. Moreover, the liberal regime requires more financial support from bank loans in its transition stage (which could lead to a higher inflation rate). The share of subsidies of total fixed capital declines significantly under the liberal regime, whereas the investment funds from bank loans and retained profits become major financial sources. Labor productivity increases owing to the introduction of a bonus incentive scheme

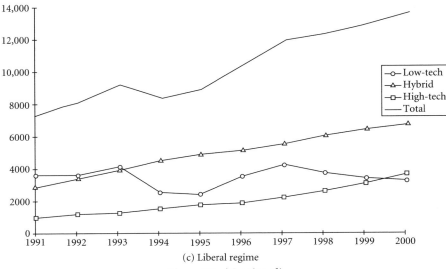

(c) Liberal regime

Figure 7.8. (*Continued*)

and technological advancement. During the early part of the first period, labor was cheap, material and energy were supplied by the government distribution system at artificially low prices, and retained profits were not large enough to finance the capital-intensive, high-technology investment. Thus, the old technology, although inefficient, still dominated the steel industry.

In the latter part of the 1980s, labor became more expensive, material and energy costs increased as the government reduced the quota input supplies, and the inefficiency of the old technology became obvious, forcing the firm to choose more advanced technologies. In the meantime, more financial sources from bank loans and the retained profits were available for the firm to invest in more capital-intensive but more efficient technologies. The reform program had successfully pushed technological progress. Nevertheless, large differentials between the planned and market prices remained, creating new problems for the reform program. Moreover, although the firm chose more capital-intensive and less labor-intensive technologies, the previously hired labor force could not be reduced, creating new inefficiencies.

Figure 7.9 depicts labor productivities under the alternative regimes. The liberal regime allows firms to lay off excessive labor, which yields the highest labor productivity. Under the base regime, excessive labor cannot be laid off when firms face financial troubles or demand shocks. Low profitability

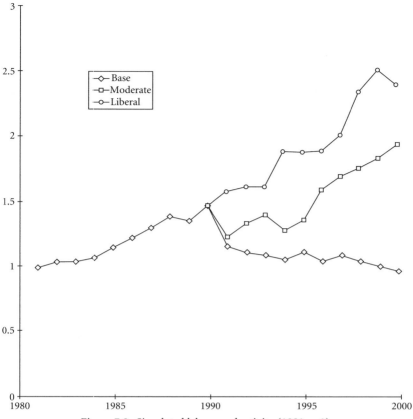

Figure 7.9. Simulated labor productivity (1981 = 1).

with excessive labor will substantially reduce the bonus received by workers, in turn reducing labor productivity in the next period given declines in x-efficiency. Thus, it is more difficult for the firm in the base regime to recover from financial troubles or demand shocks. Continuous financial troubles also induce the firm to invest in capital-saving, low-technology production. Accordingly, continuous declines in labor productivity may occur as simulated by our model. The moderate regime allows the firm to channel a limited amount of excessive workers into other industries through its multisectoral operation. The resulting labor productivity lies between the labor productivity of the liberal regime and that of the base regime.

Figure 7.10 shows capital productivity. Given an acceleration of capital deepening and increased investment costs, capital productivity declines. This decline is more pronounced under the moderate and liberal regimes

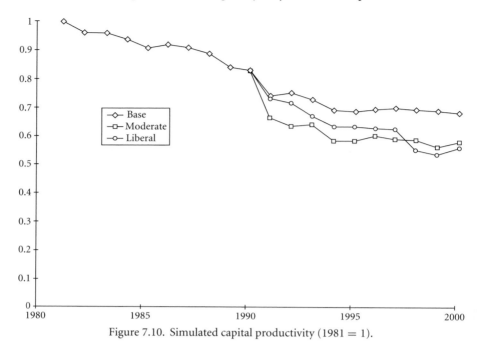

Figure 7.10. Simulated capital productivity (1981 = 1).

than under the base regime because, with a reduction in material supply quotas in the former firms, they are encouraged to use material-saving but capital-intensive technologies.

7.6 Summary and Conclusions

The type of model presented herein provides a promising framework for describing economic adjustments when market forces are operating but when individual enterprises are constrained by various types of policy instruments and when market valuations are augmented by taxes, subsidies, and prices administered through government bureaus. It is especially well suited for accommodating multiple products and alternative technologies that allow for substitution effects while also reflecting the discrete differences that exist in reality. It is designed to mimic economic behavior by boundedly rational decision makers who adapt over time to market forces and policy instruments. Although such models possess competitive equilibria in principle, in practice they generally portray growth and fluctuations out of equilibrium as enterprises adapt and the economy evolves.

Although many details have been omitted in the current model and we have carried out simulations for the steel industry with only a few alternative policy regimes, the framework is flexible enough to incorporate other important features of the business enterprise and of government policy. For example, many alternative production activities in which aggregate output can be broken down into individual iron and steel products would be possible. A more detailed breakdown of imports could be included. Simulations could be conducted to compare alternative tax rates, credit availability, bonuses, investment credits, and so forth over time.

Finally, the model can be developed along multisectoral and intertemporal lines to show macroeconomic implications. But these developments are beyond the scope of this essay.

References

Byrd, W. A. 1987. "The Impact of the Two-Tier Plan/Market System in Chinese Industry." *Journal of Comparative Economics* 11:295–308.

Chow, G. 1985. *The Chinese Economy.* New York: Harper & Row.

Day, R. H. 1971. "Rational Choice and Economic Behavior." *Theory and Decision* 1:229–51.

Day, R. H. 1996. "Satisficing Multiple Preferences in and out of Equilibrium." Chapter 1 in R. Fabella and E. de Dios (eds.) *Choice, Growth and Development: Emerging and Enduring Issues, Essays in Honor of José Encarnación.* Quezon City: University of the Philippines Press.

Day, R. H., and A. Cigno. 1978. *Modelling Economic Change: The Recursive Programming Approach.* Amsterdam: North-Holland Publishing Co.

Day, R. H., and I. Singh. 1977. *Economic Development as an Adaptive Process: A Green Revolution Case Study.* Cambridge: Cambridge University Press.

Day, R. H., S. Morley, and K. R. Smith. 1974. "Myopic Optimizing and Rules of Thumb in a Micro Model of Industrial Growth." *American Economic Review* 64:11–23.

Diao, X. 1987. "The Role of the Two-Tier Price System." In B. L. Reynolds (ed.) *Reform in China: Challenges and Choices.*

Jefferson, G. H., and W. Xu. 1991. "The Impact of Reform on Socialist Enterprises in Transition: Structure, Conduct, and Performance in Chinese Industry." *Journal of Comparative Economics* 15:45–64.

Jiandong, J., X. Shaoji, and S. Shuxin. 1991. *China's Financial Market,* China's Finance Press.

Malinvaud, E., and M. O. L. Bacharad. 1967. *Activity Analysis in the Theory of Growth and Planning.* London: Macmillan; St. Martin's Press.

Naughton, B. 1985. "False Starts and Second Wind: Financial Reforms in China's Industrial System." In E. J. Perry and C. Wong (eds.) *The Political Economy of Reform in Post–Mao China.* Cambridge: Harvard University Press.

Perry, E. J., and C. Wong. 1985. "Introduction: The Political Economy of Reform in Post-Mao China: Causes, Content, and Consequences." In E. J. Perry and C. Wong (eds.) *The Political Economy of Reform in Post-Mao China.* Cambridge: Harvard University Press.

Shen, Y. 1987. "General Situation of the Circulation of China's Production Materials." In the Editorial Committee of the *Almanac of China's Economy, 1987.* Beijing: Economic Management Press.

Tian, Y., and Q. Chan. 1987. "The Distribution System Reform in 1986." In the Editorial Committee of the *Almanac of China's Economy, 1987.* Beijing: Economic Management Press.

Wong, C. 1985. "Material Allocation and Decentralization: Impact of the Local Sector on Industrial Reform." In E. J. Perry and C. Wong (eds.) *The Political Economy of Reform in Post-Mao China.* Cambridge: Harvard University Press.

World Bank. 1983. *China: Socialist Economic Development.* 3 Volumes. Washington, DC: World Bank.

World Bank. 1985. *China: Long-Term Development Issues and Options.* Baltimore: Johns Hopkins University Press.

Wu, J., and R. Zhao. 1987. "The Dual Pricing System in China's Industry." *Journal of Comparative Economics* 11:309–18.

Yi, G. 1991. "The Monetization Process in China During the Economic Reform." *China Economic Review* 2:75–96.

Zou, G. 1992. "Enterprises Behavior under the Two-Tier Plan/Market System." McNamara Report. Washington, DC: The World Bank.

Zou, G., Z. Wang, and C. Yu. 1990. *Analysis on China's Microeconomic Situation.* Beijing: People's University Press.

PART THREE

EPOCHAL DEVELOPMENT

EIGHT

Economic Development and Migration

With Yiu-Kwan Fan

8.1 Introduction

Economic development is a process of change, a process of getting out of the existing state. Newly developing economies may have as examples the paths already trodden by their advanced counterparts. Each economy has distinct initial conditions, however, and each has to find its way onto the trodden path or to seek out a new, unbeaten path altogether. Either way is difficult and irreversible. Each may be far from optimal in retrospect.

When an economy undergoes change, it generates signals that motivate adjustments by the various economic agents and sectors. These adaptations induce still further adaptation. In each period the actors arrive at "optimal" decisions, taking into account their own perceived constraints and current objectives based on available information flowing through the economic environment from previous periods. Individuals, caught up in a turbulent current of economic activity, keep adapting to a changing environment and making the best decisions they can given the uncertainties and their limited foresight. Their decisions jointly determine the next state of the economy through a structure only accounted for in part in the individual plans. The economy as a whole searches its way through a complex terrain, stretch by stretch, and as it moves along it undergoes an irreversible metamorphosis.[1] This adaptive point of view yields a new perspective on

---

[1] The use of suboptimization with feedback (recursive programming) to represent economic development has many precedents. Our application is a direct descendent of Day and Singh (1977). Koopmans (1967, p. 12) endorsed the approach when he observed that "the problem [of economic growth] takes on some of the aspects of the ascent of a mountain wrapped

Reprinted from Richard H. Day and Cigno, *Modeling Economic Change: The Recursive Programming Approach*, copyright 1978, with permission from Elsevier Science.

the relationships among producing sectors and migration during economic development.

The experiences of economically advanced countries indicate that the degree of urbanization is highly correlated with the level of economic development. Today, less developed countries (LDCs) are experiencing rapid urbanization resulting basically from heavy rural–urban migration, but evidence seems to show that the prevailing pattern of urbanization is unhealthy for the development of these economies. The heavy influx of people into the urban areas gives rise to socioeconomic problems in the cities, and because the expansion of urban employment fails to catch up with the urban population growth, urban unemployment and underemployment have become serious problems. Rapid urban growth, coupled with slow industrial development, has given rise to the "urban traditional sector" in the cities of less developed economies. Urban unemployment and underemployment appear not in the urban modern sector but primarily in the swelling urban traditional sector.[2]

On the theoretical front, the role of migration in economic development has long been recognized, but only recently has the migration process been explicitly incorporated in development models. It has been common practice to treat migration as a labor transfer between sectors. In many cases, such as the Fei-Ranis and Jorgenson models, this transfer is assumed to be costless and instantaneous and governed by a smooth process determined by interregional wage differentials. Important as these studies are in other regards, they assume away the problems that arise during the transfer between sectors. In particular, the questions (1) What initiates the transfer? (2) How does the transfer occur? (3) How is the process sustained? (4) What are

---

in fog. Rather than searching for a largely invisible optimal path, one may have to look for a good rule for choosing the next stretch of the path with the help of all the information available at the time." Leontief (1958) had already sketched out such a model a decade earlier. His model was elaborated by Day (1969) and by Day and Fan (1976).

[2] The relationship between rural–urban migration and rapid urbanization in the LDCs is described in various United Nations studies such as UN–ECAFE Secretariat, *The Demographic Situation and Prospective Population Trends in Asia and the Far East* (1964). On the socioeconomic problem created by rapid urbanization, see Laquian and Dutton (1971) and United Nations (1970). On the problem of unemployment in the LDCs, see Baer and Herve (1966) and Morawetz (1974). On the population problem in relation to the urbanization process, see United Nations, *Urbanization in the Second United Nations Development Decade* (1970).

It is difficult to give a rigorous definition of the "urban traditional sector." Todaro (1969) described the sector as one that "encompass[es] all those workers not regularly employed in the urban modern sector, i.e., the overtly unemployed, the unemployed or sporadically employed, and those who grind out a meager existence in petty retail trades and services."

the limits to the transfer process? and (5) What is the relationship between labor transfer and labor absorption? are not considered.[3]

By way of contrast, rural–urban migration is given an explicit dynamic role in the Harris–Todaro model, which is the first of its kind to explain urban unemployment. The authors, however, observe that "despite the existence of positive marginal products in agriculture and significant levels of urban unemployment, rural–urban labor migration not only continues to exist but indeed appears to be accelerating" (Harris and Todaro 1970, p. 126). This appears to be inconsistent with the "equilibrium urban unemployment rate" determined in their model by the probability of finding a job in the city. In reality the low and ever-decreasing probability of finding an urban job has not stopped rural migration. Like other equilibrium development models, the Harris–Todaro model interprets disequilibrating changes as equilibrating marginal adjustments.

In contrast to these formulations, the adaptive approach explicitly accounts for disequilibrium changes. One can readily incorporate important factors, including noneconomic ones, affecting the decision to migrate, the feedback influence of migration on population growth and labor market conditions and the linkages among migration, production, income distribution, and quality of life in rural and urban areas. As will be shown, the characteristic features of rural–urban migration in the LDCs are rapid urbanization accompanied by little industrial growth, a heavy stream of rural–urban migration with a sizable counterstream of urban–rural migration, increasingly unbalanced spatial distribution of population, ever-worsening distribution of income before it gets better, unemployment and underemployment in both rural and urban areas, and so forth. We will show how these features arise from the multisector structure of economic adaptation in disequilibrium.

Our strategy is to explore a simplified, adaptive model of a hypothetical economy that possesses some of the central features of several overpopulated, underdeveloped but rapidly changing economies that seem to be evolving in a maladaptive manner. The result, while of considerable interest and shedding new light on the development process, must be regarded as a provisional step in the application of a general, quite flexible methodology.

---

[3] On the theoretical analysis of migration and development, see Ravenstein (1885, 1889), Redford (1926), Kuznets et al. (1957, 1960, 1964), and Sjaastad (1961). Development models explicitly embodying migration include Todaro (1969); Harris and Todaro (1970); Williamson, Kelley, and Cheetham (1972); Galbis (1972); Fan (1973a). For a critical survey of migration models in the context of economic development, see Fan (1973b).

8.2 A Hypothetical Economy

Imagine a small economy in which traditional agriculture is the predominant economic activity. "Grain" is the main crop, and most of it is produced by labor-intensive traditional farming that requires no machinery and little industrially produced agricultural materials. Modern farming has been introduced in the economy and has been adopted on a relatively small scale in the production of grain and export crops. The export crop is grown solely for foreign markets. Fiber is also grown, and its production is land- and labor-intensive. However, most of the fiber produced is exported, for the domestic consumer goods industry can only use a small amount (10 percent) of the crop as raw material. The industrial sector is very small. The value of industrial output amounts to a tiny fraction of the gross domestic product (GDP) (1 percent), and industrial consumer goods output accounts for most of that meager share (85 percent). Domestic output of agricultural and industrial machinery is very small.

Most of the population live in the rural area (87 percent). Slightly more than 80 percent of the rural labor force are engaged in agriculture, which is the preferred occupation, and the remaining are in nonagricultural productive activities. In the urban area, only 2 percent are industrial workers. The bulk of the urban modern labor is made up of civil workers (37 percent) and workers in financial intermediaries (26 percent). About 35 percent of the urban workers seek their livelihood in the "urban traditional sector," engaging in traditional services that require little more than their own labor.

This is a subsistence economy. The real wage in agriculture is at the rural subsistence level. Per capita agricultural income is slightly above the subsistence line. Rural nonagricultural workers are living on an income below subsistence. The urban residents are a bit better off. The institutional wage for workers in the manufacturing industries, the public sector, and the financial intermediaries is 2.4 times the subsistence level, and the per capita real income for these modern workers is about 2.2 times that of agricultural workers. The real income for urban traditional workers is below the urban subsistence line, and the government has to spend 1.5 percent of the total tax revenue on urban relief.

The economy is almost self-sufficient in grain but has to import agricultural machinery, agricultural materials, and industrial consumer goods. These imports are paid for by exporting fiber, an export crop, and to a very small extent, industrial machinery. The economy is running a substantial balance of trade deficit.

The government in this economy plays a minimal role in affecting the production activities of the private sectors. It levies income taxes and excise taxes to derive its revenue. On the expenditure side, besides the transfer payments to the urban poor and the wage bill to civil workers, there are programs related to agricultural and industrial development to enhance production efficiencies, and public services to maintain and improve the "quality of life" in rural and urban areas.

The quality of life is different between rural and urban areas. If we attempt to itemize the difference, we can find that, although education, health care, and housing conditions are better in the urban than in the rural area, pollution, crime, and alienation are also more serious in the cities than in the rural communities. Responding to the economic forces and quality-of-life differences, people migrate. In this economy, most of the rural–urban migrants are pushed from the rural area in the face of starvation. There is very little urban-to-rural migration. Such is the initial state of our hypothetical economy.[4]

According to the preceding description, there are two distinct "areas" and six distinct "sectors" to be represented: the Agricultural and Nonagricultural Sectors in the Rural Area (Sectors A and Z),[5] the Manufacturing Sector and the Urban Traditional Sector in the Urban Area (Sectors M and V), the Financial Intermediaries Sector (Sector F), and the Public Sector (Sector G). Production, investment, employment, and financial activity levels for a given period within the agricultural and manufacturing sectors (A and M) are represented by linear programming models, one for each sector. Activities within the other sectors are represented by behavioral equations involving adjustment to prevailing conditions. Feedback relations involving capital accumulation, income flows, labor supplies, and working capital connect sectors. The linear programming models include adaptive flexibility constraints to represent cautious behavior.

The financial intermediaries provide services to smooth out the economic activities of the sectors. The employment slacks in the rural and urban areas are taken up by the nonagricultural and urban traditional sectors, respectively. Whereas the prices of the agricultural and manufacturing products are set exogenously in the world markets, the prices of nonagricultural produce and urban traditional services are determined in the domestic commodity market by market clearing and demand functions. Sectoral income and wages are jointly determined by institutional elements and the prices and volumes of sectoral outputs.

---

[4] For a discussion of noneconomic factors affecting the migration decision, see United Nations (1953). Also see Lee (1966) and Mabogunje (1970).

[5] Our hypothetical economy is meant to represent a composite of real economies in Asia. The data used in structuring the model and the references from which they were drawn can be found in Fan (1974).

Qualities of life in the two areas are described by indexes representing education, health facilities, housing conditions, pollution, crime, "bright lights," and alienation. These indexes are influenced by the population densities and by government expenditures. Relative sectoral income levels and relative differences in rural and urban quality of life jointly generate the migration streams from one area to another. Such migration streams affect the distribution of population and, hence, the distribution of labor force between the rural and urban areas. These effects diffuse throughout the entire system through the sector linkages and feedback relations, helping to shape the new state of the economy in the subsequent period.

Table 8.1 summarizes the various activities, commodities, and input–output relationships existing in the model economy.

8.3 Seventy-Five Years of Simulated History

How does this hypothetical economy evolve? What patterns of development emerge? What problems are encountered? It would be nice if these questions could be answered by a general analysis that would show what qualitative set of trajectories is implied by any given configuration of parameters, but the model is too complex to unravel analytically. Not that it could not be done in principle using the established phase theory of recursive programming, but the undertaking would be a tedious one that would exhaust anyone's patience. Instead, we have simulated the model using the initial conditions already described and a specific set of parameter values. Trajectories for all the model variables were obtained for a 75-year period.

For actual economies, these parameter values should be estimated econometrically. In this exercise, however, most of the numerical values are fictitious ones that fall within bounds of "reasonable" guesses intended to represent a composite Southeast Asian economy. Consequently, we focus on the purely qualitative aspects of the results.

Figures 8.1 and 8.2 display the trends in agricultural and industrial production and capital stock. The classic sigmoid or S-curve of long-run growth is seen in the time path of modern grain farming and in that of agricultural capital. The counterpart of these curves is the eventual decay, after two decades of expansion, of traditional farming techniques. Exponential growth followed by an exponential decay in a remarkable phase switching is seen in fiber and export crop production and, with a later switching, in urban production of industrial machinery, farming machinery, and agricultural materials. A more complex pattern is observed in the growth of traditional services, whereas consumer goods production exhibits the neoclassical exponential growth pattern.

Table 8.1. *Production, consumption, and trade relations between rural area and urban area*

Area	Sector	Production		Consumption	Trade	
		Input	Output		Import to area	Export from area
R u r a l	A	Land Rural labor Farming machinery Agricultural materials	Grain Fiber Export crop	Grain Industrial consumer good Z-Good	Industrial consumer good Farming machinery Agricultural materials	Grain (D[a] & F[b]) Fiber (D & F) Export crop (F) Z-Good (D)
	Z	Rural labor	Z-Good			
U r b a n	M	Urban labor Industrial machinery Fiber	Farming machinery Agricultural materials Industrial consumer good Industrial machinery	Grain Industrial consumer good Z-Good Urban traditional services	Grain Fiber Z-Good	Industrial consumer good (D & F) Farming machinery (D & F) Agricultural materials (D & F)
	v	Urban labor	Traditional services			
	F	Urban labor	Banking services to A. M. G			
	G	Urban labor	Public services for maintaining and improving the quality of life and productivity in rural and urban areas			

[a] D: Export from area to domestic market in other area of the economy.
[b] F: Export from area to foreign markets.

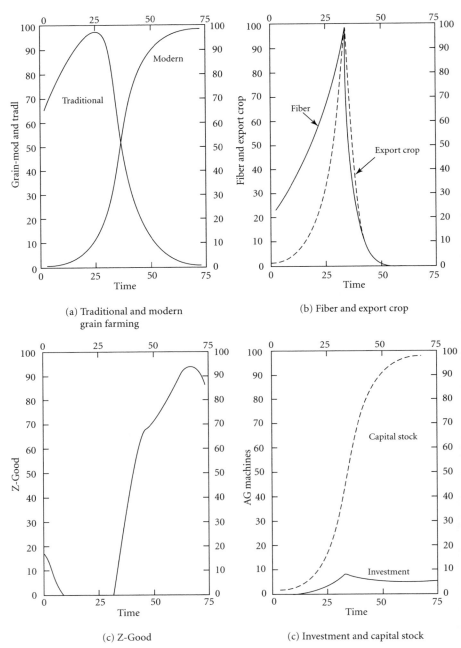

(a) Traditional and modern
grain farming

(b) Fiber and export crop

(c) Z-Good

(c) Investment and capital stock

Figure 8.1. Indexes of rural production and capital stock (100% = maximum level).

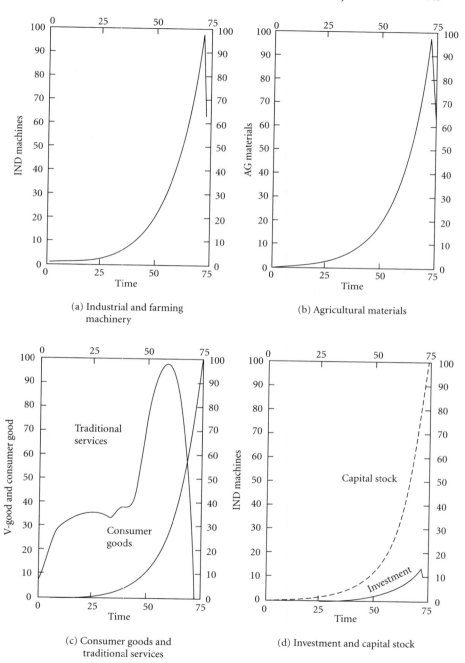

(a) Industrial and farming machinery

(b) Agricultural materials

(c) Consumer goods and traditional services

(d) Investment and capital stock

Figure 8.2. Indexes of urban production and capital stock (100% = maximum level).

The story revealed in these diagrams is of a complex transition in the qualitative profile of economic behavior and of sharp and dramatic reversals in trends associated with switches in development phase. The pattern is in stark contrast to a pattern of balanced growth. Instead, growth is unbalanced and accompanied by decay in obsolete economic activities.

This counterpoint of growth and decay is reflected in corresponding movements in migration and labor markets, as shown in Figure 8.3. The economy has evolved from a predominantly rural society to one in which more than half of its population resides in the urban area. Rural–urban migration, of course, is the vehicle bringing about this rapid urbanization.

Although agriculture declines, it plays an important role in the industrialization process. The shift of grain production from low-yielding traditional farming to the high-yielding modern technique enables the economy to feed its rapidly expanding urban population and helps to provide foreign exchange for imports. The rapid growth of fiber and export crop production in the first three decades also contributed significantly to the transformation.

The explanation for the drastic decline in the production of fiber and export crops after the first three decades or so is to be found in the constraint on agricultural land. When it becomes impossible to extend the agricultural acreage further, these activities – especially fiber production, which is very land-intensive – give way to modern grain farming, which has become the predominant production activity in the rural area.

The time path for the production of the Z-good reflects the employment situation in the rural area. In the first 30 years, agriculture rapidly absorbs almost the entire rural labor force. Then there is an upsurge in nonagricultural labor as more and more land is devoted to modern grain production and agricultural labor is increasingly displaced from agricultural activities. Agricultural employment becomes nearly constant as the agricultural transformation draws toward completion, and any increase in rural labor force has to be accommodated in Sector Z. The relatively slow increase in nonagricultural labor in the last few decades is the result of heavy rural–urban migration.

The income of nonagricultural rural workers is always below subsistence, fluctuating with the employment situation in the rural area. As agricultural labor is increasingly displaced, the nonagricultural wage falls to its floor as more and more workers have to seek survival in the Z-sector. It should be noted that, in this economy, mechanization in agriculture enriches those who can stay in agriculture and impoverishes those who are displaced.

The production of urban traditional services varies with the amount of urban labor being harbored in the urban traditional sector. For two decades or so since the beginning years, urban traditional labor constitutes over

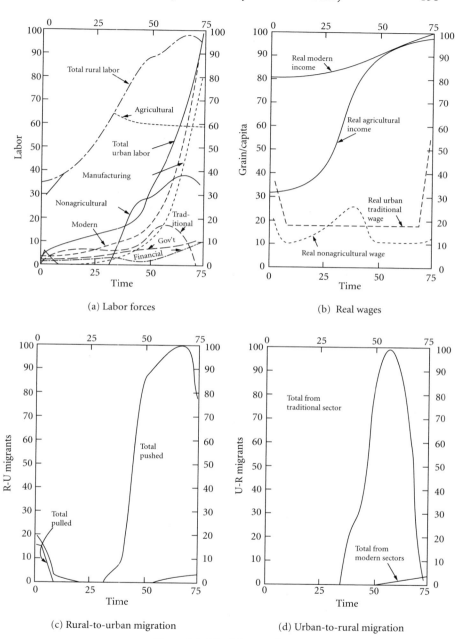

(a) Labor forces

(b) Real wages

(c) Rural-to-urban migration

(d) Urban-to-rural migration

Figure 8.3. The labor market.

50 percent of the entire urban labor force. Six decades pass before the urban traditional sector begins to disappear as more and more of its members are absorbed by manufacturing. As industrial labor in the urban area increases, the share of civil workers and workers in financial intermediaries in the urban modern worker pool falls. The swelling of the urban traditional sector drives the real wage of the traditional workers to its floor, and it is almost the end of the period before the real wage surges up again.

The development of the economy can be summarized by the time paths of real GDP and real GDP per capita, as shown in Figure 8.4. Agricultural development dominates the growth of real GDP in the first four and one-half decades, whereas industrial development dominates the later part of the curve. Per capita real GDP has increased at an average rate of 1.4 percent per year, and the general standard of living has increased by 2.6 times over the 75 years. The dip in per capita real GDP during the 1940s and 1950s is the result of the tapering off of agricultural growth while industrial growth is still slow. It is interesting to observe how these generally favorable aggregate trends mask the dramatically changing relative fortunes of the groups making up the economy.

If we examine the relative changes in various aspects of the quality of life between the rural and urban areas over this period as shown in Figure 8.4, we find that the relative advantages of urban over the rural quality of life are steadily eroded, whereas the unfavorable aspects of urban life become increasingly prominent. The gaps between urban and rural education, health care, and housing conditions close fast, whereas the differences in the levels of pollution, crime, and alienation between the areas are widening. As to bright lights, the urban area has the lead, although the gap tends to shrink slightly during the period of relatively slow urban growth when rural–urban migration is light.

The process of rural–urban migration is divided into two parts. In the first two decades we witness the working of both push and pull forces to induce rural residents to migrate. At the beginning, the push forces dominate the pull ones. However, the push component quickly diminishes as agricultural development absorbs the entire rural labor force into agriculture. Then the pull forces are weakened also by the rising income and wages in the rural area and to a lesser extent by the gradual erosion of attractiveness of city life. At the end of the second decade, rural–urban migration falls to a negligible level when agricultural development brings prosperity to the rural area.

Such a state of negligible rural–urban migration continues for about a decade. Then at the beginning of the fourth decade, the displacement effect of mechanization in agriculture begins to be felt. As rural nonagricultural

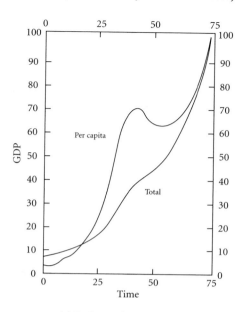

(a) Real gross domestic product

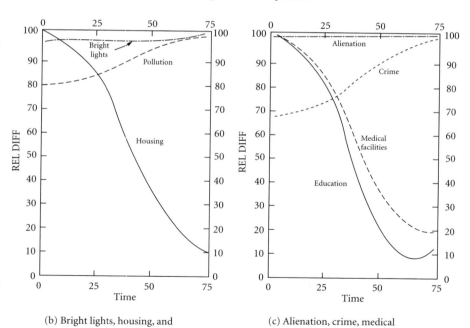

(b) Bright lights, housing, and
pollution

(c) Alienation, crime, medical
facilities, education

Figure 8.4. Indexes of quality of life.

wages fall, the push forces of rural–urban migration reappear and intensify. Displaced rural workers are pushed out of the countryside to join the city poor. The volume of rural–urban migrants grows as the nonagricultural sector expands. The pull forces play no part at all during this period of heavy rural–urban migration: those that manage to stay in agriculture are enjoying prosperity, and the relative differences in quality of life between the rural and urban areas have been reduced to such an extent that city life has lost its attractiveness to rural workers.

For the first two decades or so, there is hardly any urban-to-rural migration. The migration stream is in one direction, and rapid urbanization is under way. But rapid urbanization also brings about deterioration in the urban quality of life. By the early 1920s, this effect on the urban quality of life becomes strong enough to induce urban–rural migration among those in the urban modern sector. The volume is relatively small, and yet it grows steadily as rural life continues to improve and urban life continues to deteriorate.

The urban–rural migratory flow from the urban traditional sector is, however, more volatile. During the period of heavy rural–urban migration, an increasing number of urban traditional workers and their families are moving back to the rural area. It is conceivable that most of these are return migrants who joined the urban traditional sector in the previous periods.[6]

Toward the end of the period, there is a drastic fall in the number of urban–rural migrants. The urban traditional sector has virtually disappeared because almost all of its previous members have been absorbed by the industrial sector.

Here ends the 75-year history of our economy.

8.4 Reflections on the Development Story

What can we learn from the simulated economic development of this hypothetical economy?

---

[6] Hymer and Resnick (1969) used the term Z-good to denote the variety of nonagricultural activities in the rural area such as "process, manufacturing, construction, transportation, and service activities to satisfy the needs for food, clothing, shelter, entertainment, and ceremony." Following their lead, we also adopt the term Z-good here to represent the non-agricultural activities in our economy, but with the special connotation that they are less attractive productive activities for the rural community. The idea here is that agriculture is *the* occupation in the rural area; for the same wage rate, people prefer agricultural work to nonagricultural activities, and only when people fail to find employment in agriculture do they look for alternatives in the Z-good sector. This more distinct dichotomy on the one hand reflects the social philosophy of the rural populace, and on the other hand sharpens our analysis.

Judged from many angles, the experience is a success story. The economy has transformed itself from an agricultural economy to an industrial one. Its agriculture is mechanized. Its labor is transferred from subsistence farming with low productivity to industrial jobs with high productivity. Per capita real income is up. Capital stocks in agriculture and industry have accumulated to high levels. In sum, the economy has changed from an "underdeveloped" to a "developed" one.

Such an evaluation overlooks many problems and difficulties that can be exposed only by examining the dynamic details of the system. Agricultural development has had an adverse effect on the distribution of income. It is true that all the displaced rural workers will eventually be absorbed into the urban industries (if industrial growth continues). But this eventuality may take a long time: in our example, it takes seven decades for the urban traditional sector to disappear. At its peak, these poverty-stricken people amount to nearly 40 percent of the rural population. And during this time agricultural income is rising! It is only toward the end of the sixth decade that the percentage of rural poor begins to decline. Within this period, things are no better in the urban area: the urban traditional sector harbors 30–40 percent of the urban population living on subsistence income.

The mechanization in agriculture and the concentration of industries in the urban area have herded an increasingly greater proportion of the population into clusters of high density. Many economists and sociologists equate this urbanization with economic development. In terms of GDP and per capita GDP, a positive correlation exists. But such a correlation is misleading. In the experience of our economy, until industrial development has taken hold, urbanization simply means the swelling of the urban traditional sector in which people can barely survive, which is hardly a favorable development.

In our economy, urbanization also tends to lead to relative deterioration in the urban quality of life. It is interesting to note that, contrary to conventional wisdom, the pull forces of migration cease to be important beyond a certain point. Rather, it is mainly the lack of employment opportunities in the rural area that sends migrants to the urban area. That is, the migrants flock to the cities not so much for a better quality of life but simply for a better chance of survival. The policy implications of these observations, if they are true of real as well as our hypothetical economy, appear to be obvious.[7]

---

[7] This pattern conforms with the findings of Goldstein in Thailand and of Sovani and Bose in India. See Goldstein (1970).

8.5 Concluding Remark

This exercise in economic modeling is meant to demonstrate a promising approach to the study of the process and problems of economic development in LDCs. It is true that this approach tends to generate complex models that render algebra inadequate for their solution, but it also highlights the complexity and interdependence of the building blocks of the economic system and the complex multimode, multiphase structure of development that evolves.

Objections may be raised against drawing conclusions from simulation models whose results depend to some extent on the values of parameters and initial conditions being used. The answer to these objections can come only with better empirical studies and more accurate estimation of the values of parameters and initial conditions for specific settings of time and place. As it is, we think we have shown that adaptive models are richer than conventional theoretical frameworks. They appear even now to represent the real world better, and it is with the real world that our ultimate interest should lie.

References

Baer, W., and M. Herve. 1966. "Employment and Industrialization in Developing Countries." *Quarterly Journal of Economics* 80:88–107.

Day, R. H. 1969. "Flexible Utility and Myopic Expectations in Economic Growth." *Oxford Economic Papers* 21:299–311.

Day, R. H., and Y. K. Fan. 1976. "Myopic Optimizing, Economic Growth and the Golden Rule." *Hong Kong Economic Papers* 10:12–20.

Day, R. H., and I. J. Singh. 1977. *Economics As an Adaptive Process*. New York: Cambridge University Press.

Fan, Y. K. 1973a. "A Model of Migration and Growth for Densely Populated Economies in Less Developed Countries." Social Systems Research Institute Workshop Paper No. 7309. Madison, WI: University of Wisconsin.

Fan, Y. K. 1973b. "On Rural–Urban Migration and Economic Development in Less Developed Countries." Social Systems Research Institute Workshop Paper No. 7324. Madison, WI: University of Wisconsin.

Fan, Y. K. 1974. "A Multi-Sector Adaptive Model of Economic Development and Migration." Unpublished Ph.D. Dissertation. Madison, WI: University of Wisconsin.

Galbis, V. 1972. "A Contribution to the Theory of Labor Migration and Interregional Differentials." Unpublished Ph.D. Dissertation. Madison, WI: University of Wisconsin.

Goldstein, S. 1970. "Urbanization in Thailand, 1947–1967." The Population Research and Training Center, Chulalongkorn University, Bangkok.

Harris, S. R., and M. Todaro. 1970. "Migration, Unemployment and Development: A Two-Sector Analysis." *American Economic Review* 60:126–42.

Hymer, S., and S. Resnick. 1959. "A Model of an Agrarian Economy with Nonagricultural Activities." *American Economic Review* 59:493–506.

Koopmans, T. C. 1967. "Objectives, Constraints and Outcomes in Optimal Growth Models." *Econometrica* 35:1–15.

Kuznets, S., and D. S. Thomas et al. 1957, 1960, 1964. *Population Redistribution and Economic Growth – United States, 1870–1950.* 3 Volumes. Philadelphia: American Philosophical Society.

Laquian, A. A., and P. Dutton. 1971. *A Selected Bibliography on Rural–Urban Migrants' Slums and Squatters in Developing Countries.* Monticello, IL: Council of Planning Librarians.

Lee, E. S. 1966. "A Theory of Migration." *Demography* 3:47–57.

Leontief, W. W. 1958. "Theoretical Note on Time–Preference, Productivity of Capital, Stagnation and Economic Growth." *American Economic Review* 48:105–11.

Mabogunje, A. L. 1970. "Systems Approach to a Theory of Rural–Urban Migration." *Geographical Analysis* 2:1–18.

Morawetz, D. 1974. "Employment Implications of Industrialization in Development Countries: A Survey." *Economic Journal* 84:491–542.

Ravenstein, E. G. 1885. "The Laws of Migration." *Journal of the Royal Statistical Society* 48:167–227.

Ravenstein, E. G. 1889. "The Laws of Migration." *Journal of the Royal Statistical Society* 52:241–301.

Redford, A. 1926. *Labor Migration in England, 1800–1850.* London: Manchester University Press.

Sjaastad, L. A. 1961. "Income and Migration in the United States." Unpublished Ph.D. Dissertation. Chicago: University of Chicago.

Todaro, M. 1969. "A Model of Labor Migration and Urban Unemployment in Less Developed Countries." *American Economic Review* March:138–48.

United Nations. 1953. *The Determinants and Consequences of Population Trends, A Summary of the Findings of Studies on the Relationships Between Population Changes and Social Conditions.* New York: Population Studies, No. 17, Department of Social Affairs, Population Division.

United Nations. 1964. *The Demographic Situation and Prospective Population Trends in Asia and the Far East.* New York: ECAFE Secretariat.

United Nations. 1970. *Urbanization in the Second United Nations Development Decade.* Department of Economic and Social Affairs. (UN Document ST/ECA/132). New York: United Nations.

Williamson, J. G., A. Kelley, and R. Cheetham. 1972. *Dualistic Economic Development, Theory and History.* Chicago: University of Chicago Press.

NINE

Instability in the Transition from Manorialism

A Classical Analysis

A classical economic analysis of productivity and population growth is used to explain the rise in well-being during the expansion of feudalism, the emergence of class conflict, the demise of the manorial system, and the establishment of precapitalism. These events are given a new interpretation that involves a specific sequence of endogenously generated economic pressures. An indeterminacy remains, however, that allows for alternative histories in particular settings of time and place through the interplay of political and other institutional forces.

9.1 On Theory and History

The pure classical economic theory provides an endogenous explanation of how economic conflict might emerge and how a switch in socioeconomic regime might occur through the interaction of population growth and productivity. This little-appreciated implication of the basic Smith–Malthus model is here used to illuminate (1) the expansion of manorialism, (2) a period of shifting class interests in alternative distribution mechanisms, (3) the demise of the traditional share system, (4) the emergence of precapitalism, (5) successive surges in population growth, and (6) varied effects of the plague, including accelerated growth of the labor market or, contrastingly, a prolongation or temporary restoration of manorialism.

Reprinted from *Explorations in Economic History*, Vol. 19, pp. 321–38, Copyright 1982, with permission from Elsevier Science. The initial version of the paper reproduced here was written in 1979 while the author was a member of the Institute for Advanced Study on leave from the University of Southern California. I am indebted to several historians, colleagues at the Institute, who were kind enough to read the paper and who pointed out opportunities either for improving its historical content or for avoiding serious factual errors. These include John Barker, Bryce Lyon, Joan Scott, and Tom Haskell. Persio Arida, Albert O. Hirschman, and Douglas C. North also contributed useful suggestions on several technical and stylistic points.

These events are given a new interpretation involving a specific sequence of switching economic pressures and class conflicts. This interpretation is not drawn from empirical research but is obtained a priori, as it were, from the classical model. There is evidence already in the literature, however, that would seem to provide a basis for believing in its relevance. I present a few brief samples of this evidence but do not expect it to be an easy task to determine under just what conditions of time and place the argument is germane. That task must be the subject of arduous historical research well beyond the scope of the present inquiry. The idea that socioeconomic conflict emerges endogenously through the interplay of technology and economy will not surprise the Marxian historian or the radical economist. My treatment of this process, however, is decidedly non-Marxian. The classical economics of Smith, Malthus, and Ricardo is not augmented here with alienation, exploitation, or similar elements not already contained in the classical writers themselves. Indeed the Smith–Malthus model, which is the basis of the present contribution, was anathema to Marx as is well known. The central ingredient in the present version of the classical growth model, initially increasing returns to expanding population, is bound to elicit objections. This is not the place to review all the pros and cons pertaining to the existence of such a phenomenon. Although many of the best minds in economics contributed to that controversy, an agreement was never reached. My point of view is that it is well within the classical purview and that there are compelling reasons to believe – as did Adam Smith – in its relevance, and I will sketch a justification based on the historical setting. Its implications are so dramatic that it strikes me as something of an oddity that it has been eschewed by economic historians who have already applied orthodox economics to the interpretation of history.

On its face, it would appear outrageous to try to capture the magnificent tapestry of feudal history in the few simple equations and diagrams of classical growth theory, and that is not, in fact, our purpose. Indeed, it is the purpose of theory (in part) to simplify perception to make an understanding of reality possible. The implications or deductions that follow may then be used to raise new questions of an empirical nature that must then, in a complete historical analysis, be tested against the full array of relevant details. Even on its own terms, however, the pure theory does seem to capture

In the meantime I have received helpful suggestions from John Bowman, Rondo Cameron, Jan deVries, Stefano Fenoaltea, Fred Pryor, William N. Parker, and Peter Temin. Because I have not accepted their criticisms in every case, none of these individuals should be held responsible for what of necessity must be a controversial application of pure classical economic growth theory to economic history.

some of the salient features of the rise, transition, and demise of manorialism. Of special interest is the endogenous switch in regime brought about by the ongoing process of development. At the same time, as we shall see, room is left for political and other noneconomic forces to cause a variety of alternative outcomes mediated by the interactions among the living actors of special times and specific places.

9.2 The Feudal Transition

For centuries manorialism[1] grew and flourished alongside a gradual development of trade, commerce, and cities, reaching its acme during the twelfth or thirteenth century. Then, as Wallerstein (1974, pp. 18–20) puts it,

> sometime in the 14th century, this expansion ceased... and throughout feudal Europe and beyond it, there seemed to be a "crisis," marked by war, disease and economic hardship. . . . Edouard Perroy sees the issue primarily as one of an optimal point having been reached in an expansion process, of a saturation of population ... [while Hilton finds central] the "climate of endemic discontent," peasant insurrections which took the form of a "revolt against the system as such."

An explanation of these events in terms of an interrelationship between labor productivity and population growth appears to have been attempted first by Dobb (1946) and further explicated by Bowman (undated). They attribute the crisis to the efforts of the lords to extract greater rents as productivity fell below established wages. A similar but more comprehensive explanation was offered by North and Thomas (1970, p. 11) who argue that

> population pressure undermined the economic basis for the institutional organization of feudalism by reversing the relationship of prices as a result of diminishing returns. . . . The result was that landlords now found it in their interest to commute labour dues to payments in kind and cash ... a continuous pressure rose to eliminate the common-property use of land and to achieve private exclusive ownership.

---

[1] Historians distinguish carefully between feudalism, a system of political, social, and judicial relationships among the elite, and manorialism, which was the economic basis of the feudal institutional structure. This paper, strictly speaking, deals directly with manorialism and only indirectly with feudalism. Moreover, many crucial historical events and numerous relevant details of time and place are not taken up, not because the author is unaware of their importance, especially for tailoring the argument to differing regional settings, but because it would divert us from the central task at hand. This is to show what the pure classical economic theory of productivity and population implies for the interpretation of historical events.

The assumption of constant or diminishing returns to scale used by these authors, however, is inconsistent with the long trend in rising real per capita incomes commented on recently by Cameron (1975). Adam Smith was aware of this general if gradual improvement and attributed it even "in the early stages of development" (where agriculture must have predominated) to the increasing specialization and coordination that groups and growing numbers afforded. The implication of Smith's view (expressed in the opening paragraph of *The Wealth of Nations*) is that production must have displayed, at least for a time, increasing returns to an expanding population.

A classic account of the relationships between technological progress, population growth, specialization, and coordination in prehistoric and ancient times is found in Childe ([1936], 1951, pp. 14–15). That population increase might yield increasing returns in the early stages of manorial growth seems entirely plausible on a moment's reflection. Initially, population is clustered in agricultural villages in a limited area. Only land that can be secured in the neighborhood of these settlements is available for cultivation. As population expands, new villages in more remote areas can be established. These villages bring in new lands, some of which will be even more fertile than the best of the old, and make possible a superior adaptation of available crop varieties to local conditions. On this point, see Parker (1980, p. 4).

As transportation routes develop, agricultural specialization, coordinated by trade, facilitates the further geographical adaptation of production and commerce. In addition, an increasing population, organized into a feudal hierarchy and combined with the king's growing power to crush individual raiding bands, made for increasing peace and civil order – a process given great emphasis by Bloch (1961).

So it is that agricultural productivity might increase, at least under some conditions, with an expanding frontier. The sources of improvement here cited are generally referred to as "externalities." In a macrofunction that relates social product to population, they imply initially increasing returns to expansion in the aggregate manorial economy.[2]

---

[2] An alternative explanation for increasing well-being is the gradual improvement of technology. Certainly, invention and diffusion occurred, and any quantitative analysis of the record must take them into account. For qualitative purposes, however, I believe it is preferable as a first approximation to leave such exogenous factors aside and to suppose with Adam Smith that such improvements in labor productivity that did occur can be attributed primarily to the fruits of specialization and gradually improving transportation, communication, and civil order, all of which lead to lowering transaction and coordination costs and increasing productivity even in the absence of industry and concentrated urban production.

With the closing of the European frontier in the twelfth or thirteenth century, however, such economies as could be achieved by further specialization and rational adaptation to an expanding resource base must have contended in the aggregate with diseconomies brought about by limitations in the supply of choice land. From the macroeconomic point of view, therefore, the aggregate production function must have at least two distinct regimes: first, one of increasing returns, and then, after a given population P^* is reached, one of diminishing returns.[3]

Even in the simplest possible terms manorial society cannot be represented by less than two classes, the incorporation of which, along with our assumption about technology, leads to some striking implications. They follow from the fact that a marginal product scheme cannot govern the early progress of income distribution in a two-class society until the critical population level P^* is reached, where diminishing returns take over. Correspondingly, we initially assume the existence of an alternative distribution mechanism, which we here call the "traditional share."

We now have the ingredients to explain the long period of rising feudal prosperity alluded to above, which covered roughly the fifth through twelfth centuries. Moreover, by allowing for eventual diminishing returns, an endogenous mechanism is provided for the emergence of a distributional crisis.

A further hypothesis – and this is the substance of our argument – is also implied: that the pressure for a market in labor comes first from the peasants (as implied by Hilton) and only later from the lords (as argued by Dobb, Bowman, North, and Thomas). This is because the newly feasible marginal product wage will initially be above the traditional share. By the time the aristocracy wishes to grant freedom from the obligations of the manor, numbers have expanded so far that the wage has plummeted below the traditional share. The interest of the peasant class reverses. When this happened historically, the peasants probably did not attempt to regain traditional roles. But we would expect them to have pressed for improved wages and working conditions and, failing in that effort, to have resorted to political pressure or rebellion in an attempt to regain previous income levels.

---

[3] It might be useful, and perhaps more realistic, to allow a segment of constant returns to intrude between the initial segment of increasing and the final segment of decreasing returns. Although this is easy enough to accomplish, our argument is changed little by doing so. We leave this as an exercise for the interested reader.

9.3 A Classical Model[4]

Let us now consider our abstract model economy, which I call "Manoria," in order to distinguish it from the real-world economy whose development we wish to understand. As we have said it consists of two economic classes, the elite or aristocrats and the peasants. The elite (nobility and clergy) control the land and provide various services to the peasants. The peasants till the soil, producing food (i.e., wheat). The two-class assumption is, of course, a great oversimplification of the actual feudal world and forces us, in effect, to subsume within the peasant class all those workers whose specialized production contributed directly or indirectly to agricultural productivity. Likewise, the residual rent allocated to the elite must include payments to all those artisans and servants whose efforts directly enhanced aristocratic consumption and provided administrative, judicial, welfare, and police services on the manors and in the urban centers. All of the latter are here treated as a kind of social overhead.[5]

Given the interpretation of the feudal transition described in Section 9.2, the aggregate production function,

$$Y = f(P), \tag{9.1}$$

---

[4] The analysis presented in Sections 9.3–9.5 is a new version of an unpublished study by Day and Koenig (1974), who found that "in a real economy roughly approximated by our theory of Manoria we would expect societies ... to be socially unstable because of class conflict ... " (p. 17). The present analysis incorporates a more general, non-Malthusian population equation and is conducted in terms of continuous rather than discrete time. In contrast to North and Thomas, population is endogenous, as in the neo-Malthusian literature (e.g., Samuelson 1948, Leibenstein 1956, Solow 1956, Buttrick 1960, Nelson 1956, or Niehans 1963). The germ of an analysis of an agrarian economy may be found in Haavelmo (1954), Georgescu-Roegen (1960), and Baumol (1970). Sauvy (1970) incorporated increasing returns but did not develop an explicitly dynamic analysis.

[5] Peasants obviously provided most of the labor in the manorial system, but it need not be supposed that the contribution of the elite was nonexistent or negligible. Indeed, such a contribution must explain (at least in part) the emergence in primitive society of distinct economic roles and a special claim on the social product willingly given up by the workers. Presumably, the role of the elite in the feudal system was to provide managerial, entrepreneurial, and public services such as quasi-judicial functions, policing, and military functions (Thompson 1928, pp. 701–3); accumulation of knowledge of improved agricultural practices through travel and study; and other activities afforded by leisure (Lyon 1957, pp. 48, 55). These activities in turn made possible the gradual improvement in output per worker as the economy expanded. It may be supposed for simplicity that the gradual growth of towns and commerce can be subsumed within the allocation of output to the elite. Improvements in technique other than those that were mediated by the elite members of the system are assumed to be negligible in what follows.

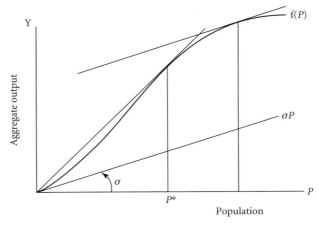

Figure 9.1. The production function. The subsistence level is σ. At the population P^*, per capita output is maximized. At population P^e, the rent is maximized.

which explains the dependence of output Y on peasant numbers P, takes the general shape shown in Figure 9.1. For peasant numbers below P^* increasing returns prevail, whereas above this population decreasing returns set in.[6]

The distribution of product for peasant populations below P^* cannot be given by the marginal product, $f'(P)$, as is assumed in neoclassical economic theory, for the total product would be more than exhausted. Only at constant and declining marginal product for populations beyond P^* is such a wage system possible. It is therefore assumed that an alternative scheme exists in a traditional share function which, for simplicity, is here assumed to be a constant fraction τ of average product; that is,[7]

$$w = \omega_T(P) := \tau f(P)/P. \tag{9.2}$$

The function $\omega_T(\cdot)$ may be called the "traditional" or "manorial distribution function."[8]

---

[6] More exactly, there exists a P^* so that $f''(P) > 0$ when $P < P^*$ and $f''(P) < 0$ when $P > P^*$; also, that $f(0) = 0$ and $f'(P) > 0$ for all $0 < P < P^m$ for some $P^m > P^*$. An interesting discussion of the empirical evidence against decreasing returns is by Gunderson (1975). Parker (1980) has made a strong case for the increasing-returns regime, and further evidence bolstering this assumption will be found in Boserup (1965) and Simon (1977). It should be noted that, if the aristocrats are taken to be productive, at least to some extent (see note 5), in an overhead sense increasing returns can be obtained in the sense of average product even if decreasing returns to direct labor were to hold throughout.

[7] The notation := indicates a definitional equation or identity.

[8] This raises the interesting, important, and difficult issue of the determination of the so-called traditional share. We will have to put this issue aside in the present study.

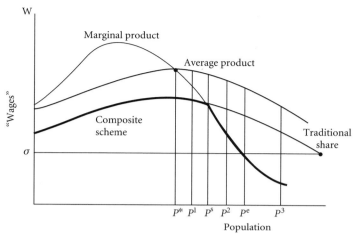

Figure 9.2. Marginal product, average product, and traditional share relationships.

For peasant populations above P^*, a marginal-product wage distribution scheme (and a "free" labor market) is technically feasible. Hence, we may, as an alternative to Equation (9.2), consider the "marginal product distribution function":

$$w = \omega_M(P) := f'(P).\qquad(9.3)$$

Now there exists a point P^s greater than P^* but less than P^e, where the marginal product is just equal to the traditional share. Between P^* and P^s, a market-determined marginal product wage will be to the advantage of peasants and to the detriment of the elite. For populations above P^s, the opposite is true. The population P^s is, therefore, a critical "switch point" at which class interests in the two alternative distribution schemes reverse. These qualitative relationships are brought out in Figures 9.2 and 9.3. Figure 9.2 illustrates marginal product, average product, and traditional share relationships, and Figure 9.3 shows the implied total wage bills under these alternative distribution schemes.

Let us imagine the development of Manoria beginning at some initially quite small population, say P^0, at a time when the traditional share distribution system reigns. As peasant numbers expand, both the per capita peasant share and the residual rent rise. Such a period, during a regime of increasing returns to the expanding system, would be one of more or less harmonious relations between the classes and general support for the system. During the course of this expansion, however, the peasant population P^* is eventually surpassed. As a consequence, a marginal product wage becomes technically

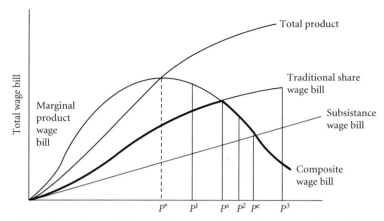

Figure 9.3. The total wage bill implied by a marginal product wage ($f'(P)P$), a traditional share ($\tau f(P)$), and subsistence (σP).

feasible. Moreover, the marginal product wage lies above the traditional share!

Obviously, the real world, being immeasurably complex, would not reveal its character in the stark fashion implied by the diagrams. But if our model economy even crudely approximates it, then we could imagine that some individuals among the peasants might perceive the situation and initiate pressures to introduce a competitive (market) wage system based on marginal worth. Because the cost to the elite of such a new scheme would initially lie above that of the traditional distribution system, such efforts would be resisted. Repressive measures would very likely be introduced to keep the system on course.

Repression, however expedient for a time, eventually becomes uneconomic from the lord's point of view (a point fully appreciated by North and Thomas), for with the continued expansion in peasant numbers, the marginal product must eventually fall below the traditional share. This is the critical switch point. From here on we must expect the elite, perceiving the new advantage themselves, to acquiesce to the demands for change – indeed to assume the lead in advocating a competitive wage system.

If for simplicity we suppose that the lords bring about a shift to a marginal product wage all at once – as soon as it becomes advantageous to them at population P^s – then we have the composite distribution scheme shown by the heavy line in Figures 9.2 and 9.3 and given by the equation

$$w = \omega(P) := \min\{\tau f(P)/P, \ f'(P)\}. \tag{9.4}$$

The real income of peasants must now decline much faster with the expansion of their numbers than it would have under the traditional share scheme. It must further come to pass that peasants will recognize the free market in labor, for which they formerly agitated, as a growing detriment to their interests, and they will come to oppose efforts by their lords to impose it. No longer needing to offer inducements for peasants to remain, the aristocracy must now employ aggressive means, such as enclosure, to separate peasants from their manorial privileges (cf. Cohen and Weitzman 1975).

In reality, the competitive wage system was not brought about suddenly. It is doubtful that its advantage to the elite and its disadvantage to the peasants would have been perceived by all at the same time. But we should guess that the pressure for transition grew in force and that the enclosure of land and the expulsion of peasants replaced whatever measures had been adopted previously to repress the mobility of labor.

If the system did grow initially along the path governed by the traditional wage, then later enclosure and expulsion would have made possible a gradual shift toward the marginal product. A landless class of wage earners would have emerged whose source of income must have come ultimately from feudal rents – perhaps indirectly through work performed in the growing urban centers.

It is worth remembering, too, that in the long run the fate of the peasants is the same, regardless of the distribution scheme; namely, they must eventually approach the subsistence wage. The fate of the elite, however, is quite different. With equilibrium at P^e (under the marginal product wage) a maximum surplus exists from which might be drawn the resources to support the arts and mechanical invention and to found the beginnings of industry. The switchover in distribution scheme should therefore make a difference in the subsequent emergence of capitalistic production.

9.4 "Exogenous" Events and Switching Regimes

Of the many complicating factors well established in the historical record but ignored in our theoretical treatment so far, one of the most significant must surely be the fourteenth-century plague. Consideration of such an event within the classical framework suggests several possible scenarios.

Consider first the situation that would have existed had a precapitalistic labor market not developed, perhaps because the elite was slow to perceive its advantages as population expanded beyond the switching point P^s.

Referring to Figure 9.2, suppose population is as high as P^3 but as a result of the plague falls to P^2. The peasant's wage will rise according to the traditional share scheme. Since this would occur after the preceding decline, when population passed P^*, continuation of the traditional scheme would seem favorable to the peasants. If, however, the elite could impose a marginal product scheme, wages would not rise; if they did rise, they would not do so by as much as they would if the traditional system were continued. The outcome of the implied difference in interests cannot be determined within the framework of the model, but the effect of plague on a manorial economy with a preplague population beyond the switch point could well be an acceleration of the pressure for a market on the part of the elite and an escalation of class conflict.

If from the same initial situation at P^2 the population fell even further, to P^1 for example, a quite different set of class pressures would have evolved. In this case the marginal product, although feasible, would increase wages above the traditional share. The pressure for change would now come not from the elite but from the peasants, who, with such evidently high marginal products, might welcome a competitive market. The result is the same as before, namely, an acceleration in the pressure for a market and an escalation of class conflict, though this time the motive force lies with the peasants.

Now consider an entirely different scenario in which the conversion to a labor market is already achieved or well in progress through enclosures and the like and the initial population is P^2 (again see Figure 9.2). A postplague population of P^1 would now give the elite an incentive to attempt a restoration of the manorial system. Because shares would rise under the old system, and the old system (at the initial population P^1) would have been desired by the peasants, who would have seen market wages falling drastically before the plague occurred, the peasants might very well support a restoration.[9] Feudalism – or at least its manorial underpinnings – could have received a new lease on life.

There is nothing in the classical model that could indicate which of these outcomes might occur. It would depend in part on developments prior to the plague (in terms of population levels and the labor market), on the political strength of the contending groups, and perhaps on the sagacity of their leaders. Evidently, all of the cases described (and others that are left to the reader to construct) might have occurred, each one in a particular

---

[9] Further plagues would have perpetuated the old system once reestablished. Even so, with the eventual recovery in peasant numbers, incentive for the commutation of wages would have eventually resumed its importance.

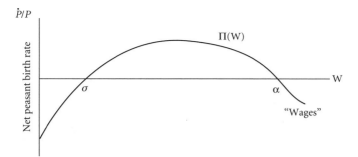

Figure 9.4. Net birth rate as a function of income (σ is a subsistence level and α a ZPG affluence level).

period and geographical setting. It may be emphasized here, however, that it is the emergence of class conflict and the switching of class interest that is explained by the endogenous forces of economic development. How those conflicts were resolved and what were the political forces unleashed by such economic turnabouts are questions that go beyond the classical economic analysis to which we are here confined.

9.5 "Endogenous" Population Growth

The pure classical theory of economic growth is completed by incorporating an endogenous explanation of population growth. Let it be supposed – again, as a first approximation – that, in view of the clergy's celibacy and the nobility's internecine warfare, aristocratic numbers are more or less held in check.[10] Peasants, however, will be assumed to multiply according to a smooth function of real per capita income,

$$\dot{P}/P = \Pi(w), \tag{9.5}$$

as illustrated in Figure 9.4, where $\dot{P}$ is the rate of change in population per unit of time. The parameter σ is the classical subsistence level – psychologically or culturally determined – at which the net rate of growth is zero: below it population declines, and above it population grows until some level of affluence, here denoted by α, is attained. The allowance for a decline in population growth rates as real income rises sufficiently overcomes one of

---

[10] This assumption is not innocuous because it is precisely the rapid growth in the number of claimants to feudal rents that plays a key element in the turbulence of the fourteenth and fifteenth centuries, as pointed out in private correspondence by deVries and Parker.

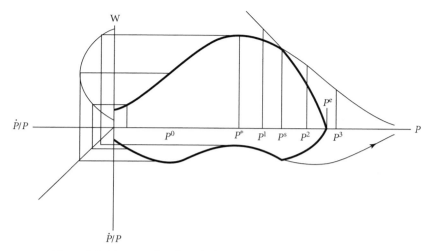

Figure 9.5. Constructing the relative population of growth function.

the most frequently raised objections of the classical model.[11] It leads to a further hypothesis of a wavelike appearance in demographic growth, which could have occurred even in the absence of the plague.

Substituting Equation (9.2) into (9.5), we obtain

$$\dot{P}/P = \Pi[\tau f(P)/P]. \tag{9.6}$$

This substitution and the resulting implications can be illustrated graphically, as shown in Figure 9.5. There Figure 9.4 has been tilted on its side in the upper left quadrant, and Figure 9.2 (drawn to a different scale with some of the unnecessary details omitted) occupies the upper right quadrant. By drawing a 45° line in the lower left quadrant we can project onto the lower right quadrant the functional relationship between the relative population growth rate $\dot{P}/P$ and the population level implied by the underlying sociotechnical relationships that define the model economy.

The story we have already summarized can now be retold with the help of the phase diagram of Equation (9.6), which we have transposed from Figure 9.5 to Figure 9.6 in the form

$$\dot{P} = P\Pi[\tau f(P)/P]. \tag{9.7}$$

---

[11] Writers in the neo-Malthusian tradition who have used a similar function in different contexts include Buttrick (1960) and Leibenstein (1956). Day and Koenig (1974) used a pure Malthusian equation and obtained cycles of population and fluctuating class interests by developing their analysis in discrete time.

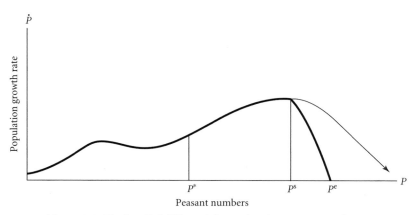

Figure 9.6. The implied differential equation for peasant numbers.

Beginning with a small enough population, we find that peasant numbers grow at an increasing, then declining, rate as their real income per capita increases. As population continues to expand, however, average productivity and the peasant share of it declines, bringing about a second surge in population growth and then a renewed decline. Eventually, an equilibrium level is reached with peasants living at a subsistence wage. This wavelike appearance of population growth rates is not a necessary but a possible consequence of the population growth equation (9.5) with the shape assumed in Figure 9.4. Various alternative profiles of population growth can be obtained by changing the position and shapes of the underlying growth rate and distributional equations. Nonetheless, it is not without interest to see that, even without the advent of the Black Death, population in the Middle Ages could well have exhibited ascending surges of growth (cf. Cameron 1975).

During the course of the development, the switch P^s would be surpassed. If for simplicity we suppose that the lords bring about a shift to a marginal product wage all at once as soon as it becomes advantageous to them at population P^s, then we have, instead of Equation (9.7),

$$\dot{P} = \Pi[\min\{\Pi f(P)/P, \ f'(P)\}]P. \tag{9.8}$$

This equation is obtained by substituting the composite wage function (9.4), comprising the minimum of the two schemes, into Equation (9.5). The story is very much the same as before except that the real income of peasants must decline much more quickly with the expansion of their numbers and a lower equilibrium population must be reached much sooner. This is also shown in Figures 9.5 and 9.6.

It has already been emphasized that, in reality, the switch in regime would not take place suddenly but would depend on perception lags, relative political strengths, and the dialectical uncertainties of conflict and conflict resolution. Moreover, plagues would interrupt normal trends, possibly accelerating the demise of the manorial system, or alternatively perhaps, under some condition of labor markets, even stimulating the restoration of manorial obligations and benefits.

9.6 Implications for Interpreting History

In summary, the classical growth model leads to the following interpretation of the economic history of a manorial economy and its transition to precapitalism and a competitive labor market.

1. The manorial system grew and flourished for a considerable period (in reality from the fifth to the twelvth centuries) because of the increasing and sustained material benefits to its primary classes. These benefits were brought about through economies achieved in reality by means of increased specialization and coordination as the frontier was settled and peasant numbers expanded.

2. As population grew and settlement continued, decreasing returns set in that led peasants to seek a release from manorial ties and to obtain the liberty to sell labor for what it was worth in a market that had been technically impossible in former, less populous times; rebellions against the prevailing system would presumably have followed. No doubt this pressure was resisted through various forms of repression by the lords.

3. The further expansion in population reversed class interests to harmonize with what might be assumed to be the monopoly power of the land-controlling elite; the result was a rapid fall in wages, either through a direct increase in feudal taxes and aristocratic rents or through the gradual relaxation of manorial obligations with a substitution of market wages for the traditional shares, and the vesting of land as property to be enclosed as a means of forcing a break in the established regime. In this way, peasants must have been expelled into a market they had previously sought to bring into existence. Where such a scenario did not develop it must have been due to a lag in economic perception or to political and cultural preferences for the established regime.

4. The incidence of plague may have greatly accelerated the pressure for a marginal-product market wage system either from the aristocracy or,

alternatively, if the population reduction was great enough, from the peasants.

5. Where a labor market had already emerged, a reduction in population, if drastic enough, could have led to a restoration of feudal traditions in an effort to hold wages within bounds that would support aristocratic interests. Because the traditional share at the reduced population would also have benefited the peasants, such a reactionary movement might have succeeded.

6. Even in the absence of plague, population may have expanded in at least two successive surges due to the relationships between the net birth rate, the real wage, and the level of population.

Scholars are well aware of the manifold forces influencing development – forces that were complex even in ages past when the sophistications of modern political and economic systems were not yet in existence. They will not need reminding that the classical economic model is no more than a parable, a mere cartoon designed to highlight essential economic ingredients for a complete story and to suggest hypotheses or conjectures for further investigation. But for a mere cartoon, the insights are surprisingly rich and the hypotheses surprisingly sharp and powerful. Moreover, there is evidence already in the literature that the theoretical analysis of possible developments in the transition from feudalism to precapitalism is in fact relevant.

Certainly, from the fall of the Roman Empire through the classic feudal period in the late Middle Ages, Northern Europe (France, Germany) had a developing frontier with eastward colonization up to Russia ending around the thirteenth century. Along with expanded settlement came improvements in trade and measures for enhancing the protection of merchants on highways. Bloch makes much of this, and Fenoaltea (1975) attributes virtually all increases in productivity to increasing pacification. According to Thompson (1928, p. 701), in a standard work, "there can be no doubt feudalism as a whole was a phenomenon of social progress...." Although there is scarcely unanimity on this point, it is "virtually certain," according to Cameron (1975, p. x), "that each of the accelerating phases of population growth was accompanied by economic growth in the sense that both total and per capita output were increasing." Here Cameron is referring to a first surge from the ninth through twelfth centuries and to a second one from the mid fifteenth and sixteenth centuries – surges he regards as established. Through 1200, the number of villages grew nearly as fast as population (Thompson 1928,

p. 796), reflecting the frontier nature of the economy and the possibility that migration would prevent excessive exploitation. Indeed, according to Thompson (1928, pp. 797–8), "the boldest elements refused longer to be bound by servile ties ... the lords were forced to hold out inducements to make them stay." This suggests that the pressure for a competitive market indeed came first from the peasants – as (retroactively) predicted by our theory – who rebelled against excessive measures to repress increasing mobility. Thus, "by 1300 the serfs ... had ascended to freedom ... the economic revolution had forced emancipation" (Thompson 1928, p. 799).

As for the effect of the plague on the transition, "the black death set the stone rolling in the direction of commutation. The lords consented more and more readily to arrangements based on money [which] merely accelerated a precedent of movement" (Thompson, 1931, p. 394). This is the first scenario obtained in Section 9.4.

Surely though, progress was not uniform and the direction of change must have varied from place to place, depending on political forces. Thus, Barker (personal communication, 1979) believes, in line with the second scenario of Section 9.4, that the upheavals caused by the shortage of labor in the wake of the plagues

prompted governments and dominant economic interests (land holders, capitalist town leaders) to clamp down and either reimpose old obligations or formulate new ones. For monarchial regimes, it was a logical trade-off to secure the greater loyalty and quiescence of the aristocracy by backing the latter in its re-assertion of rights and benefits in the exploitation of the peasantry. It was often in reaction to this clamping down that the terrible peasant risings of the latter half of the 14th Century occurred.

There are of course still more subtleties to the story. For example, Lyon (1957) has emphasized the importance of the development of free rural communes within "the vast land reclamation characterizing the eleventh and twelfth centuries." Such developments are thought to have played a major role in the emancipation of the common man and, according to our theory, must have occurred sometime after P^* but before P^s was reached because the expensive reclamation of land could only be initiated after richer, more easily settled lands were occupied. These developments, of course, do not imply that rents were not exacted from the "free" rural holders by the ecclesiastical and noble establishments. In fact, according to Lyon (1957, pp. 52, 53), such rents were paid. The significance of the development is rather that political and economic freedoms were achieved by such communities at their inception and not as the outcome of rebellion or the breakdown of manorial traditions.

Nonetheless, in periods of great labor shortage, such as might have occurred in those areas most grievously affected by the plagues, the privileged classes may well have attempted to establish onerous taxes and rents, supported by legal means, that would have repressed market competition for labor more or less as described by Barker in the quote earlier and as explicated by means of our theory in Section 9.4.

These "empirical" remarks are merely meant to be suggestive. One referee remarked on an earlier version of this study that "there is a literature of oceanic proportions from which one can find material illustrative of the theoretical issues raised [here in]" and then suggested beginning with the well-known works of Postan (1970, 1972) and Miskimin (1969). A further exegesis of this literature in terms of the theory we have presented here must, however, await another occasion.

9.7 Conclusion

Obviously, economic analysis alone is insufficient to explain all the details of historical development. Indeed, we have shown that the purely economic forces that must underlie historical evolution leave room for alternative "solutions" to the problems of class conflict and switching material interests in various socioeconomic groups. Nonetheless, the classical model of development, even in the pure and quite simple form exploited here, is a useful instrument for illuminating the economic factors involved. It is sufficient by itself to explain how the endogenous development of an economic system contains within it the sources of conflict that must arise in the course of its evolution, and points to the reasons why great political as well as economic changes erupt as a natural (endogenous) consequence of the interactions of demographic, technological, and distributional elements of economic life.

References

Baumol, W. F. 1970. *Economic Dynamics*. 3rd Edition. London: The Macmillan Co.
Bloch, M. 1961. *Feudal Society*. Chicago: University of Chicago Press.
Boserup, E. 1965. *Conditions of Agricultural Growth*.
Bowman, J. D. (undated) "On Dobb and the Breakup of European Feudalism." Manuscript.

Buttrick, J. 1960. "A Note on Growth Theory." *Economic Development and Cultural Change* 9:75–82.

Cameron, R. 1975. "Excursus, the Logistics of European Economic Growth." *Journal of European Economic History* 2.

Childe, V. G. 1936. *Man Makes Himself.* New York: New American Library, 1951. Originally published in England in 1936.

Cohen, J. S., and M. L. Weitzman. 1975. "A Marxian Model of Enclosures." *Journal of Development Economics* 1:287–336.

Day, R. H., and E. Koenig. 1974. "Malthusia: Population and Economic Growth in the Preindustrial State." Social Systems Research Institute, Working Paper No. 7411. Madison, WI: University of Wisconsin.

Dobb, M. 1946. *Studies in the Development of Capitalism.* 3rd Edition. New York: International Publ.

Fenoaltea, S. 1975. "The Rise and Fall of a Theoretical Model: The Manorial System." *Journal of Economic History* 35:386–409.

Georgescu-Roegen, N. 1960. "Economic Theory and Agrarian Economics." *Oxford Economic Papers* 12:1–40.

Gunderson, G. 1975. "Economic Trends in the Late Middle Ages: A Test for the Common Case for Diminishing Returns." Unpublished. Presented at the 1975 Cliometrics Conference. Madison, Wisconsin.

Haavelmo, T. 1954. *A Study in the Theory of Economic Evaluation.* Amsterdam: North-Holland Publishing Co.

Hilton, R. 1976. *The Transition from Feudalism to Capitalism.* London: New Left Books.

Leibenstein, H. 1956. *A Theory of Economic-Demographic Development.* Princeton: Princeton University Press.

Lyon, B. 1957. "Medieval Real Estate Developments and Freedom." *American History Review* 62:47–61.

Miskimin, H. A. 1969. *The Economy of Early Renaissance Europe 1300–1460.* Englewood Cliffs, NJ: Prentice-Hall.

Nelson, R. 1956. "A Theory of the Low-Level Equilibrium Trap in Underdeveloped Countries." *American Economic Review* 46:894–908.

Niehans, J. 1963. "Economic Growth with Two Endogenous Factors." *Quarterly Journal of Economics* 77:359–71.

North, D. C., and R. P. Thomas. 1970. "An Economic Theory of the Growth of the Western World." *Economic History Review* 23:1–17.

North, D. C., and R. P. Thomas. 1971. "The Rise and Fall of the Manorial System: A Theoretical Model." *Journal of Economic History* 31:777–803.

Parker, W. 1980. "Economic Development in a Millennial Perspective." Unpublished manuscript.

Postan, M. M. 1970. "The Chronology of Labor Services." In E. Minchinton (ed.) *Essays in Agrarian History.* Newton Abbot, England: David and Charles.

Postan, M. M. 1972. *The Medieval Economy and Society.* Berkeley, CA: University of California Press.

Samuelson, P. 1948. *Foundations of Economic Analysis.* Cambridge: Harvard University Press.

Sauvy, A. 1970. *General Theory of Population.* New York: Basic Books.

Simon, I. 1977. *Economics of Population Growth.* Princeton: Princeton University Press.

Solow, R. 1956. "A Contribution to the Theory of Economic Growth." *Quarterly Journal of Economics* 70:65–94.

Thompson, I. W. 1928. *An Economic and Social History of the Middle Ages: 300–1300.* New York: Century Co.

Thompson, I. W. 1931. *Economic and Social History of Europe in the Later Middle Ages 1300–1500.* New York: Century Co.

Wallerstein, I. 1974. *The Modern World System.* Text Edition. New York: Academic Press.

TEN

Do Economies Diverge? Economic Development in the Very Long Run

With Oleg Pavlov

... there are no examples so frequent in history as those of men withdrawing from the community they were bred up in, and *setting up new governments* in other places; from whence sprang all the petty commonwealths in the beginning of ages, and which always multiplied, as long as there was room enough, till the stronger or more fortunate swallowed the weaker; and those great ones again breaking into pieces, dissolving into lesser dominions. (paraphrased)
John Locke, *Two Treatises on Government 1690*

... for time does not stop its course for nations any more than for men; they are all advancing towards a goal with which they are unacquainted.
Alexis de Tocquville, *Democracy in America 1832*

Our purpose here is to describe and illustrate in the simplest possible way a multiple-phase theory of economic growth and development that helps explain why human evolution has not been characterized by steady progress but by fluctuating growth and changing forms, sometimes progressing to higher levels of complexity and sometimes reverting to earlier stages of organization. In the form outlined here (in terms of macroeconomic growth theory) it is convenient to think of the analysis as involving the "very long run." But for reasons that will be suggested in the conclusion, the very long run is of great interest for interpreting events in the "very short run," in particular the processes of integration and disintegration currently at work in the world. Moreover, we can propose with some confidence an answer to the question posed in the title of this chapter. Yes, indeed, economies diverge!

The first author developed the ideas incorporated here for a course on economic dynamics given at the University of Wisconsin in the early 1970s. Subsequently, he came in contact with

10.1 Background

The classical economists understood that a long-run stationary state at some culturally determined "subsistence" income level could be avoided through inventiveness and improved productivity. They emphasized that the latter in turn depends on a favorable institutional infrastructure that fosters education, private initiative, and factor mobility; that maintains and enforces property rights; that adjudicates disputes; and that provides an acceptable legislative system for establishing the character of the system as a whole.

In response to trends in the early industrial economies from the mid-nineteenth to mid-twentieth centuries, economic theorists abstracted from infrastructural prerequisites to obtain quantitative models of resource allocation and capital accumulation consistent with the macroeconomic picture of more or less steady, exponential growth. Historians of the nineteenth century, however, noticed that, before the industrial takeoff, economies had passed through distinct stages of development characterized by differences in production technology and in the organization of exchange and governance. Archaeologists, aided by modern methods of dating materials, have extended this picture backward in time, giving a proximate but coherent chronology of major developments on a worldwide basis that stretches back to the earliest evidence of a human presence.

To social scientists accustomed to the extensive data resources of "advanced" economies, the archeological record, no doubt, appears sketchy and essentially qualitative. For purposes of understanding socioeconomic evolution, however, there is a certain advantage in the very-long-run

Jerry Sablov, then at Harvard, who later organized an advanced seminar at the Center for American Studies in Santa Fe in the fall of 1978 including archeologists M. Aldenderfer, L. Cordell, G. Low, C. Renfrew, and E. Zubrow; a mathematician, K. Cooke; a philosopher, J. Bell. The goal was to see how the fascinating prehistory of our species that had been so patiently constructed by archaeologists in the preceding hundred years could be understood in formal terms and simulated numerically. See Sabloff (1980). It was not until he came across Ester Boserup's *Population and Technological Change*, quite by serendipity, that he actually set down in writing his theory of macroeconomic evolution, subsequently delivered at the conference on Evolutionary Dynamics and Nonlinear Economics sponsored by Ilya Prigogine's Center for Statistical Mechanics and the IC^2 Institute in Austin in 1985. A version, coauthored with a young French mathematician, Jean-Luc Walter, who spent a year visiting USC, was published in the proceedings. See Day and Walter (1989). All of the computation and graphics for this essay were prepared by the second author while a graduate student at the University of Southern California.

perspective it affords: salient features of the process stand out in bold relief.

Briefly, the great variety of human societies can be grouped into a relatively small number of forms or *stages* based on production technology and social infrastructure. Any such grouping is to some extent arbitrary and, by taking account of more and more details, a progressively finer array of types can be identified. To describe the major developments throughout the entire span of *Homo sapiens sapiens* and to take advantage of the known archaeological information a reasonable minimal specification would be as follows:

1. Hunting and gathering
2. Settled (village) agriculture
3. Complex societies and city-state civilizations
4. Trading empires
5. Industrial states
6. Global information economies

Various geographical areas traversed these stages at very different times, and the advance through them did not increase uniformly from lower to higher index. Rather, progress from one to another, especially in earlier times, was interrupted by reversions to lower-level stages. Moreover, fluctuations in income, population, and capital have been typical. The overall picture is one of growth at fluctuating rates with sometimes smooth, sometimes turbulent transitions when jumps and reversions occurred until a "higher" stage became firmly established. It is obvious that many complexly interacting forces are responsible for all this. Nonetheless, it is possible to capture the economic essence of the process by augmenting the pure classical growth theory with an explicit representation of diseconomies, infrastructure, and multiple socioeconomic regimes.

Because the vast changes under consideration have occurred over the millennia, it is tempting to presume that the long-ago past has little relevance for the present. Nothing could be farther from the truth. The past provides evidence of fundamental ingredients of socioeconomic structure that would seem to be involved at all times and all places; those fundamental ingredients must be playing a central role in what is going on now. Indeed, given an ability to explain the past in terms of the theory, implications for understanding present and possible future developments can be derived with some confidence.

10.2 Beyond Classical Growth

10.2.1 Household Behavior, Technology, and the Classical Story

Consider the classical time unit of a human generation – a quarter century, say. Each period is represented by a population of adults and their children who inherit the adult world in the next generation. Assume that each generation must provide its own capital goods, which only last the period. The possible output is then a function of the number of adults. The number of children who survive (that is, who become adults in the next period) depends on the per capita production of goods. The first relationship is the production function, which is assumed to possess eventually diminishing marginal returns to population. This function gives rise to the familiar curve of total output, which rises monotonically as population grows but at a declining rate. The second is the family function, which shows that (in our overlapping generation terms) the number of children of a given sex surviving to adulthood is nil below some very low income threshold η; this number then rises rapidly, reaching a bound given by Ricardo's natural rate of growth, and then at very high levels of income declines.[1]

Putting these ingredients together and assuming no advance in productivity, we obtain the standard classical results: If the threshold $\eta = 0$, then population, beginning at a small enough level, rises at an exponential rate during a phase of relative abundance; eventually, as diminishing returns lower the marginal and average productivity of labor, a regime of scarcity is entered; the average standard of living declines; population growth slows and converges to a stationary state at which the level of well-being is sufficient to motivate and sustain the formation of families just big enough to replace themselves generation after generation. If a continuous, exponential advance in output on augmenting productivity is incorporated, then the steady state gives way to "geometric" growth. The iron law of wages is then postponed indefinitely, which is a fact appreciated already by the classical writers.

Recently, a less well known conjecture of Malthus has been established theoretically; namely, that population growth could overshoot the stationary state and be followed by fluctuations in output, income, and population

---

[1] See Day, Kim, and Macunovich (1989) for the derivation of such a function from household preferences. See Easterlin (1978) on thresholds. However, see Day and Pavlov (2001), who extend the present analysis to include this phenomenon.

numbers. It is sufficient for the threshold η to be positive (and large enough).[2]

10.2.2 Internal Diseconomies, Economic Space, and Viability

The classical economists emphasized that, given a fixed technology, marginal productivity declines as production expands because of the scarcity of land, water, and other resources. But the scarcity of material resources is not the only cause of diseconomy in the production process. Another source is the increasing complexity of planning, communicating, and coordinating as output expands.[3] Diseconomies also accrue because the social goods and services on which market productivity rests become increasingly difficult to provide. We may call these *internal diseconomies* of population size. Recognizing these diseconomies yields absolutely diminishing returns to population within an economy. Instead of a monotonic production function, a single-peaked function emerges in which production rises to a maximum as population increases; if population continues to rise, however, production diminishes.[4]

Setting aside technological advance for the time being (it will be reintroduced in due course), we easily see that internal diseconomies could cause convergence, or fluctuations (cyclic or irregular), or, in the extreme, collapse! In that case, the standard of living would fall below η and the demise of the economy would occur – a prospect even more dismal than envisaged in the iron law of wages. This possibility poses a consideration for growth theory that goes beyond classical concerns, namely, that of *viability*: the conditions that enable an economy to persist cannot be taken for granted.

For analytical purposes it is convenient to assume that, for any given economy, output cannot be sustained if population exceeds some bound. Such a bound is most obvious for hunting and food-collecting peoples, but it is not unreasonable to suppose it would exist for any given socioeconomic

---

[2] For the conjecture concerning fluctuations, see Malthus's *Principles of Population*, Day (1983), and Day and Min (1996).

[3] A classic reference to internal diseconomies is E. A. G. Robinson (1958).

[4] A negative-sloping segment in production cannot occur if resources are freely disposable, but people are not freely disposable; thus, the "free disposal axiom" is not germane. It could be argued that people would never reproduce to such an extent as to depress absolute production, but this is a view supported more by faith than by facts. Overpopulation within the context of a given technology or given stage of development seems to have occurred and very likely is occurring in many places, and thus its analysis seems relevant indeed.

system – This upper bound determines the *economic space* within which a given economy is viable.

10.2.3 Infrastructure and Viability

An economy's technology can only be effective if a part of the population forms a social infrastructure upon which the use of the given technology depends. Such an infrastructure mediates the human energy devoted to coordinating production and exchange and to providing social cohesion for effective cooperation, for training and inculturating the workforce, and for producing the public goods, such as waste disposal and public safety, required for the well-being of the workforce. Call this part of the population the *infrastructural force*. Boserup (1981) called the knowledge on which the infrastructure is based the *administrative technology*.[5] It must augment the *production technology*. Together they form the socioeconomic technology of a society. We refer to the combination of infrastructure and socioeconomic technology of a given economy as its *socioeconomic system*. Every viable society depends on the existence of such a system. In this study the six examples given in Section 10.1 approximately span all of humanity's existence.

Given that the social infrastructure requires a significant block of human resources, it follows that, for an economy to be feasible, the population must exceed a lower bound. The effect on the production function is to shift it so that output can become positive only when the human resources have accumulated beyond a certain level. Combined with the possibility of internal diseconomies the problem of viability is clearly exacerbated, for population must not fall below the numbers required to keep the infrastructure intact. If it does, the economy is no longer viable.

This formulation raises the question, How could a society reach the required threshold in the first place? The answer is obvious: only by having already passed through a growth process within a system or through a sequence of systems that required a less elaborate infrastructure and hence lower thresholds for positive production. Actually, there is somewhat more to the story than this, but let us develop it a step at a time.

---

[5] Infrastructure in the sense defined here exists inside individual businesses as "management" and in the public sector as administrative, judicial, and representative bodies. The role of infrastructure in economic development has been receiving increasing attention. See North (1981) for very broad aspects and the World Bank (1994) for numerous details. For a suggestive attempt to quantify infrastructural effects on productivity, see the working paper by Charles I. Jones and Robert Hall, "Measuring the Effects of Infrastructure on Economic Growth," Stanford University.

10.2.4 Replication, External Diseconomies, and Reorganization by Fusion

Very early human societies were built around very small groups so that families themselves could provide infrastructural requirements without the need for elaborate hierarchical organizations. The hunting and gathering band thus takes its place early in the process of economic development. Archeologists have now traced its diffusion throughout the world. The mechanism that mediated this diffusion is that of *fission*. If, and as, a band gradually grew, it would eventually deplete the sources of game in its neighborhood. The productivity of search became greatly reduced. By splitting, two much smaller, more or less independent bands could be formed that, moving apart, could greatly increase the total area supplying food while greatly increasing productivity with no significant change in technology or organization. This growth and replication process can proceed until no vacant terrain is left.

One need not go back into prehistory to find this process at work. Indeed, the splitting up of a city-state into independent parts with one forming a new colony was described already by Herodotus. It has now been established as a common process by which civilized societies spread throughout the Mediterranean world and in this way overcame the internal diseconomies of population size. Such a process can continue until again the known world is full of such units. It is at this point that the Malthusian process of overshoot and undershoot might be expected to occur. Continuing growth is not possible without fundamental (structural) technological change.

To see what is meant by the term "full", to the internal diseconomies that operate within a given socioeconomic unit, take account of the *external* ones that derive from the total population of all the economies together. These are, for example, caused by the exhaustion of the environment's waste-absorbing capacity. This capacity can – for a given technology – be stated in terms of the *environmental space* available, which in turn depends on the population density. In addition, as resources become scarce and the cost of extracting and refining them grows, diminishing absolute returns to the workforce in all of the economies can eventually come to pass as the total world population gets large. The internal diseconomies can be overcome by fission; the external ones cannot.

Once the world is full in the sense that external diseconomies become important, the replication of economies with the same basic structures must come to an end. This is as true of the city-state as it is of the hunting and gathering band. If a collapse occurs due to a very powerful drop in productivity, the population may reorganize itself by fusing into a smaller number of city-states. Then the stage is set for renewed internal growth of the individual economies and further fission until the limits are reached again. Fluctuations not only in total population but in the numbers of economies (or societies) could ensue as well, perhaps in a highly irregular way, for a considerable span of time.

In summary, one avenue for economic growth that can overcome the limitations that bound an economy with a given socioeconomic system is replication. We refer to a collection of economies that possess the same system as a *culture*. Thus, in these terms "cultural growth" has a precise meaning.

10.2.5 Development Blocks, Integration, and Disintegration

Because of external diseconomies, and in the absence of fundamental technological change, growth of a given culture must ultimately be limited. But now consider the role of "ways of life" or "development blocks," represented by the different socioeconomic systems that underlie the great stages of development. Each of these is structurally distinct and depends on different production and administrative technologies that correspond to very different infrastructural requirements. Moreover, the infrastructural requirements have grown as one proceeds through the order. That is, each successive stage requires a greater overhead of human capital as a prerequisite for civil order and effective production. This implies that, once the limits of a given culture have been reached, for a switch to a more advanced stage to occur, existing economies must integrate to form larger, reorganized and elaborated infrastructures. Further growth in the total population is possible only if the external diseconomies are greatly diminished by such a change, or, to put it differently, only if the environmental space is greatly expanded by virtue of the different socioeconomic technology. Then, for each successive system a much larger worldwide population can be reached before external diseconomies become acute.

If the environmental space is expanded enough by the switch to a new regime, the process of growth through fission can resume until the new limit is reached. On the other hand, convergence could, in principle, occur to a fixed number of economies and a fixed population, or fluctuation in total population or numbers of economies (or both), or even collapse. What actually occurs depends on all the system parameters.

10.2.6 Learning by Doing

The continuing advance of productivity based on experience or learning by doing is still another mechanism to be considered that enhances growth potential. It can only occur within the currently adopted socioeconomic systems. As experience within a given system accumulates, output per unit of labor increases. Each distinct technology is assumed to have a maximum potential productivity parameter. The difference between that potential and the current level of the productivity index represents the potential improvement possible through learning by doing. The rate at which learning enhances productivity is assumed to be proportional to the potential for improvement.

10.3 The Multiphase Dynamics

Now let us put together all these ingredients to obtain a theoretical model of long-run economic development.

10.3.1 The Organizational Options

Begin with the menu of alternative socieconomic systems or regimes. Each will be described by parameters of household behavior, production, productivity improvement through learning by doing, infrastructure, and economic and environmental spaces. A given economy that belongs to one of them has several options as follows:

1. It can continue to grow with the same socioeconomic system.
2. It can divide so as to form two similar, more or less independent economies, each with the same system.
3. It can merge with another similar economy to form a new economic unit with the same basic system as before.
4. It can integrate with one or more economies to form a new, much larger economy with more elaborate infrastructural requirements, a much larger social space, and possibly much larger economic and environmental spaces than before.
5. It can disintegrate into several smaller economies, each with a less elaborate socioeconomic system and each with smaller infrastructural requirements than before.

10.3.2 Selection and Phase Switching

The "choice" among these options is guided in the present manifestation of the theory by the sole criterion of the average standard of living in terms of output per family for the current generation. This is in contrast to the optimal population growth theory, which characterizes an economy using an intertemporal optimization that takes into account (and determines) the standard of living and demoeconomic behavior of all future generations forever. Whatever one may think of the desirability of an infinite planning horizon, I take it as obvious that doing the best for the present generation, given its current population, is already a considerable intellectual and organizational challenge and, no doubt, in itself an exaggeration of actual capabilities.

A system change occurs if average productivity is enhanced by doing so. This does not mean that each successive technology is uniformly more productive than its predecessor but only that, at the total population at which the switch to a new regime occurs, the standard of living at that population level will be enhanced. In other words, "local efficiency" is sufficient to drive the selection process of technological regime switching in much the same way that it drives the process of replication through fission.

Given the infrastructural requirements and the limits implied by social and environmental spaces, growth cannot continue forever within any given economy but can only do so as long as there is a possibility of replication within a given system or if integration and switching to more advanced systems is possible. Every switch in the number of economies or in the socioeconomic systems changes the structure of the system and occurs endogenously on the basis of the standard of living.

Growth, however, is not the inevitable outcome of the dynamic process implied by the theory. Instead, other options involving fluctuations in population and the numbers of economies and in jumps and reversions among socioeconomic regimes can occur. Very complex demoeconomic histories are quite possible. In other words, human history can be as complicated in theory as it has been in fact. A comprehensive theoretical analysis of these possibilities and the parametric conditions under which each can occur is carried out elsewhere.[6]

---

[6] For a mathematical analysis of the various trajectories that can be generated by the model, see Day and Walter (1989) and Day, Chapters 21–23 (1999). Of course, capital required for the infrastructure and for production and capital accumulation should be incorporated in the theory, but I will not go into that aspect of the story here. For discussion of capital accumulation with multiple phases, see Day and Zou (1994).

10.4 Mimicking Economic Development in the Very Long Run: Results of a Simulation

10.4.1 The Socioeconomic Systems

We now describe a simulation with a specific model based on the theory just outlined. Remember that the division among the six socioeconomic systems merely reflects the roughly dominant forms of social organization and economic activity. The regimes incorporated in the theory are idealizations. It is not implied, for instance, that hunter-gatherers only hunt and forage or that agrarians neither hunt nor gather wild foods. Nor do we wish to imply by the term "city-state" that citizens never engaged in hunting or that hunter-gatherers were entirely absent in later stages. The mechanisms of replication and merging and of integration and disintegration are also idealized reflections of historical fact. In addition, it is supposed that at any one time the world population is dominated by a single culture and thus that all of its economies at a given time are based on the same family function and the same administrative and production technologies. Let us refer to the collection of such economies at a given time as a *culture*. The essential empirical characteristics of cultures can be summarized as follows.

1. The several cultures form an advancing sequence of increasingly complex infrastructures and expanding social spaces.
2. Demoeconomic conditions are a part of the prerequisites for the advance from one system to another. Thus, for example, hunting and food-collecting people do not adopt agriculture until the declining productivity of their own culture makes a switch desirable. They integrated to form more or less settled villages when the economic conditions became relatively favorable for agriculture.
3. Disintegrations can occur that cause a reversion to a simpler socioeconomic system in the sequence. They can be followed by an eventual reintegration that facilitates a jump back to a more complex stage.
4. Continuous productivity improvements take place in a given socioeconomic system when it is operative.
5. Reversion to a smaller number of economies with the same system or to an earlier system in the sequence is accompanied by population declines.

Historical development through the stages has actually taken place in fits and starts and at different times at different places. This is partly because the world is very heterogeneous in terms of topography and resource endowment, which means that similar technologies can have different productivities, and partly because many societies were more or less isolated from one another, which, in combination with even tiny perturbations in technology, social parameters, or both, can make huge differences in the sequencing and timing of the major transitions. For the present purpose these are details that are not dealt with at all.

10.4.2 A Model-Generated History

The history generated by a given model based on the theory is, in effect, a scenario described by the episodes that make it up. An *episode* is a period of time during which the number of economies and the system governing them does not change. The following variables describe a given model history:

The time and duration of each episode
The socioeconomic system used in each episode
The number of economies sharing the current system
Population
Aggregate production
Average standard of living per family
Average number of children per household who survive to adulthood
Average family size
The technology levels
The size of the aggregate infrastructure
The size of the total labor force

The specific mathematical forms and parameter values for the family and production functions are given in the references cited. On their basis, a simulation was begun with an initial population of 100 families ($x_0 = 100$) and was continued for 4,185 periods or generations – a span of a little over 100,000 years. The graph of population for this run, as shown in Figure 10.1, is virtually a vertical line over the present caused by explosive growth after a takeoff a few centuries ago. Very close to the present, fluctuations can be observed, but, in terms of sheer numbers, human population is utterly insignificant until the most recent centuries. This picture, however, is quite misleading, as can be seen by blowing up the time scale and plotting the data for shorter time spans. This is done in Figure 10.2. Panel (a) plots the simulated size population for the hunting and food-collecting culture. We see that rapid growth appeared only after some 25 millennia. Then, irregular fluctuations of increasing magnitude appear. Panel (b) plots population for systems 2, 3, and 4 also in millions for some 300 generations. Prominent fluctuations are featured, which is an exaggerated yet well-known qualitative

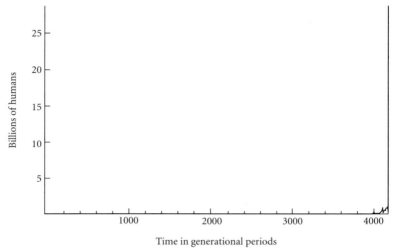

Time in generational periods

Figure 10.1. A simulated population history. Time is measured in "generations" of 25 years; population in billions.

feature of reality. Panel (c) plots population in billions for systems 4, 5, and 6 and brings the story well into the twenty-first century with the switch to the global information culture.

The implied structural evolution, as shown in Figure 10.3, displays the dominant system index at each time. The initial population in our simulation adopted the first system and remained with it for well over 3,000 generations. Growth during this long epoch thus occurred by means of fission and by improvements in the hunting and food-collecting technology.

A more detailed presentation of epochal evolution is presented in Figure 10.4. Panel (a) gives the system indexes from late in the System 1 epoch through to the "permanent" switch to System 4. Early in this evolution, a temporary jump to System 2 occurs. It involves the integration of the very large number of hunting bands into a smaller number of village agriculture economies that disintegrate, however, and revert within a generation back into the original hunting and food-collecting culture. Then successive integrations and disintegrations occur until the society locks into settled agriculture in period 3,784 or about 8050 B.C. Growth by replication then continues within this village agriculture system for 182 generations or 4,550 years. A similar sequence of structural fluctuations occurs between Systems 2, village agriculture, and System 3, the city-state and System 3 and System 4 trading empires with corresponding fluctuations in the number of economies as integrations and disintegrations bring about system jumps and reversions.

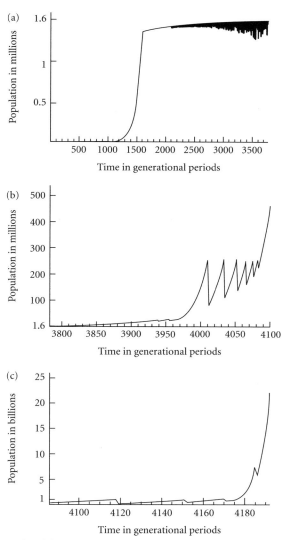

Figure 10.2. Details of the population dynamics. (a) System 1, population in millions. (b) Systems 2, 3, and 4, population in millions. (c) Systems 4, 5, and 6, population in billions. Note the changing time scale from (a) to (c).

In panel (b) the story is continued. The switch to System 4 shown in panel (a) was not permanent. A reversion occurred to System 3, followed by reintegration; integration and disintegration also occurred between Systems 4 and 5, the nation-state. The run terminates with a jump to System 6, the

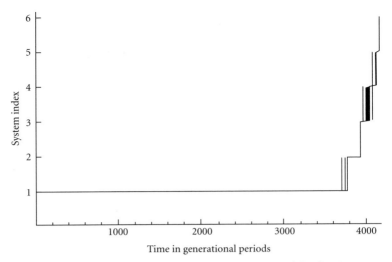

Figure 10.3. Simulated history of structural change in terms of the dominant systems index.

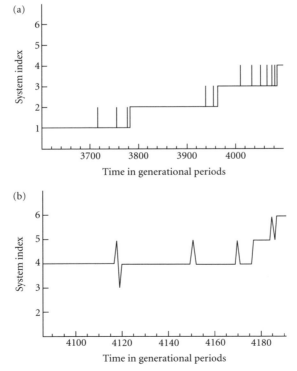

Figure 10.4. The evolution of socioeconomic systems. (a) Systems 1, 2, 3, and 4. (b) Systems 4, 5, and 6. Note that structural fluctuations occur between 1 and 2, 2 and 3, and 4 and 5.

global information economy, which takes place through an integration of industrial economies, and then a reversion followed by another jump. Note that the time scales used in diagrams (a) and (b) are different. This obscures the fact that the great instabilities in a structural sense are compressed into the 10,000 years since the advent of agriculture.

10.4.3 The Archeological and Historical Record

In reality, various geographical areas traversed these stages at very different times. The advance through them did not increase uniformly among the areas from a lower to a higher index. Rather, progress from one to another was interrupted and reversions to lower level stages occurred at varying times. Moreover, fluctuations in income, population, and capital have been typical. Inspite of these differences the overall picture is one of growth at fluctuating rates with sometimes smooth, sometimes turbulent transitions when jumps and reversions occurred until a "higher" stage became firmly established. This is what our theory would "predict" and what the example shown actually does.

Now consider behavior within epochs and in the transitions between them, beginning with hunting and food collecting. It is well known that the diffusion of hunting and food-collecting cultures throughout the world occurred through a process of fission and migration with relatively little elaboration of infrastructure but with advances of technology that involved a gradual improvement in utensils, weapons, and other material artifacts. Our theory both reflects and explains this fact.

The reason for the cessation of this expansion and the subsequent settlement of people into more or less fixed agricultural villages is less obvious and still debated. If Binford (1968), Boserup (1981), Cohen (1977), and others are right, then the regime switch was not due to the discovery of agriculture, which must have occurred long before the switch. Rather, it was due to the necessary decline in the productivity of the earlier way of life when the world became "full." Given the levels of population that had been reached and the decline in the population of prey species farming became relatively more efficient.

Our theory explains the early growth in terms of replication through fission, a well-established fact, and the switch to agriculture in terms of the reorganization of production due to the relatively greater productivity of labor in the new regime given the larger population and its greater social and environmental spaces. Thus, more people can live cohesively in a village than in a hunting band, and far more people can live on earth under agriculture.

The process of expanding agrarian settlement from 9000 to 3000 B.C. and the subsequent emergence of city-states in the ancient Near East has been described in meticulous terms by Nissen. Of special interest is his explanation of the internal conflicts that led to a reversion to individual village organizations and the continuing fluctuation between these forms for an extended period. Saggs, who gives a survey of civilization before the classic period, explained why, because of the unusually favorable conditions for wild animals and plants along the Nile, people in Egypt settled down later than elsewhere. He also describes how, as population grew, towns began to form from 5000 B.C. onward and then integrated to form a unified state, unifying upper and lower Egypt about 3000 B.C.

Scarre observes how a similar transition occurred in Greece about 1800 B.C. when the cluster of villages making up Attica combined to form the city-state of Athens.

Much is known about the vast extension in administrative infrastructure associated with the regime switches involving city-states and trading empires in Mesopotamia, Egypt, and Greece – developments only possible with sufficiently large and productive populations divided between production per se and administrative functions.

Of special interest to the present theory is the process of the repeated integration of villages to form the complex societies of Burundi and Polynesia and their disintegration back to collections of independent villages. This history, described by Sagan, involves a switching and reswitching between levels of socioeconomic organization that is predicted by our model for well-defined conditions of infrastructural requirements and productivity.

Another possibility that occurs generically in our theory is that of collapse and demise, a developmental outcome known to have occurred at various times and places in the archaeological and historical records. Iseminger summarizes an example discovered relatively recently in the broad plain east of St. Louis. During the period 9500–600 B.C., hunter-gatherers set up seasonal villages and, later, permanent settlements. By 1200 A.D. a substantial city that archaeologists call Cahokia came to dominate the surrounding territory. Two centuries later it was abandoned and no "ties have been established between the great city and any historical tribe." Possibly in this case the collapse involved a switch back to the hunting and food-collecting stage, which left no artifacts to distinguish it from other hunting and food-collecting tribes that dominated North America for many centuries before and since.

A few years ago, Katie Pollard, a young mathematics major at Claremont, simulated our model using data depicting the reconstructed history of the

Anasazi Indians in Chaco Canyon described by Lightfoot. Her model traces these people through their initial "hunting and gardening," village agriculture and centralized (city-state-like) systems, the fluctuation between these regimes, and the ultimate collapse and disappearance.

The replication mechanism that played such an important role in the diffusion of the hunting and food-collecting culture is also evident in the diffusion of the city-state. The classic description of the process is Herodatus's story of the division of Lydia's population and the subsequent colonization of North Africa and Italy. He also relates the belief of people in a city near the Bosporus whose citizens claimed that they were founded by a colonial expedition from Egypt.

Throughout the world, trading empires eventually arose through the widespread political and economic domination of surrounding territories by larger, more powerfully organized, and more effectively coordinated agglomerations of people. We might include the feudal era through the Renaissance in this epoch which is distinguished by repeated integrations and disintegrations of smaller city-states and principalities as empires rose and fell. All this can be explained in terms of the theory at hand and mimicked by computational simulations. One thinks of Egypt, Persia, Greece under Philip and Alexander, Rome, China, and India.

Obviously, a great variety of geographical, social, and even psychological factors were involved in these examples and none were alike in detail. Yet, all the historical details had to work themselves out within a framework of interacting technological and demoeconomic forces roughly modeled by the present theory.

With the Industrial Revolution, a vast expansion in the resources devoted to infrastructure took place: elaborate educational and scientific establishments; multiple levels of representative government; bureaus for monitoring economic activities of many kinds (banking, trade, production, etc.); elaborate systems for adjudicating economic and social conflict; public goods for recreation, communication, transportation, and so forth. And integration and disintegration continued.

10.5 The Lessons for the Present and Future

Our grossly aggregative theory would seem to provide too course a sieve to filter out the salient features of modern history involving such intricately elaborated and interconnected institutions among so many levels of organization as now exist. Yet, if the facts have been interpreted correctly, our theory contributes to an understanding of the evolution of humanity through its various cultural forms – not in detail, of course, but in some of its principal aspects. If that is so, then we are entitled to draw implications for understanding events in our own time and for considering policies that will shape events in the future. Let us summarize some important examples.

10.5.1 Infrastructure and Productivity

The theory is based on a crucial link between population size, infrastructure, and productivity. The productivity of a society by any measure (its wealth, political power, size, and welfare distribution) depends on an effective workforce whose productivity depends in turn on the existence of an appropriately developed infrastructure with sufficient resources to sustain the population as a whole. As population grows, infrastructure must also. It is not just the size of the infrastructure but its functions and organization that must change. When population begins to become excessive relative to its infrastructure, productivity must fall. To avoid fluctuations or even collapse, population must be stabilized or the infrastructure transformed.

Associated with the rise of the nation-state (System 5 in the simulation) is an explosive increase in population and a considerable instability in the composition of the individual economic units. From the point of view of the present theory, it is not mere fluctuations in business that characterize this institutional instability but rather the integration and disintegration of political economic units throughout the nineteenth and twentieth centuries.

10.5.2 Integration and Disintegration: Europe and the Soviet Bloc

The development of NATO after World War II was an initial step in the integration of the industrial nations of Europe, a response to the forced integration of Eastern European countries by Soviet Russia. Subsequent efforts to develop closer ties among the Western European countries have led to an expansion of the economic, legislative, and judicial infrastructures making up the European Union.

The Soviet Bloc, however, suggests something like the kind of reversion our theory predicts: a large, complexly organized economy disintegrating into several smaller ones. In terms of the theory spelled out here, the causes are clear: the system outgrew the infrastructure required to continue growing in an effective manner. A population of such great size cannot persist within that kind of socioeconomic system. A new one is required, and that is what the transition is about. The presumption, both inside the former Soviet economies and outside, is that the new regime should be based on democracy, markets, and private property, that is, on a different administrative technology.

Private property and the market economy depend on the state – the right kind of state – that has created the right kind of public infrastructure within which private initiative can thrive in a way that enhances the system as a whole. This means an accumulation of laws defining the rights, obligations, opportunities, and limitations of public and private actions; a system of courts for interpreting the law and adjudicating disputes about its application; an effective system of representative government to adjust the law in response to changing conditions so as to engage the willing participation of most of the people most of the time; a large scientific and educational establishment to provide competent participants in private and public institutions; and a system of monitoring to ensure standards of quality on the basis of which specialized production and trade can flourish. Most of all, the market economy needs institutions that create a sense of common purpose and commitment so that the population forms a cohesive body that spends most of its energies on symbiotic activity rather than on destructive social conflict.

We know of the great cultures that have accomplished enough of these things to have played a powerful role in shaping the world as we know it. We also know that all of them have eventually failed in providing some of these crucial ingredients. In the midst of the transition to another regime from a culture that has failed, it is difficult, indeed, to anticipate the outcome. Certainly, the situation in Eastern Europe reflects this problematic aspect of the transition process. Will it go through a sequence of integration and disintegrations as chaotically as has occurred at various places and times in the past?

10.5.3 Infrastructure and America in Transition

In the midst of our own spectacular American transition into the global information economy, we recognize the decline in the aspects of welfare by which the ascendant quality of American life in the first half of the twentieth century was measured: infant mortality, literacy, educational attainment, material well-being, public safety, longevity, and the sense of unlimited individual opportunity. The fact is, our situation has substantially worsened in these terms both absolutely and relative to many other countries in the last quarter century or more. No doubt, many causes have contributed. The theory developed here suggests that we look at infrastructure and population as key elements in an explanation. Let us take one prominent example: the modern city, and consider one case in point, Los Angeles.

Los Angeles has a population roughly the same magnitude as Denmark's. Yet it has a single mayor, a single police chief, and a single superintendent of schools – in short, a single layer of government. Denmark, by way of contrast, has several layers of government, many mayors, and many police chiefs. In this sense, it has far more infrastructure than Los Angeles has.

Or, consider this: when the first census of the United States of America was taken in 1780, the population of the country was about 4 million or roughly that of Los Angeles now. But the U.S. population was divided into 13 states with 13 governors, 13 legislatures, and 13 state supreme courts, not to mention hundreds of county and city governmental institutions and officials. Contrastingly, Los Angeles has one mayor and a single city council! Can it be that the United States has outgrown its governmental infrastructure and outgrown it by far? Is this the reason representative government is seen to be unrepresentative by a growing body of alienated citizens? Can the basic problem facing this country be one of *too little representation* and not one of too much government?

10.5.4 The Global Economy

Population in the global simulation portrayed in Fig. 10.1 reached 25 billion in the late-twenty-first or early twenty-second century, more than four times its current level. With the rate of growth slowing down among some peoples, this number might never be reached. Indeed, some projections now estimate that the maximum number attained will be between 10 and 12 billion, which is still a very large number. But given the socioeconomic systems in place some areas of the world are already hideously overpopulated. If no other evidence convinces one of the relevance of the present analysis, surely the evidence in these places should. The world's population is rapidly expanding despite these regional disasters.

Immigration into the countries with relatively slowly growing indigenous populations has been greatly facilitated by the forces of globalization, providing some temporary relief to those who succeed in relocating. But present events show that humans have not learned to live any more peacefully with one another than in the past. With total world population still expanding rapidly, the problems of development, assimilation, and conflict are likely to grow still more acute.

Theoretically, it all boils down to economic and environmental space. Can more be created, and how? There would seem to be four means of doing so. First, reduce or reverse population growth, which, seemingly, is unlikely given past experience. Second, slow down or reduce the decline in economic and environmental spaces by conserving resources, recycling, and reducing pollution. Third, expand research on new production technologies. Fourth, develop behavioral rules, modes of organization, and living arrangements that can more effectively produce social cohesion and civil order within populous urban agglomerations, including the development of local, representational community governance and public services at the local level that are essential for representative, republican institutions, participatory democracy, and private enterprise.

Noteworthy has been the elaboration of infrastructure at a global level: earth satellite systems, international courts and assemblies, trade agreements, and the vast complex of research organizations that feed technical advances. With the spread of jet aircraft, airport facilities, satellite communications, and the World Wide Web we have entered a new global information economy that facilitates and coordinates communication, the dissemination of knowledge, the flow of people, and the exchange of goods throughout the world. Will these developments succeed in overcoming the attending economic and political conflicts?

10.5.5 Do Economies Diverge?

A look at the facts of economic growth in the very long run indicates that yes, economies do diverge. They may approach steady states but eventually depart and head off in a new direction after perhaps a turbulent period of switching and reswitching with jumps and reversions among socioeconomic systems. Such divergences from any fixed pattern are explained by instabilities in the way demoeconomic forces interact in the presence of diseconomies, infrastructures, and multiple socioeconomic systems. Convergence could in principle come about. But the facts suggest that the qualitative properties of technology and behavior that would lead to such an outcome are not the relevant ones. How prescient, then, is de Tocquiville's plaintive observation, "for time does not stop its course for nations . . . they are all advancing towards a goal with which they are unacquainted."

References

Binford, L. 1968. "Post Pleistocene Adaptations." Chapter 21 in M. Leane (ed.) *New Perspectives in Archaeology.* Chicago: Aldine Publishers.

Boserup, E. 1981. *Population and Technological Change.* Chicago: University of Chicago Press.

Boserup, E. 1996. "Development Theory: An Analytical Framework and Selected Application," *Population and Development Review* 22:505–15.

Cohen, M. 1977. *The Food Crisis in Prehistory.* New Haven: Yale University Press.

Day, R. H. 1983. "The Emergence of Chaos from Classical Economic Growth." *Quarterly Journal of Economics* May:201–13.

Day, R. H. 1999. *Complex Economic Dynamics, Vol. 2: On Introduction & Dynamic Macroeconomics,* Cambridge: MIT Press.

Day, R. H., K.-H. Kim, and D. Macunovich. 1989. *Journal of Population Economics* 2:139–159.

Day, R. H., and J.-L. Walter. 1989. "Economic Growth in the Very Long Run: On the Multiple-Phase Interaction of Population, Technology, and Social Infrastructure." Chapter 11 in W. Barnett, J. Geweke, K. Shell (eds.) *Economic Complexity: Chaos, Sunspots, Bubbles and Nonlinearity.* Cambridge: Cambridge University Press.

Day, R. H., and M. Zhang. 1996. "Classical Economic Growth Theory: A Global Bifurcation Analysis." In T. Puu (ed.) *Chaos, Solitions and Fractals* 7(12):1969–88.

Day, R. H., and G. Zou. 1994. "Infrastructure, Restricted Factor Substitution and Economic Growth." *Journal of Economic Behavior and Organization* 23:149–66.

Easterlin, R. A. 1978. "The Economics and Sociology of Fertility: A Synthesis." Chapter 2 in Charles Tilly (ed.) *Historical Studies of Changing Fertility.* Princeton: Princeton University Press.

North, D. 1981. *Structure and Change in Economic History.* New York: W. W. Norton & Co.

Robinson, E. A. G. 1958. *The Structure of Competitive Industry.* Chicago: University of Chicago.

Sabloff, J. 1980. *Simulations in Archaeology.* Albuquerque: University of New Mexico Press.

World Bank. 1994. *World Development Report 1994, Infrastructure for Development.* Oxford: Oxford University Press.

PART FOUR

TOWARD A GENERAL THEORY OF DEVELOPMENT

ELEVEN

Economics Far from Equilibrium

What drove these transformations from one level to the next remains largely
unknown but at least we have achieved a non-contradictory description of
nature rooted in dynamic instability.

> Ilya Prigogine, *The End of Certainty: Time, Chaos and the New
> Laws of Nature*

Nature changes quite abruptly at any point when a quantitative modification
leads to a sudden emergence of a new quality.

> Konrad Lorenz, *The Natural Science of the Human Species*

Such is the continuous market, which is perpetually tending towards equilibrium without ever attaining it.... like a lake, there are days when it is almost
smooth... [and others] stirred to its very depths by a storm, so also the market
is sometimes thrown into violent confusion by crises.

> Léon Walras, *Elements of Pure Economics*

During the last quarter of the twentieth century, great progress was made in
explaining physical, biological, and human social processes that, in former
times, were thought to be too complex to be explained in terms of mathematical models. This discussion is concerned with these developments in
economics. As a prelude, the basic properties of complex dynamics that
have so far been shown to have a significant bearing on economic processes
are outlined. Then two applied studies are summarized: one representing macroeconomic development over many centuries, one representing
microeconomic development within a decade or generation. These studies
imply that economies evolve far from equilibrium.

Lecture presented at the interdisciplinary lecture series, *Facing the Uncertain*, organized by
Ilya Prigogine, the University of Texas at Austin, April 14, 1998.

11.1 Complex Economic Dynamics

Economics is a naturally quantitative subject, dealing, as it does, with prices, incomes, amounts of various goods and services, inputs, and outputs of production processes, all of which bear clear algebraic relationships among one another. Early economic theorists formulated macroeconomic concepts of demand and supply and of adjustments to their imbalances. Later, they developed microeconomic models of actions based on the rational pursuit of needs and wants within possibilities determined by technical, economic, social, and psychological constraints. Mechanisms were also formulated describing how individuals and business firms pursue goals even without comprehending the working of the system as a whole. It has become clear that the situation in which the various individuals and organizations in the economy find themselves depends in an intricate way on what is going on in the economy as a whole but in a way that individuals and organizations – at best – can only comprehend in part and – at worst – cannot fathom at all. Much of the intellectual effort aimed at understanding those characteristics of a decentralized, private ownership economy has been dominated by concepts of optimality and equilibria – the condition under which states of perfect coordination exist with relatively little attention allocated to the mechanisms that bring about such states. Indeed, within a prominent line of macroeconomic theory the assumption is made that an economy is always perfectly coordinated and that the more or less randomly changing equilibria are optimal responses to random shocks that become the cause of fluctuations in output and employment.

A contrasting category of work to which my own studies belong views the observed fluctuations and instabilities as being intrinsic to the development process, that economies do not converge to stable stationary situations or to ones of steady uninterrupted economic growth, and that they can be explained in part by the formal representation of adaptive economizing and market mechanisms that function out-of-equilibrium.

In the course of this work, four properties of behavior emerged from model solutions that reflect fundamental qualitative properties of real-world history in an abstract, analytical manner. These properties are (1) irregular fluctuations of economic data, (2) structural change in economic systems, (3) overlapping waves of technical adoption, and (4) structural breakdown. Let me elaborate briefly on the first two of these properties here. The last two are dealt with in the applied studies described in Sections 11.2 and 11.3.

11.1.1 Irregular Fluctuations

Irregular, more or less unpredictable fluctuations occur in stock market prices as anyone who follows the financial pages knows. They also occur in many data series such as interest rates, commodity prices, number of people unemployed, industrial capacity utilization and gross domestic product, foreign exchange rates, and so on. For a long time these kinds of irregular fluctuations were treated by economists as the result of random disturbances coming from outside the system of endogenous economic relationships. But models of supply and demand, of economic growth, and of interacting agents have now been shown to exhibit similar properties without the assumption of random perturbations and purely on the basis of deterministic connections among the endogenous variables.[1]

Certainly, economists are entitled to take account of influences coming from "outside" whose causes correspondingly originate outside the economy itself. And, indeed, it may not lie within the economist's interest or capability to explain such exogenous events. That random-like irregularity, however, can also be generated by the way the economy works means that part of the vicissitudes of history can be explained in comprehensible economic terms even though they cannot be predicted. I say "part of the vicissitudes" because, obviously, the economy *is* influenced by outside forces. To assume that those forces have the character of random shocks is a reasonable way to conceptualize them for analytical study. However, it is our ability to explain the economically generated part of the chaotically irregular that is new.

11.1.2 Structural Change

While theorists such as Marshall and Walras were formalizing the basic concepts of economic analysis, economic historians such as Schmoller and Gräss and somewhat later institutionalists such as Veblen and Commons were busy describing economic development as an evolutionary process, that is, as a sequence of institutional structures that changed over time with a given system of economic and social relationships giving way to another – a process of morphogenesis seemingly at odds with the program already

---

[1] Examples of this theoretical work will be found in Day (1994, 2000), Hommes (1991), and Lorenz (1993).

under way of mathematizing economic theory. Thus, a schism emerged, separating institutionalists and theorists.[2]

In other sciences, the possibility that the objects of inquiry could self-organize into structurally differing states, each exhibiting distinct properties and behavioral patterns, was already well understood in the transformation of the states of matter and in the development of living organisms. Some economic theorists such as Marshall, and especially Schumpeter, began to see the economic process in similar terms in the sense that the technologies, institutions, and ways of life of a given time develop the preconditions that lead to their replacement by other technologies, institutions, and ways of life at later times. That similar processes of self-organization and structural transformation are at work in all of nature – physical, biological, and social – seems to have been the unique vision of Prigogine (1997, 1998), who it may be noted has more than anyone devoted his energy and resources to the development of this new point of view.

The mathematical analog of structural change lies in the concept of *multiphase dynamics*, in which a complex system is described by a partition of its state space into *phase zones* and by a set of dynamic relationships or *phase structures*, one for each zone. Each such phase structure describes how the system behaves in the corresponding zone. Each phase zone–structure pair is a *regime*. Using such a system, we can describe evolution in terms of the switching of the process from one such zone to another, implying, as it does, a transition from one formalized structure to another. This way of thinking about structural change, already known in physics and engineering, was introduced into economics by Leontief and by Georgescu-Roegen in the 1950s. Their work was the basis for my development and application of the theory of multiphase dynamics in economic processes (1963, 1995, 2000).[3]

The idea of a *punctuated equilibrium*, introduced by Gould into evolutionary biology and discussed by Wilson (1999), is a particular kind of multiphase process. A graphical metaphor of this idea is illustrated in Figure 11.1. The phase space is divided into zones **a**, **b**, and **c**. From initial conditions x_0, y_0, z_0 within the zones, the time paths wander about and then converge to, or remain close to, "equilibrium" situations labeled A, B, and C in the three zones, respectively. Each zone and each equilibrium within it

---

[2] Veblen and Commons based their evolutionary theories on the detailed study and careful description of individual firms, labor organizations, legislative bodies, and legal processes. Economic theorists such as Marshall, Walras, and Fisher focused on isolating quantitative principles and their graphical or mathematical representation and analysis.

[3] Similar concepts based on continuous time have been studied in engineering and have received an elegant treatment by Aubin (2000).

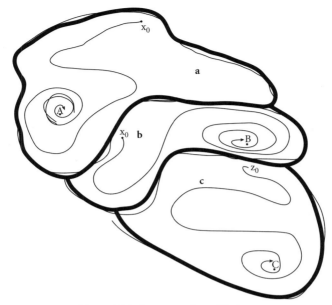

Figure 11.1. Punctuated equilibrium.

is stable. Some randomness may occur within a given zone when relatively small outside disturbances perturb the state, and thus the time path may not converge to a steady state but fluctuate around one.

In such a system, structural phase switching could occur only if a relatively large perturbation were to take place (by some unexplained process) that shifts the state into another of the phase zones. Such a shock creates a new initial condition in another phase zone. Then a different yet stable dynamic structure takes over and the path eventually converges to, or fluctuates near, a new equilibrium. Punctuated equilibrium is thus described by a sequence of relatively stable changes punctuated by some kind of significant exogenous event that precipitates a structural change. It has also been called *path dependence* by Paul David because the path the system takes and the equilibrium to which it converges depend on the history of shocks to which it has been exposed. The term would seem to be equivalent to the property of a path generated by any open dynamic system influenced not only by the internal working of its endogenous variables but also by external conditions as described by exogenous variables that impinge upon it – a property that Samuelson in his (1947) classification of dynamic systems referred to as "historical."

An alternative to this exogenous way of generating evolution occurs if a regime is *unstable*, that is, from any position within a given phase zone the structural equation leads the state of the system to cross a boundary and into another zone. The new structural equation, starting from the state it has inherited, then generates the path of the system until it crosses a boundary again. Such a process has the property that the evolution of structure from one form to another occurs endogenously as a result of the way the system functions within each zone. Each switch into a zone is caused by conditions brought about in its predecessor; each new structure "emerges" from the old. Change occurs within the new zone until a phase switch again occurs. Structural change continues unless, and until, a stable zone is entered. In the latter event only an outside shock could cause a resumption of the phase-switching process. If no stable phase zones existed, evolution would almost surely never cease, with regimes switching between each other or, if their number were not finite, possibly continuing from one unique structure to another indefinitely. By "almost surely" is meant "with full measure" or "with probability one." These are delicate, mathematical phrases recognizing the "existence" of special stationary situations that could only occur if the system in question were to begin in one. A zone made up of states in which the process could not exist at all is called the "null phase zone." It consists of all those states in which the equations of change are inconsistent. If the dynamic process carried the system into this null phase zone, then the evolution would come to an end and the system would be said to have "broken down," "collapsed," or "self-destructed."

This endogenous representation of evolution can also explain the appearance of punctuated equilibria. By projecting a higher dimensional space onto a flat page, as in Figure 11.2, a trajectory can be displayed that begins in zone *A*, wraps around an "equilibrium" without quite reaching it, then veers away and rapidly enters into zone *B*, where a new equilibrium is approximated with perhaps relatively modest fluctuations around it, and then, again with a rapid transition, enters into zone *C*. This system would appear to be in, or close to one or another, equilibrium most of the time with a rapid but endogenously generated transition occurring at occasional intervals. It then mimics Walras's description of a continuous market, seemingly always tending toward some kind of more or less steady state, or gently fluctuating about one, but occasionally interrupted by crises like a lake amid a summer storm.

Given continuous differential equations of motion, the endogenous transition from one regime to another requires adding at least a third dimension to explain how the path can fluctuate closely around an equilibrium and then veer away without intersecting itself; although for a discrete time representation, this would not be necessary. This kind of property can occur in a nonlinear system when some variables move relatively

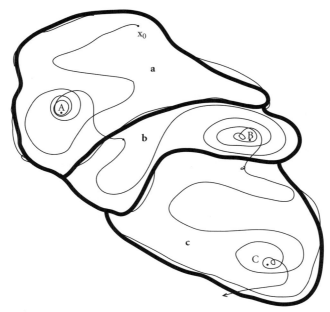

Figure 11.2. Multiple-phase dynamics generating the appearance of punctuated equilibrium.

slowly whereas others move relatively more rapidly – an idea discussed in a suggestive article by Starbuck (1973), which drew in part on a mathematical paper of Pontryagin (1961). If, indeed, the underlying system were continuous and higher dimensional, but its projection on 2-space were observed only at discrete intervals, the process might appear as if it were described by stable phase equations punctuated by a shock driven by some "outside" influence. In this case, the limited empirical picture would deceive us about the underlying endogenous self-organizing, and self-disorganizing mechanisms.

I take the fundamental task of science in any field of inquiry, and not the least in economics, to be that of extending the domain of endogenously explained processes, gradually replacing explanations in terms of random shocks and exogenous forces wherever possible. Multiple-phase dynamics with unstable, "chaotic" properties are contributing to this advance. Still, we must recognize the inevitable intrusion of unexplained perturbations as the price of our ignorance.

One might presume that an attempt to reduce the richly varied panoply of human development to a set of mathematical equations would be fruitless. Such a view is quite understandable, for it would seem obvious that, indeed, this cannot be done. However, it may be possible to identify salient causal relationships that have played a fundamental role in this history. Such an objective is shared by all scientists: the physicist who understands the manifest variety of the physical world as the dynamics of "energy" in its various forms without in any way enhancing our immediate apprehension of sense experience, or the biologist who derives the variety of living forms from the process of genetic variation, inheritance, and selection without adding one whit to our understanding of the conscious sense of being alive. Yet, the variety of physical, biological, and mental processes we experience and observe, and that we know have taken place in the past, must all be consistent with the underlying mechanics of physical and biological dynamics.

Likewise, the rich, infinitely varied fabric of human history must be consistent with underlying laws of population, productivity, economizing behavior, and human welfare. Thus, mathematical models of population, industry, and polity may be able to describe certain laws of socioeconomic evolution with which all the particular and variegated developments of human activity must be consistent. As with their physical and biological counterparts, they may suggest new ways of conducting human activity so as to avoid the crises that inevitably occur if these laws are ignored.

At this point, I propose to summarize two examples of this kind of research with which I have been involved myself: one investigating structural change at the macroeconomic level, the other structural change at the microeconomic level. In the course of the discussion we will see how complex economic dynamics, overlapping waves of technical adoption, and breakdown emerge from multiple-phase dynamic processes.

11.2 Production, Population and Polity: Macroeconomic Development in the Very Long Run

At a given stage of development, the "structure" of a society consists of institutions that govern and coordinate the interactions among its constituents, that determine the scope for individual initiative, that create incentives and conditions for cooperative endeavor, that formulate the rules and regulations for dealing with conflict, and that operate processes for inculturating the common values and understanding forming the basis of its culture. Generally speaking, these institutions, together with the people and capital goods required for their functioning, compose the *infrastructure* of the society. A part of this infrastructure forms the *polity* of the society, that is, its public, civic institutions and activities; a part of it resides in more or less independently formed households and privately organized enterprises that make up its *private sector*. Together they embody the *administrative technology* that makes productive work and specialized exchange effective. Without this infrastructure, society would not exist. Archaeological, anthropological, and historical research clearly demonstrates that, without an effective infrastructure, social life degenerates into chaos, and those who wish to destroy a given social system understand their task to be one of destroying that effectiveness.

Each production technology demands certain functions of infrastructure, such as a cadre of teachers who can inculcate the principles of mechanisms and social behavior that production of goods and services requires, a moral code and a system of law to encourage appropriate behavior, and a system of governance that induces the willing participation of most of the people to be socially productive enough of the time. Thus, some effort in any society at any stage of development is devoted to producing the public goods and collective services that form its infrastructure and some is devoted to producing private goods and services that satisfy the individual needs and wants of its members.

The hunting and food-collecting societies that provided the dominant form of human social and economic organization were incredibly simple compared with the current globally interacting information economy that has emerged in our own era. Yet, they depended in an equally important way on the appropriate combination of infrastructure and production technology. From a few bands – or perhaps a single band of a very few individuals who apparently emerged at least 100,000 years ago and probably much earlier – this form of human society spread throughout the earth, its productivity gradually advancing with the improvement of tools and weapons. It did so by the replication of its basic units through fission, that is, growth within a given band followed by splitting to form two bands that moved away from one another, each of which resume growth as more or less independent units. In this way, the basic social unit remained quite small, consisting of one or two dozen families. Work tended to be specialized between the sexes: the men engaged in hunting and fabricating weapons and tools and the women in collecting and processing food and fabricating clothing. Infrastructure consisted of priests or shamans who governed religious ceremony and medical practice, leaders of the hunt, councils for group decision making and dispute adjudication, scouts or intelligence gatherers, social clubs, recreational games, and so forth – all together, providing a framework for effective cooperation in carrying out the work of the band.

This mode of socioeconomic organization persisted through at least 90 percent of our species' existence. This long epoch was not an equilibrium or steady-state situation, however, though it may have approximated one. Population grew very slowly for many millennia, very likely fluctuating owing to the endogenous effects of crowding and to "outside" environmental changes. As new regions were discovered, growth could resume until virtually all the habitable regions of the world were occupied. Productivity within the same basic technological paradigm also grew – sometimes in spurts when more efficient weapons and tools were invented and disseminated and knowledge of foods and plants accumulated. This upward trend in productivity, combined with the replication mechanism of fission, enabled growth to continue until the earth became "full." Because this culture required a very low population density, growth within the hunting and food-collecting culture could not continue. Eventually, crises occurred at various places in the world – not simultaneously, of course, but more or less in the same way – and the transition to settled agriculture occurred, precipitating a period of faster population growth.

During the next 10 millennia or so, a sequence of transitions occurred among a set of very different cultural paradigms that can be grouped into several crude categories:

1. Hunting and food collecting
2. Settled (village) agriculture
3. The city-state
4. Trading empires
5. Industrial, nation-states
6. The global information system

The transition from one such stage to the next involved the integration of essentially independent economies at one stage into more populous economies at the next stage with elaborated infrastructures and with more refined specialization of production and administration activities.

The process of integration has often been accompanied by economic upheaval and violent social conflict. Moreover, it has not advanced uniformly but has been interspersed by disintegrations and temporary reversions to less complex socioeconomic systems followed eventually by new integrations and transitions to the more complex forms.

Nor has this evolutionary process come to an end. In our own time, we observe various moves to integrate more or less independent nation-states, as in the European Union, and at the same time the disintegration and reversion of the Soviet Empire into a collection of more or less independent states. Despite these contrasting movements, at the same time an array of institutions and physical constructs are creating the entirely new form of worldwide integration into what may be called the global information economy.

I described a model of this process elsewhere in considerable analytical detail. For our present purpose, it is sufficient to summarize its content in very general terms.[4]

Consider first the attributes of a given essentially coherent, independent economy. Family formation and reproduction are determined by cultural values, individual preferences, environmental, cultural, and economic factors. A function depending on these cultural parameters and on the standard of living attained by the parents' generation determines the average number of children per family who will survive to adulthood and form the adult population of the next generation. It is measured by the number of families.

Part of the adult effort within a given generation is devoted to the production of goods and services that make up the "standard of living" or "income"; another part is devoted to the activities of infrastructure within the family, within private groups, and within the public domain. The former part of the effort is labor; the latter is called "administration." An appropriate infrastructural, administrative body is a prerequisite for the adoption of a given system. The material output of the economy is determined by the labor force, which exhibits eventually diminishing returns as the labor force grows. The productivity of labor is at the same time enhanced by experience within the given system of administrative and production technology. In common parlance this process is known as learning by doing. Given that system, the average standard of living per family is the resultant of the size of the labor force and its accumulated experience.

The average standard of living increases for a time, but if learning slows down or does not increase fast enough, population eventually surpasses the optimum level and the standard of living declines – eventually declining enough to bring about a decrease in population, which will have the effect of increasing the standard of living in the next generation, thus leading to fluctuations; or, the economy will divide itself into two more or less similar units through the replication process cited earlier in this section; or, if a more "advanced" system is available, several economies may merge, form a new integrated and elaborated infrastructure, and adapt the corresponding production technology, which will result in a standard of living higher than would have been possible under the "old system" and high enough to permit continued population growth.

A computer simulation of this model has been used to describe economic development over the entire span of "modern" human existence beginning

---

[4] A detailed description is presented in Day (1999). The approach has been extended by Pavlov (2001). [See Chapter 10 above.]

with the hunting and food-collecting band, traversing by successive transitions the next four systems but punctuated from time to time by disintegration and reversion, and arriving finally at the global information economy. In this way the model explains the long progression of humanity in mathematical terms through its successive structural stages that exhibit periods of growth followed by fluctuations interrupted by abrupt transitions that are generated endogenously by the inherent instability of each regime.

An analysis of the model's qualitative characteristics shows that this picture is robust with respect to initial conditions and parameter values, though when any are altered, the detailed timing of phase switching and the duration within given phases can change drastically. The model represents cultural evolution as a growth mechanism involving an interaction of population, productivity, and infrastructure. Whenever population "outgrows" its infrastructure or its environmental space, it must experience a crisis with fluctuations. It may then advance to a qualitatively different, more productive regime or, failing that, it may disintegrate into a larger number of economies with smaller infrastructural requirements. The model cannot explain the details of the transition from one system to another, or the detailed socioeconomics-political processes for bringing one about. It merely explains why a particular kind of transition must take place. Combined with a careful reading of the historical and archaeological records, the model tells us something fundamental about the history and points to future problems that must in all likelihood emerge along the path our species is taking.

11.3 Adaptive Economizing and Technological Change: The Microeconomic Transformation of Production and Work

The level of detail that can be incorporated in models intended to explain salient features of historical experience depends, among other things, on the time scale involved. Over the vast span of time that has just been considered, a single generation of 25 years is a very short period, and the data available to construct a moving picture of development are fragmentary – especially until the most recent centuries. That a highly aggregative model can capture the most dramatic features of the incredibly complex system of interactions taking place among individuals, their organizations, and environments seems to have been realized in the multiphase macroeconomic model of long-run development just described.

Motivated by the Great Depression of the 1930s and subsequently by World War II, government agencies, private trade associations, and industry institutes undertook a vast machinery of data collection, data processing, and information dissemination. By midcentury micro- and macroeconomic data could be marshalled to give a highly detailed picture of production, technology, resource utilization costs and returns, and commodity prices in agriculture and various industrial sectors. In contrast to the intergenerational time scale used in the very-long-run development model, these data make it possible to study the complex dynamics of change and transition that occur within a single generation and at the microeconomic level for individual production sectors such as agriculture, steel, coal, petroleum, and so forth.

The moving pictures of individual sectors that can be assembled from all these data display many common features. First, in every case production facilities of varying vintages and technological characteristics existed and were utilized at the same time; some were more labor intensive, others less; some were more capital intensive and others less; some used more of some materials and energy, less of others, and so forth. Second, new techniques were initially introduced with relatively small amounts of capacity and, if they proved more profitable, grew for a time more or less exponentially, gradually displacing older, less profitable alternatives until they in turn were gradually driven out by still newer techniques. Following a succession of innovations, overlapping waves of production techniques for particular commodities were created, each wave representing the innovation, adoption, and eventual abandonment of a particular production process. Third, in a corollary of this process of technological innovation, adoption, and substitution, the derived utilization of the several forms of energy and the various materials changed correspondingly. Fourth, (and in particular) labor-saving, capital-intensive production processes replaced more-labor-intensive, less-capital-intensive processes, greatly reducing the demand for labor used in individual processes, which, when added up, led to considerable reduction in the aggregate amount of labor used in the sectors involved.

A series of studies of several specific sectors were undertaken with the purpose of explaining in mathematical terms the economic process that generates these empirical developmental experiences.[5] The then-new methods of activity analysis made it possible to incorporate, in principle, as many goods and as many production techniques as time, energy, and computing power would allow my students and me to accommodate. Production, investment,

[5] [See Chapters 4–8 above.]

and resource utilization were represented as deriving from an explicit choice based on profit maximizing or cost minimizing of alternative available production processes subject to "technical" constraints on existing capacity and labor utilization and on behavioral constraints that limit the economizing search to an adaptively adjusted neighborhood of existing practice. These adaptive neighborhoods are called "zones of flexible response."

The cost and profit expectations were based on extrapolation of contemporaneous experience with prices and costs and were updated period by period. Likewise, the zones of flexible response were adjusted to the most recent practice; they were stretched in the direction of the most successful processes and contracted in the direction of the least successful.

The models in this way adjusted action to experience, guided by expectation and constrained by caution in a manner approximating the actions of the real-world firms making up the sectors under study but here formalized in a recursive programming model of adaptive economizing. The models were simulated for various periods. The model-generated production and process levels were then compared with available data series.

Even with the considerable detail incorporated, each model was still a rather coarse representation of the sector in question. Yet, each one tracked the record reasonably well, mimicking the characteristics of the microeconomic development outlined earlier in this section: (1) a heterogeneity of production processes within each sector; (2) the evolution of individual processes in overlapping waves of adoption, diffusion, and abandonment; (3) the corollary changes in the aggregate demand for, and utilization of, capital, energy, and materials; (4) the displacement of labor-intensive by labor-saving, capital-intensive methods of production with the corollary decline in the aggregate demand for labor.

These results help us interpret many of the developments that have taken place in the last half century: the measured increase in aggregate labor productivity over time, the vast migration of people from rural to metropolitan areas, the shift of labor demand from the steel- and coal-producing sectors to others, and the dramatic aggregate effects on the standard of material living and social functioning in the industrial economies.

The dynamics of this microeconomic story and its macroeconomic implications work at a speed utterly incomprehensible compared with the evolution of human culture over most of its duration. Indeed, these microeconomic, adaptive economizing models generate essentially complete transformations of production technology and work in a decade or two, which is reflected in the detailed historical record of the individual industries modeled.

Such speeds of structural transformation find their explanation in the way the decentralized components of the market economy adapt to existing conditions and new innovations comprehended in terms of a multiple-phase dynamic process. The term adaptive is to be emphasized. Decision makers, of course, think about the future and try to adjust to anticipated conditions, but they only know current conditions (in part), and they can only utilize some of the available data about the present and past to estimate them. Moreover, it seems that decision makers are often unaware of, unconcerned with, or not involved in dealing with the aggregate implications of the process. But these implications are profound, for displaced farmers and agricultural workers flooded into urban areas by the tens of millions; thousands of steel workers were forced into other regions within the industry or out of the industry altogether. All the high-grade iron ore deposits were depleted, and foreign ore and manufactured steel and steel products began to take over a growing share of the domestic market.

What is true of people within a given industry is true of outsiders as well. Urban leaders seemed to be as oblivious to macroeconomic consequences as the industrial managers involved in bringing them about. For example, as the cities began to absorb the flood of rural migrants in the wake of agricultural mechanization, their political leaders were seemingly unaware of the speed at which it was happening and in *every case* failed to prepare for or to adapt effectively to it. In particular, the strain on urban infrastructure that resulted was not anticipated, nor has it yet been dealt with effectively decades after the transitions themselves have run their course.

This development experience and our analysis of it suggests that detailed microdynamic modeling could play a role in understanding the process of microeconomic change and in anticipating its aggregate effects. In this way, models could provide private and public decision makers throughout the economy with prognoses that could serve as the basis for a more effective regulation of, and response to, accumulated effects of microeconomic evolution.

11.4 Economic Processes Far from Equilibrium

The term *economic equilibrium* connotes a state of perfect coordination enabling all the participants in the economy to carry out their intentions without reason to regret having done so. The concept has been extended to an economy working over time so that all actions are always perfectly coordinated. Such a process is said to be an intertemporal equilibrium or a recursive, competitive equilibrium.[6]

The concept of equilibrium as a paradigm for explaining macroeconomic data came into vogue during the last quarter century. Because this concept presumes individuals to perform cognitive and administrative miracles, it can be justified as a scientific theory only as a highly stylized approximation, and then only when it is shown to yield reasonable results in specific empirical studies. Even if one grants the relevance of the equilibrium point of view for certain theoretical and practical purposes, its use as the foundation for empirically based theory must be suspect, for conclusions that follow from obviously implausible premises must always be challenged, whereas implications drawn from seemingly plausible premises must always compel serious consideration.

Of course, models are not the real world; they are mere abstractions. Aside from the pure intellectual pleasure in their invention and manipulation, they can be useful only to the extent that they characterize salient features of empirical experience in terms of what we know of causal structure and of how economic data behave. The multiphase, adaptive economizing approach used as the basis for the work described here is highly plausible in this sense. It incorporates the possibility that economies may sometimes approximate states of near coordination and may remain near such states for some periods of time. But this approach suggests that the endogenous processes of economic evolution inevitably bring about unanticipated consequences to which the participants must adapt one way or another. Sometimes this adaptation can be accomplished with little loss in efficiency and minimal disruption. From time to time, however, such great changes accumulate that the usual and normally successful strategies of adaptation are overwhelmed. Crises are precipitated by the working of the current system that carries the economy far from equilibrium and sets in motion forces that precipitate very rapid restructuring of socioeconomic life.

From this point of view, equilibrium clarifies the problems of coordination and efficiency an economy needs to solve. The concept does not describe how people in a real economy attempt to solve those problems; it

---

[6] The term *equilibrium* in general means "a balance of forces." Such a balance may imply a stationary or steady state. A steady state in physics denotes a stationary distribution of randomly moving particles or, in economics, a balanced growth path. In economics, even chaotic paths can be shown to emerge from a balance of economic forces over time in what would seem to be a contradiction in terms. However, the idea is actually similar to the ergodicity that describes systems in a stochastic equilibrium.

cannot characterize the crises and transformations a real economy generates along its path. These aspects of real economic life can only be described by approaches that explicitly incorporate the adaptive modes of economizing, that embody the potentials for structural change, that incorporate the fundamental instabilities which precipitate phase switching and that characterize the unintended, unanticipated macroeconomic implications of actions determined at the microeconomic level. How else are we to understand what has happened in the economic world? How else are we to anticipate problems that are emerging and that will emerge as a result of what is being done now? How else are we to fashion instruments of policy for business and government to overcome those problems?

References

Aubin, J.-P. 2000. *Dynamic Economic Theory: A Viability Approach.* Studies in Economic Theory Series. Berlin: Springer-Verlag.

Day, R. H. 1963. *Recursive Programming and Production Response.* Amsterdam: North-Holland Publishing Co.

Day, R. H. 1994. *Complex Economic Dynamics, Volume I, An Introduction to Dynamical Systems and Market Mechanisms.* Cambridge: MIT Press.

Day, R. H. 1995. "Multiple Phase Economic Dynamics." T. Maruyama and W. Takahashi (eds.) *Nonlinear and Convex Analysis in Economic Theory: Lecture Notes in Economics and Mathematical Systems* 419:25–45. Berlin: Springer-Verlag.

Day, R. H. 1999. *Complex Economic Dynamics, Volume II, An Introduction to Macroeconomic Dynamics.* Cambridge, MA: MIT Press.

Hommes, C. 1991. *Chaotic Dynamics in Economic Models: Some Simple Case Studies.* Grönigen: Walters-Nordhoff.

Lorenz, H.-W. 1993. *Nonlinear Dynamical Economics and Chaotic Motion.* Berlin: Springer-Verlag.

Lorenz, K. 1997. *The Natural Science of the Human Species.* Cambridge, MA: MIT Press.

Marshall, A. *Principles of Economics.* 8th Edition.

Niles, E., and S. J. Gould. 1972. "Punctuated Equilibrium: An Alternative to Phyletic Gradualism." In T. J. M. Schopf (ed.) *Models of Palisbiology.* San Francisco: Freeman.

Pavlov, O. 2001. *Demoeconomic Dynamics: Evidence from Historic Europe.* Ph.D. Dissertation. Los Angeles: University of Southern California.

Pontryagin, L. S. 1961. "Asymptotic Behavior of Solutions of Different Equations with a Small Parameter in the Higher Derivative." *American Mathematical Society Transaction Series* 8:295–319.

Prigogine, I. 1997. *The End of Certainty.* New York: The Free Press.

Prigogine, I. 1998. *The Networked Society.* Vienna: IST.

Samuelson, P. (1947). *Foundations of Economic Analysis,* Cambridge: Harvard University Press.

Schumpeter, J. 1934. *The Theory of Economic Development*. Cambridge: Harvard University Press.

Starbuck, W. 1973. "Tadpoles into Armegeddon and Chrysles into Butterflies." *Social Science Research* 2:81–108.

Veblen, T. 1904. *The Theory of Business Enterprise*. New York.

Walras, L. 1926. *Elements of Pure Economics or the Theory of Social Wealth*, Definitive ed. Trans. William Jeffré. Homewood, IL: Richard D. Irwin, Inc.

Wilson, E. O. 1999. *The Diversity of Life*. New York: W. W. Norton.

TWELVE

The Dialectical Republic

Toward a General Theory of the Coevolution of Market and State

> Existence is either ordered in a certain way, or it is not so ordered, and conjectures which harmonize best with experience are removed above all comparison with conjectures which do not so harmonize.
>
> Thomas Hardy

Various kinds of simple dynamic economic behavior are well understood: the existence and character of stationary states, steady or balanced economic growth, and periodic business cycles. Each of these types of behavior has its corresponding explanation or set of alternative explanations. Theories of general equilibrium explain stationary states or steady, balanced growth. Theories of business cycles explain periodic oscillations in the economy. Unfortunately, simple dynamic behavior is not exhibited by typical economies of record. Instead, they manifest complex dynamics: irregular fluctuations, overlapping waves of development, structural change, and institutional evolution.

If there were a tendency for economies to converge to simple dynamic paths within a fixed institutional framework, the irregularity of economic behavior would be unimportant because the departure from balanced growth or cycles would eventually abate; theories of the steady state and of cycles would approximate with ever greater accuracy the path of actual events, and society would settle down once and for all to a fixed organizational structure. But this is not the case. If anything, the pace of change has accelerated

This chapter is based on Richard H. Day, "The General Theory of Disequilibrium Economics and of Economic Evolution," in D. Batten, J. Casti, and B. Johansson (eds.), *Lecture Notes in Economics and Mathematical Systems: Economic Evolution and Structural Adjustment*, Springer-Verlag, pp. 46–63, 1987 with permission of the publisher.

with the advance of human progress; the durations of growth and decay periods have correspondingly shortened. Fluctuations have dampened for a time only to erupt again and, in spite of the remarkable development of statistical estimation methods, progress in forecasting is negligible at best, economic change being as erratic, or even more so, than ever.

The ubiquity of complex behavior has not dissuaded theorists from extending the theory of equilibrium from the mere explanation of stationary states and balanced growth to a rationalization of the business cycle. This is not because theorists eschew an interest in the empirical facts of change. Indeed, some of the most beautifully motivated and influential work in this direction has been aimed precisely at the explanation of the stylized facts of the business cycle. But to square theory with reality it has been necessary to augment the equilibrium concept and its underlying convergence postulate with an assumption of perturbing exogenous shocks. These presumed shocks fall in two classes. In one class are structural changes such as alterations in government policies, the reorganization of private and public institutions, or the adoption of new technologies that induce a new wave of development. In the second are more or less random shocks such as weather, political tampering with policy variables, earthquakes, and so forth that continually perturb economic motion and give it the irregular character universally observed in the data. Given the presence of such shocks, complex change is roughly in accord with equilibrium and the convergence postulate when applied to the past century or two of macroeconomic data.

From the point of view of pure theory this is an unsatisfactory state of affairs, however, because it rests on two ad hoc assumptions: that of convergence and that of exogenous shocks. Without denying the practical necessity in empirical work of incorporating exogenous variables and the perturbing influence of random shocks, we note that there is still the open question of how an economy would behave when the former are constant (or some other simple function of time) and the latter are absent altogether. If the convergence postulate does not hold, then complex dynamics may very well persist, and whether or not it holds and under what conditions are considerations open to discussion.

Somewhere Paul Samuelson observed that economic equilibrium is a state that, if brought about, would have certain properties. His colleague, Frank Fisher, in a cogent review of the literature, pointed out the deficiencies in the theory of how such equilibria might be brought about. He went on to consider a disequilibrium foundation for equilibrium economics in an attempt to address the theoretical lacunae. But I think it would be more instructive – as often seems to be the case – to turn the argument around and to recognize in equilibrium a foundation for a disequilibrium theory of economic change. This is because disequilibrium theory implies that, if an economy is out of equilibrium, it must change, and, of course, by hypothesis, it must change out of equilibrium. This leads to a modeling problem: How do economies work in disequilibrium? And this leads to several analytical questions: Under what conditions will an economy in disequilibrium converge? When will it perpetuate change in disequilibrium? When will that change be complex? This chapter presents the beginnings of answers to these questions.

12.1 Changing Economies

Let us begin by identifying salient features of actual economies that must be the basis for any theory of change. Consider that time is decomposed into elemental periods (days, weeks, months, seasons, years). At the beginning of each period, states of technology, resource availability, social organization, and individual preferences prevail and, of course, a history of past consumption, production, and technological practice has occurred. On the basis of all this, individuals and organizations in the economy make their plans, modifying or retaining old plans, or drawing up altogether new ones, and they carry out various actions. In the next period, the situation has changed. Resources have been depleted, capital may have been augmented, prices and other indexes of value and wealth will have been modified, and so on. The system is poised for a new round of planning and action.

Observed over a sequence of periods, the economy will exhibit a history of specific activities that were and were not pursued, of specific technologies and resources that were and were not utilized, and of specific constraints that were or were not binding. In the course of this process, the consumption and production activities actually utilized change, or the constraints actually impinging on choice and actions switch. Some variables that appeared relevant will no longer seem so; other variables that once seemed of no importance at all will now appear to play an active role in development; some technologies may be abandoned, different ones taking their place; some resources once available in plenty and perhaps thought of as free goods now become scarce and attain value in exchange; still other once crucial resources are abandoned, perhaps even before they are exhausted, again becoming valueless.

Viewed in the aggregate, waves of growth or decline in productivity and output will occur, and in the long run, various "epochs" or "ages" dominated by characteristic activities and resources will appear. In the short run, one will see individuals and organizations occasionally change what they do and how they do it. In general, the economy's regimes will switch; its consumption and production patterns will change; its technological structure, behavioral patterns, and organizations will evolve.

The economy will not appear to converge to states that have the earmarks of equilibrium. Individuals will rarely be seen to do their best; they often experience regret, and from time to time they are forced to change their plans or even to act contrary to plan. Markets rarely balance, and individual plans are often incompatible. Normally, some people are becoming better off, whereas others are becoming worse off. Even aggregate indexes of activity will not indefinitely follow or converge to steady states of balanced growth.

In summary, economizers rarely achieve optimal plans; their plans are often inconsistent; the flows their actions generate are out of balance; their fortunes fluctuate along divergent paths; the economy is a disequilibrium process.

12.2 The Individual as an Adapting Process

A fruitful starting point for a theory of the evolving disequilibrium economy is the adaptive process, a dynamic system in which a behavioral unit of interest, the agent (firms, households, government bureaus, and individuals in them), responds to its own internal conditions and to prevailing circumstances in its environment. Because agents and environment influence each other, interactive feedback is involved. With respect to each agent, other agents are part of the environment. The economy may then be thought of as being made up of a set of interacting adaptive processes, that is, as a complex, adapting system.

To be feasible, action must be consistent with internal states, but since the intended action of a given agent may be inconsistent with those of other agents in the environment, it may be impossible to execute them. Therefore, actions must generally be based not just on intentions but on internal and external states that have the effect of insulating the agent from inconsistencies with the outside or that make it possible for the agents to generate unbalanced flows (consumption exceeds production or vice versa, etc.). The general solution to this problem is the stock-flow mechanism.

12.3 Stock-Flow Mechanisms

Actions bring about material, financial, informational, and energy flows that modify internal and external stocks. The flows among various agents, based on individual adaptive processes, are in general imperfectly coordinated. The resulting imbalances in flows are mediated by stocks that make it possible for flows into a given agent to be unequal to flows out from the given agent. Internally, the agents can maintain strategic reserves of materials and energy potentials to allow production and consumption to take place if shortages or delays in supply occur. And they can maintain financial reserves (cash balances, liquid portfolios) to make possible a flow of expenditures that might otherwise be curtailed when sales and incomes fall.

Externally, special agents or institutions have come into being whose primary function is to mediate flows by regulating stocks. For example, stores are inventories on display that make it possible for consumers to purchase goods and producers to supply them without either knowing the plans or actions of the other. Banks and other financial intermediaries regulate the flow of purchasing power between uncoordinated savers and investors. Their ability to create credit provides a means of coordinating activities at different points in time and of facilitating exchange when current monetary stocks are inconsistent with intended investment or consumption expenditures.

Thus, it is that stock-flow adjustments may have the effect of rendering the unbalanced flows induced by disequilibrium actions feasible. But there is nothing in what we have said that guarantees that existing internal or external stocks will provide the buffers required, or, if they do for a time, that they will continue to do so.

12.4 Intended Action, Contingent Tactics, and Buffers

The process of generating intended actions is more or less elaborate and deliberate. It takes time and uses resources and is therefore costly. But actions must take place more or less continuously to avoid a catastrophic crisis of inaction. If plans cannot be carried out, a different tactic must be available that facilitates a timely remedy for intended but currently infeasible actions. It must not take too long to formulate; it must not use too many resources to execute; and, of course, it must work. By the very nature of disequilibrium and its inherent uncertainty, viability is not guaranteed, and in "the real world" there is evidence on every hand that it is not always achieved. One tactic is to postpone action and wait until intentions can be carried out, drawing down buffer stocks that can be restored later. This, of course, presumes adequate stocks of resources to tide one over. Still another is simply to do without and modify plans accordingly. But this, too, requires resources to enable the agent to do without the desired items. Thus, buffer stocks are absolutely essential for the working of an economic system.

Our concern is with resource allocation, production, exchange, and consumption. The processes that generate behavior of this kind involve economizing because they require the use of scarce resources and involve a trade-off among alternative ways of doing things. To accord with the facts of disequilibrium just outlined, economizing must incorporate a crucial distinction between intended action and contingent tactic.

12.5 Boundedly Rational Choice

Consider now how intentions and contingent tactics of economizing behavior are formed. As we have seen, economizing takes place within a complex, adapting system based on stock-flow adjustment mechanisms. It is constrained by the inherent limitations of the mind. There is the imperfect perception and knowledge of the environment. Existing states are perceived imperfectly, and the feedback structure that determines how the environment of a given agent works is only partly understood. The exercise of conscious thought involves limited memory, limited recall, and limited powers of ratiocination. These imply limits on the ability to solve complex decision problems. Moreover, individuals do not always know what they want; their preferences are incomplete or undefined. Still further, individual people possess limited capacities for interpersonal communication and cooperation – frailties that are amplified in organizations, as illustrated in the childhood game of "telephone." In short, thought and communication require effort, take time, and are imperfect.

Rational choice is the conscious, deliberate process of selecting the most preferred among perceived alternatives. As a means of arriving at good strategies, intended actions, and contingent tactics, it is bounded by cognitive limits and is imperfect. Thus, constrained individuals form simplified representations of alternative activities and constraints. Their optimization is therefore proximate. In routine situations they conceive of choice as a departure from previous activity and explicitly consider a small number of alternatives in the neighborhood of what is familiar. The willingness to depart from current practice, that is, the extent of the region searched, may depend on experience and on the behavior of other agents. Thus, adaptation to current economic opportunity may be more or less flexible. The set of alternatives that may be considered at a given time, which I call the zone of flexible response, depends on experience and imitation. This dependence means that economizing is adaptive and more or less cautious.

The choice within the constraints determined by technology, resource availability, and by the willingness to be flexible in responding to opportunity is directed by preferences represented by various goals. These are arranged according to some (perhaps temporary) hierarchy or priority order. A first goal dominates comparison of alternatives until a satisfactory solution is obtained according to this goal; then a less important goal is used to choose among the alternatives satisfying the higher order goal, and so on, until a single choice is reached.

12.6 Obedience, Imitation, Haberation, and Experimentation

Rational thought requires effort and takes time and resources itself. It can only be effected when well-defined preferences exist. But there are other options. These include obedience to an authority, which is doing what you are told, and imitation, which is doing what someone else is doing or has already figured out. Both of these may be attractive modes of behavior compared with thinking for oneself because they save intellectual effort for other mental tasks and make possibly superior forms of behavior accessible that could not have been created through one's own exercise of imagination and rationality.

An additional mode is universally involved in human economizing activity. It is to do what one has been doing. This allows for a kind of mechanical, unconscious mode of behavior that requires neither imagination nor rationality and is thus still more stingy with mental energy than imitation. It enables one to behave according to a habitual pattern. Because English does not contain a verb meaning to act according to habit, I suggest the term *habere*. If I "habere," I execute a frequently repeated sequence of actions that requires little if any conscious thought. "Habering," "habitude," or "haberation" is certainly an extremely important mode of behavior and, in a mind of bounded rationality, an indispensable faculty for economizing the mental energy that drives conscious thought.

Still another mode of behavior must be distinguished that allows for purposeful activity when the conditions of rational thought do not exist, when a habit appropriate to the purpose is yet unformed, or when the motivation for imitation is lacking. As a general mode it may be called experimentation. It may involve a systematic exploration of a controlled environment or model as a way of arriving at a decision. It may involve a trial-and-error search in a sequence of local experiments in which the direction of search is modified in response to a measure of success or failure, or it may involve vaguely purposeful exploration or even play. It can be directed at solving all sorts of mental and physical problems, or it can be essentially unmotivated. In either case, it is a free-wheeling, sometimes nearly random process that involves trials of alternative thought or action patterns when careful methods of ratiocination cannot be exercised or when the requisite skills have not been acquired.

12.7 The Economy of Mind

All of these modes play a useful role in the allocation of scarce intellectual capacity to alternative purposive tasks. They imply the existence of a higher level cognitive faculty that must direct the mode of mental activity to that governing behavior at any given time. What is implied in this description of behavior is an economy of mind: a system of mental resource allocation and of choice among alternative modes of transforming internal or mental states and information about the external world into economic choice and effective behavior. Such a higher order faculty cannot operate according to the usual laws of pure economic rationality, however, because the consequences of choosing one over the other mode of behavior are rarely known. At the risk of introducing a confusion with other uses of the term, I call this faculty *judgment*. How it works is a matter that should be of concern to economists, for its exercise must be a routine aspect of economic behavior. It is responsible for orchestrating a system of information processing, planning, and control that will lead to intended action that is practical, that is, an action that can be realized as often as possible and, in addition, to a contingent tactic, or hierarchy of contingent tactics, that can take over the governance of economizing behavior when intended actions are infeasible. Such algorithms will involve one, or more, or perhaps even all of the economizing modes we have mentioned. Since all of them involve internal and environmental feedback to the agent, we may refer to such a system as adaptive economizing with feedback.

Bounded rationality and imperfect coordination imply that every organization is a system of cooperative specialization whose functioning is only partially determinate and only more or less effective and that the outcome of every human action is uncertain. Potential outcomes are learned from experience, and experience then enters further attempts at decision making and cooperative action. Rationality enters the picture when participants in a process exploit systematic, logical methods of thought to analyze experience, formulate plans, and design or redesign organizational systems of cooperative interaction. Looked at in this way, an economy is a system of interacting individuals whose organizations and actions are the outcome of intended and unintended experiments. If I were to use Eliasson's term, "the experimentally organized economy," this is what I would mean by it. Aside from terminological differences, this seems to me how Alcian, Schumpeter, Hayek, and Simon thought about it. But given that one understands the terms, isn't this what anyone thinks is the nature of the real world?

12.8 Recursive Programming and Multiphase Dynamics

The mathematical analysis of such a dynamic, multimode, microeconomic theory has scarcely begun, but one example emphasizing boundedly rational economizing with feedback has been extensively applied. This is the recursive programming model, a dynamical system in which behavior is represented by cautious, local optimizing subject to stock and flow constraints, to constraints that define the local region of flexible response and in which the constraints depend recursively on past behavior of the agent and other agents in the environment in a way that represents the accumulation and decumulation of stocks and the effects of imitation and haberation. The solution of such a model typically exhibits changing modes of behavior, nonperiodic fluctuations, and sensitivity to perturbations in initial conditions and parameter values. In addition, the solutions exhibit changing sets of utilized activities and tight constraints. When these sets switch, the variables and equations governing the evolution of the system switch and in effect bring in a different set of causal structures and feedback loops. These structures are called phase structures or regimes. A given model may contain a single regime or a very large set of potential phases. The result is an endogenous theory of structural evolution and overlapping waves of technological development based on explicit economic trade-offs.

12.9 Chaos

Radically simplified models of this kind generate nonlinear difference equations that produce deterministic, erratic behavior very much like the irregular fluctuations observed in reality. Moreover, as recent research has shown, these characteristics can be generic; they may occur for continuously varying classes of parameters with long-term frequencies of variable values converging to stable probabilities.

The nonlinearities responsible for these results are to be expected in other dynamic economic models. They occur because of the ubiquitous presence of nonnegativity restrictions on many economic variables; because of "natural" hypotheses such as liquidity traps, increasing and diminishing returns, and so on; and because of the quadratic nature of monetary values that always involve the multiplication of price and quantity.

In my opinion, it is not too early in the development of this theory to conclude that endogenously generated irregularity of these kinds is a very important ingredient in explaining the actual fluctuations of economic data. However, much more crucial instabilities are inherent in economic processes than this one.

12.10 Global Instability and Inviability

Global instability and inviability are suggested in extensive simulation experience with empirical recursive programming models. In general, it has proven to be a nontrivial task to find parameter values that lead to convergence or even to viable solutions. Indeed, the typical model will work for a time, mimicking with more or less verisimilitude an actual history of some region or economic sector, but will then become even less stable and stop working altogether. Models that stop working are said to be inviable. Their analogs in the real world are bankruptcies, banking system collapses, hyperinflations, and complete economic breakdowns.

The latter forms of instability are relatively rare, but bankruptcy is a normal and continuing part of the working of an advanced economy. In this sense, inviability (global instability) is a further characteristic of the complicated dynamics of individuals well-captured by the theory and models we have put forward. But that poses a problem: If economies are inherently inviable, what keeps them running?

Viability in organic, life-bearing systems is not maintained for individual components, which are, for individuals, globally unstable subsystems that eventually disappear. Rather, the forces of change and development are acted out on a level that transcends individuals – a level within which the dynamics of reproduction, of birth, and of death determine the viability of populations.

Societies adopt a similar solution when they provide for bankruptcy proceedings and new technologies, new preferences, and new organizations. A quite analogous process also operates within individual organizations with respect to rules of conduct that govern behavior within them. These rules of conduct are constantly judged by the economic forces of survival, accumulation, decumulation, and demise. They are modified or replaced from time to time by innovative acts of planning and management. Indeed, human culture generally is a population of rules and regulations that originated in numerous acts of innovation and assimilation. Cultures, too, are unstable. Many have disappeared. Of those extant, only a few are flourishing.

The recursive programming model of boundedly rational economizing with feedback takes on expanded meaning once we accept the view that economic systems are unstable – and globally so. Indeed, this approach represents economic change as a counterpoint of adoption and abandonment of alternative ways of conducting economic activity and alternative objects of material form. It points to the inherent tendency toward breakdown that can only be overcome by more general evolutionary forces.

12.11 Evolution and Creative Morphogenesis

Biological evolution involves the interaction of genetic processes with forces of individual behavior and environmental selection. The economic evolution that is our subject here is, of course, embedded within the broader biological process. In addition economic evolution consists of a cognitive process of variation and selection interacting with the complex adapting system of individuals and organizations. These mental acts operate through an intricate, generative Gestalt in which the mind, processing whatever inputs it has, generates a new thought and creates a new sequence of acts embodying that thought in some new form that was not there before.

This creative faculty must lie at the foundation of rational processes of thought in general and of economics in particular. Rational thought after all requires the comparing of alternatives according to well-formed values and the perception of the limits of choice, that is, the set of feasible alternatives and the selection of a candidate from this set that best satisfies preference. This process, especially when it involves the possibilities for future action, entails "imaginative rehearsal" of possible scenarios of what might happen, that is, sequences of imagined act and consequence that form conscious stories of what might be. To choose rationally is to compare stories, to select one, and then to design a sequence of actions that will make those stories come true.

The imagination is also required to imitate what someone else has already figured out to do for himself, as in the enjoyment of a new piece of music, the adoption of a new way of allocating resources, a new technology, or a new product for consumption. Even obeying an authority requires an imaginative rehearsal that can lead to actions never taken before. Thus, imagination is an intimate part of the exercise of both rational and non-rational thought and, to the extent that people make conscious choices in their daily lives, it is routine: we can say that every human possesses it to some, however limited, degree.

This faculty of imagination, which plays its routine role in everyday life, rises to an exalted position in the functioning economy when it leads to invention and innovative ways of doing things, new things to produce and consume, new rules of conduct, new forms of information, decision and organization, and new understandings of ongoing physical and biological processes in the nonhuman world. For these are the elements of variation that feed the process of selection and evolution that keep the economy as a whole working in the face of individual bankruptcies and the breakdown of various institutional systems of action. Individuals who possess these capacities to high degree are called entrepreneurs in the world of business, visionaries in the world of politics, and prophets in the world of religion. It is their particular role to fashion into being ideas and mechanisms that allow an economy to work when its agents are boundedly rational, its transactions imperfectly coordinated, and its long-run behavior intrinsically and globally unstable.

Entrepreneurs are the result and the mediator of evolution in both its narrow biological and broader cultural senses. Once a part of human culture, their activity does not switch on and off according to well-defined accounting messages or in response to carefully anticipated need but functions nearly continuously, thereby providing an uninterrupted source of perturbation to the analytical structures that define routine production, consumption, and managerial activity. The implication is that economies will evolve whether they need to or not. Thus, the very faculty that makes economizing modes possible in general and plays an essential role, especially in rational planning, is the source of a continual flow of perturbations that would disrupt any equilibrium that might occur.

12.12 Transactions and Markets

Among the activities engaged in by individuals in the course of allocating resources are transactions. Transactions among agents are mutually interrelated actions involving the exchange of information and goods and the establishment or modification of constraints on further action. Such behavior involves further aspects of disequilibrium and instability that have not been accounted for so far. Transactions occur in several different modes: collection and redistribution in primitive economies, more or less bureaucratically administered rules within the complex organizations of modern economies, and decentralized market processes among individuals and organizations. The latter have, in traditional economic theory, been represented by bargaining between individuals in isolation, or in a sequence of bilateral negotiations among freely associating traders, or as structured auctions, bidding systems, or negotiational procedures. These bidding-negotiation-bargaining forms, which describe bilateral trade among nations, real estate transactions, and the formulation of wage contracts, are of considerable importance but, like other aspects of rational activity, are extremely time-consuming and resource intensive. Though characteristic of market economies in the early stages of development, these forms are increasingly supplanted as development proceeds by two fundamentally different processes of exchange.

Most evident on the retail scene are stores, which are essentially inventories on display, as has already been noted. Almost as evident and perhaps even more important are order-delivery-information systems that govern most wholesale, construction, and heavy investment transactions. Individuals and organizations order goods. Producers, warehouses, and stores receive orders and either fill them or delay delivery, adjusting their order backlog accordingly. Even the stock market, which is often thought of as an example of a competitive market, works in part on the basis of order-delivery-information systems with broker-specialist agents.

From a physical point of view, these inventory-order-price-adjustment market types are stock-flow mechanisms that mediate transactions among agents using periodic price-adjustment rules. No doubt the specific character of the commodities involved, such as their storability, their time period of production, and their relative cost, influences or determines what type of market mechanism is used in transactions involving them. But a noteworthy fact is that bargaining-negotiation-bidding processes are not pervasive in the real world. Indeed, one could imagine an economy in which they are absent altogether and exchange occurs using inventory-order-price-adjustment procedures exclusively. The basic virtue of these latter mechanisms is that they enable exchange to take place when supply and demand are not equated at prevailing prices. The participants need not postpone other activity while a sometimes interminable process of haggling works itself out.

When studied in highly simplified, experimental settings, direct exchange systems based on bidding-negotiation-bargaining sometimes converge rapidly to competitive equilibria. These settings may be typical of some markets, such as auctions, that are held at a single place at periodic intervals for short periods with relatively small numbers of people. Other markets, however, lack these characteristics. They are held continuously and can involve large numbers of individuals who may be separated by great distances and whose participation is not simultaneous but strung out over time. Inventory-order-price-adjustment mechanisms make such markets possible.

Certainly, markets of the latter type did not always exist. Their creation, however, introduced new avenues for exchange and with them new possibilities for specialization in production while enabling all this to happen in a decentralized, imperfectly coordinate flow of action. These markets have therefore played a crucial role in the progress of technological development and the growth of income and wealth. They provide a good example of how entrepreneurial activity has led to an evolution in the form and number of economic institutions.

12.13 Market Instability, Uncertainty, and Exposure

At the same time, the complexities of dynamic interaction introduced by these market mechanisms enhance the conditions for disequilibrium, complicated change, and inviabilities. The data of modern financial and commodity markets reflect this.

Markets both create and destroy opportunity. They widen the scope of choice; they expose participants to a widened range of uncertainties about the values of stocks and flows, of goods in exchange, and even of access to the market system itself. Because of these uncertainties and the realization from time to time of inviabilities due to exposures to an unpredictable fluctuation in values, some individuals and organizations are made worse off by the system.

A further complicating force in decentralized exchange is the routine exposure of individuals to asymmetries in the power of bargaining in part (and fundamentally) because individuals vary in their cognitive capacities as well as in the initial conditions they bring to every act of exchange. These factors lead to asymmetries and changes over time in the costs and benefits of exchange. Such asymmetries lead to dissatisfaction, not just with exchange but to the system of exchange.

12.14 Polity

Implicit in the market system is a cooperative agreement to engage in peaceful, voluntary exchange on terms specified by the system. When, despite buffers, plans cannot be realized and contingent tactics fail, individuals face the catastrophic risk of imminent demise. Moreover, asymmetries in bargaining power, when extreme enough, can cause a breakdown in the system of voluntary exchange and usher in a system based on coercion or deceit. At such times the prevailing system comes under review. Thus, market exposure creates constituencies for organizational innovation and motivates that enticing alternative to voluntary exchange called plunder – the taking by force or deception of what is possessed by another.

To prevent the destructive tit for tat of plunder or the fury of revolutionary breakdown, the participants in an economic system must develop a generative process of polity that allows for changes in the rules of economic conduct, an avenue for politicoeconomic morphogenesis, so that recourse is restored for those who stand to lose too much too often. If an equilibrating economy could be established, such a polity would (in the absence of creative thinking) wither away, leaving a fixed system of institutions and rules, or merely a collection of individuals with no institutions or rules at all, converging ever closer to a competitive or communal ideal in which all the people planned to do their best, they all carried out their plans, and no organization could be put forward that would not provoke objections. But, because individuals have limited powers of cognition and communication as well as asymmetries in knowledge, wealth, and power, and because of the complicated dynamics of prices and quantities, equilibrium behavior does not emerge. Disequilibrium persists and with it the potentially catastrophic asymmetries in the costs and benefits of participation.

One way to deal with these potential results of market exposure is to eliminate disequilibrium, to destroy the system of decentralized, discretionary action, and to replace it with one of administered rules of behavior based on tradition, imitation, and obedience to authority. To do so would be to constrain rationality, limit creative morphogenesis, and operate within the bounds of established bureaucracy.

On the other hand, a society can embrace disequilibrium in a dynamic form of organization based on an alternative principle to that of a social equilibrium. That principle has been called "willing participation." In such a society most of the people most of the time will accept its working, will contribute to its functioning, will refrain from plunder, and will defend it from any force from inside or out that would attempt to supplant volition by coercion. Rationality in such a system cannot operate exclusively according to exact laws of deterministic, dynamical systems or to unchangeable laws of political interaction. The functioning of these laws is too complicated; their intrinsic working leads to unpredictable change and again and again to inviability because the more creative participants in the economy continually perturb it with wholly unanticipated possibilities for change.

Instead, such a system of polity must rest on access to its instruments. Because people will not generally agree, it must allow access to instruments of argument, persuasion, and debate – modes of mental conduct and communication that go beyond the economizing modes of behavior and form the ingredients of democratic discourse and the basis for willing self-transformation. Such a system becomes the medium through which institutions evolve. Subject to the opportunities and limitations of political process, the people in such a system possess a freedom limited by the rules and operation of their collectively imposed and individually accepted system. Their potential participation in the continual evaluation of its components and in the process by which those components may be modified, replaced, or augmented is their exercise of liberty. It is not unlimited freedom but a limited potential. It is the basis of their willing participation in a system whose functioning they sometimes regret.

The laws of such a system are not analytical in the cause and effect sense that governed the development of my argument through the concept of global instability. Instead they are dialectical in the Aristotelian sense that understanding emerges from the free interplay of ideas and of the discussions about them. Argument, persuasion, and debate play the role at the social level that search and experimentation play in the faculty of mind that underlies individual volition. From the conflicting views of the system's boundedly rational participants their function is to synthesize changes in the rules and regulations that govern individual opportunity, changes in the understanding of how the overall system works, and even changes in the values that guide rational thought so that the new system so changed, will work – at least for a time – with minimal economic plunder and without debilitating social discord.

The system of polity that provides the framework for argument, persuasion, debate, and institutional change coexists and codevelops with a market system. It makes continuing disequilibrium possible and mediates the evolution of mechanisms that perpetuate the coevolution of market and state. Some call it the "democratic market economy" or "democratic capitalism." Its principles were encoded in the Constitution of the United States of America and, subsequently, with some variations in the constitutions of various countries around the world. I call it "the Dialectical Republic."

Index

Page numbers in italics point to figures.